Uphol

Upholding the Common Life

The Community of Mirabai

Parita Mukta

Delhi
Oxford University Press
Calcutta   Chennai   Mumbai
1997

Oxford University Press, Great Clarendon Street, Oxford OX2 6DP

Oxford   New York
Athens   Auckland   Bangkok   Calcutta
Cape Town   Chennai   Dar es Salaam   Delhi
Florence   Hong Kong   Istanbul   Karachi
Kuala Lumpur   Madrid   Melbourne   Mexico City
Mumbai   Nairobi   Paris   Singapore
Taipei   Tokyo   Toronto

and associates in

Berlin   Ibadan

© Oxford University Press 1994
First published 1994
Oxford India Paperback 1997

ISBN 0 19 564373 9

Laserset by SJI Services, B-17 Lajpat Nagar Part 2, New Delhi 110 024
Printed in India at Pauls Press, New Delhi 110 020
and published by Manzar Khan, Oxford University Press
YMCA Library Building, Jai Singh Road, New Delhi 110 001

For HASU, MADHU, BENA and TARA
who cosseted my childhood in song

and for
PUSHKERKAKA
who secured the ground for us to walk on

Contents

Mirabai	ix
Acknowledgements	xi
Abbreviations	xvii
Note on Translation	ixx
Prologue	1

INTRODUCTION

Chapter One	: Introduction: On Community and the Common Life	19

PART ONE

Chapter Two:	Opposing Loyalties: Mira's Bhakti and Rajput *Dharma*	49

PART TWO

Chapter Three :	A Community Forged: The Birth of a Song	69

Chapter Four	: A Dream Validated	115
Chapter Five	: Ordeals of Community: The Song Imperilled	150
Chapter Six	: Privation in Community	155

PART THREE

Chapter Seven	: Incorporation	173
Chapter Eight	: A Nation Cleaved: The Song Betrayed	182
Chapter Nine	: Amplification	201
Chapter Ten	: The Rainbird Thirsts	211

Epilogue: Earthly Life and its Completion — 225

Appendix: Mira's 'Janam Patri': An Epic Poem on the 'Birth and Life of Mira' — 233
Footnotes — 235
Krishna by Other Names — 240
Glossary — 241
Bibliography — 251
Index — 261

Mirabai

Mirabai is more than a historical figure. She goes beyond the shadowy realms of the past to inhabit the very core of a future which is embodied within the suffering of a people who seek an alternative.

The actual historical dates of Mira's life on this earth are not known. It is believed that she was born towards the end of the fifteenth century, within the Rathor Rajput family who held control over the land of Merta (in present day Rajasthan). It is said that, as was the custom within medieval polities at the time, a marriage was arranged between Mira and the heir apparent to the throne of Chittor in order to consolidate the allegiance of the Rathors of Merta to the Sisodiyas of Chittor. Mira however, spurned the rank and title of wife to the prince of Chittor, and refused to consummate the relationship, declaring that her love and allegiance lay with Krishna, god and king of Dwarka. The Sisodiyas of Chittor, rulers of a mighty and warring state, felt shamed by Mira's public defiance of their power and they bore her a cruel enmity all her life.

The people know that Mira suffered greatly, both for bearing a love towards Krishna, and for associating with others who shared her emotional life. They say that the Sisodiyas sent Mira a cup of poison. This turned to ambrosia. A venomous snake was then sent to her in a basket, to cause her death. This snake turned into a garland of flowers.

Mira, seeing that her own allegiance was under threat, left the fortress of the Chittor rulers and took to the life of an itinerant singer, with her love of Krishna steady in her heart. She shed the attire that marked her out as a woman of rank and took on the clothing of a mendicant. With an *ektara* in her hand, singing of her love for Krishna, she visited all the places associated with his name, and at last sought refuge in Dwarka, the town that Krishna had ruled from.

Mira did not shelter here for long though. The legend continues that the Sisodiya ruler sent two emissaries to the Dwarka temple to ensure that Mira returned to the capital of the Sisodiya state. Mira refused. The two emissaries of the Rana then staged a *dharna*, attempting to exert pressure on Mira to return. Mira then replied that she would seek Krishna's advice as to what course to follow. She went inside the sanctum sanctorum—and was seen of no more.

Mirabai's songs, added to over the years by those who love and believe in her, continue to be sung today.

Acknowledgements

As a child I was drawn intimately into the world of bhakti through the women in my family—my mother, grandmother and aunts. The familial and domestic sphere within which individuals were sustained and regenerated to face the outside world, was here marked by a deep faith. This contributed substantially to mitigating the harshness involved in the struggle to make ends meet (for ours was not an affluent family). The close knit bonds of loyalty and solidarity which were required to face daily vicissitudes were constantly being informed by the messages which flowed out of the bhajans sung around one. From these bhajans one acquired a sense of historical tradition, within which one's own suffering (*'dukh'*), grief and hardships were contextualized by the knowledge of the hardships undergone by figures such as Taramati and Harishchandra, Draupadi and the Pandavas, Nal and Damayanti etc.[1]

It was, in a dramatic way, a period of transition for the family: of migration from East Africa to Britain in the 1960's, with its concomitant changes in structure and consciousness—a period preceding the changes which accompanied mobility, particularly the entry of women into the wider world of universities, responsible jobs, of social and political involvement. Throughout all these changes, bhakti continued to provide a counter-point to virulent individualistic values and it enabled the enunciation of disjunctured hopes in the face of pain and oppression. In order to understand the complexities of bhakti better, I have had to grapple with both its resonating strengths, as well as its painful limitations in enabling one to realize one's potential. This work would thus not have been possible—indeed would not have been begun—without this experience behind me. This work is thus dedicated to my family, my grandmother, whose name I bear, being the heart of this.

This work began as a Ph.d thesis at the University of Manchester in October 1983. Throughout the years of clarification and consolidation, my supervisor Hamza Alavi, provided critical encouragement, a sharp acumen and valuable support. Teodor Shanin bears my gratitude too for seeing me through my academic travails.

Within Rajasthan, the area in which I conducted extensive field-work in an attempt to locate Mira within the particular social moorings in which she has been kept alive, Komal Kothari, Director of the Institute of Folklore in Borunda was a source of strength and inspiration. His depth of knowledge pertaining to the cultures of the communities in Rajasthan, and his active engagement in the process of retaining integrated cultural forms, enabled me to broaden the context of my own work. The Kothari family, together with Dr Bhimpuri, saw me through a bout of hepatitis while I was on field-work in Jodhpur in August 1987, for which I am grateful.

I began the task of tracing the Mira bhakti in January 1986. Arun Kumar was then editor of *Rajasthan Patrika* in Udaipur, and he provided the first support in the exploratory stages of the work. This was invaluable in giving shape to further field-work. Mr Minaria of the Maharana Mewar Institute (Udaipur) and Mr K. Shastri of the Mira Kala Mandir (Udaipur) were both helpful with sources. G.S. Bhattnagarji of Chittorgarh provided valuable insights into dominant Rajput values.

It was not, however, till February 1987 that I embarked upon a systematic study of bhajan gatherings held in villages in the area covering the former states of Marwar and Mewar (Mira was born in the former and married into the latter). In the task of studying the Mira bhakti, various organizations provided institutional support and put me in touch with rural workers. Prayas (Deogarh) brought together, one magical evening, on the tenth of February 1987, a group of bhajniks from the Mina community, and this opened to me my first experiencing of the peoples' Mira as she emerged through the bhajans. This was the beginning of many more evenings of listening to bhajans being sung in different peasant communities. The work in the villages of Rajasthan could not have been conducted without the co-operation and support of the village-based women workers of Sewa Mandir (Udaipur) and the *saathins* of Jodhpur Prodh Shiksha Samiti. To them all, and they are numerous, I owe the times of fulfillment found in a process of learning which contained many revelations.

To the bhajniks themselves, who shared their bhajans with me and who let me touch their lives, goes my deepest gratitude. I have striven, at all times in the writing, to be honest and true to them, to render their voices in a way which will best demonstrate their hopes and their visions.

It was essential to attempt to supplement the oral material with written, archival documents. For this, I turned to the Oriental Research Institutes which held collections of verses of various bhaktas, and to the Rajasthan State Archives in Bikaner, which yielded important background documents.

In Saurashtra, the work of recording bhajans in the villages around Dwarka was completed in February 1988. The village contacts in this area were made through the Sadhs of the Ramdev Pir tradition, the priests who initiate the worship of Ramdev Pir and who lead the all-night singing. The organic link they had with bhajniks made for a qualitatively richer learning. Mohanpuri Goswami, worker-writer and bhajnik based in Porbander and Narottam Palan, lecturer in Gujarati literature at Upleta were especially helpful with their insights into Saurashtrian society. Jyotsnaben Vaishnav, teacher at Mahila College, Porbander, was generous in her hospitality.

Earlier, in 1984, Bapalbhai Gadhvi had accompanied me to pilgrimage places in Saurashtra associated with the *ann-kshetras*, a strong tradition in this region. Bapalbhai's knowledge greatly enhanced my understanding of the area.

In Calcutta, Ratnavalli Ghosh gave friendly encouragement, and was a delightful companion on a visit to Chaitanya's birthplace. J.C. Swamiji worked very hard with me in Bikaner to enable me to transcribe the Rajasthani bhajans, bringing to the process a warmth and sympathy of spirit. The translations of these bhajans are my own. Satyakam Joshi in Surat came to my aid in transcribing with me the Saurashtrian bhajans, a tedious task but here performed with zest. Again the translations are my own.

Throughout the four years and more of my work on Mira, the Centre for Social Studies, Surat, provided a congenial work environment, and a pleasant home. Pradip Bose read all my earlier fumblings and gave encouragement to my thoughts. The librarian, Mrs Mac, was helpful in obtaining material, and Hina Shah, assistant librarian, was a warm and sensitive companion on one of the field-trips to Chittor district in June 1987.

Nandita Gandhi provided an open home in Bombay and gave intellectual and personal support. Nandita Shah, Gabriele Dietrich, and Lata Mani have, at crucial points, provided understanding of the work. An opportune suggestion by Lata Mani sowed in my mind the seed for the contents in the final chapter. For this, I thank her.

More prudent schema of writing had to be abandoned as they did not accord with the substance of the bhajans. I would particularly like to thank A.R. Desai for the time he took to map out a framework of chapters, which though I have not utilized, enabled me to clarify my thoughts. A.R.'s commitment, incisive understanding, and enthusiasm have been at all times strengthening. Indrannel Chakravarty offered support in enabling me to realize the work.

Shahid Amin read the first part of an earlier draft and gave valuable criticisms. Tanika and Sumit Sarkar's warm reception of an earlier draft was much appreciated.

In England, Josna Pankhania with her enthusiasm for bhajans and a keen awareness of the importance of inter-related struggles, gave valued encouragement. Indira Chawdhry, Jane Haggis, Mary Kennedy, Ajay Skaria, K.N. Chaudhri and David Arnold read the Ph.d thesis and gave helpful comments. Interacting with all those present at the conference organized by David Lorenzen on 'Popular Religion and Socio-Political Dissent in N. India' at el Colegio de Mexico, 23-24 May 1991, as well as with Peter Friedlander and his work on Raidas verses has stimulated my own work considerably. Leena, Bindu and Anju have, through their love and faith in me, ensured that I was able to bridge the changes in my life, from being a full-time activist (1979-83), to a time spent on more sustained study (1983-89), with some security. These changes, taking place in a period which has seen the retreat of alternative political movements in Britain, have not been easy to come to terms with. If the present work has taught me anything, though, it is that there is strength in the people's culture which is born of their suffering, and a hope in it which is often disregarded and ignored by the vagaries of intellectual fashions. It is a hope which needs to be paid serious attention to.

In my search for Mira and meaning attached to her life, David Hardiman has walked the same road with me consistently, over light clear days and shadowy evenings. David and Mira have, together, held me to life and to myself.

Abbreviations

B.A.	Bikaner Archives, (Rajasthan State Archives).
C.o I.	Census of India.
C.W.	*Collected Works of Mahatma Gandhi*.
D.S.	*Dwarka Sarvasangraha*, by P. Gaukani (ed.), Gujarat Itihaas Parishad.
M.G.	Mewar Gazetteer, (Rajputana Gazetteers), Mewar Residency.
M.R.H.	*Mardumshumari Raj Marwar* (Census of Marwar).
M.S.A.	Maharashtra State Archives, Bombay.
R.D.	Revenue Department.
S.P.K.	*Saurashtrani Pachat Komo*, Saurashtra Pachat Varga Board.

Note on Translation

All non-English words have been italicized (for exceptions, see below), and those which are not self-explanatory through the text have been translated in the glossary provided at the end of this work.

The analysis of 'bhakti' and 'bhajan' being central to this writing, I have not italicized these two words in the text, nor attempted to provide a precise (and hence a misleading) definition of these. I hope the reader will become aware of the complexities and permutations of these expressions in the course of being engaged with this work.

'Dalit' is a term employed which requires some explanation. Historically, various terms have been employed to categorize those groups which occupy the bottom rung in the caste hierarchy—the 'untouchables', 'Antyaj', 'Harijans', etc. The term 'dalit' is a self-conscious term of pride which has emerged out of these subordinated groups in recent decades, with for example, the growth of the Dalit Panther Party, and an increasingly strong current of dalit self-expression, through dalit poetry, etc. While I do utilize the other definitions (in their context), I have chosen the term 'dalit' in preference over the others, as it gives a dignity to these oppressed groups. Words such as 'guru', 'saree', 'hookah', etc. which are widely used and understood in the English language, have been left unmarked.

PROLOGUE

I set out for Rajasthan in January 1986, with the intention of visiting the places associated with the life of Mira, and to attempt to place her within her own social context. Having grown up in a milieu where Gandhi's evocation of Mira within the nationalist movement had established a preeminent place for her within Gujarati middle class culture, I had expected to find, in Rajasthan, visible and identifiable marks of Mira worship. However, the scholars, historians, librarians, archivists that one necessarily meets with at this stage of the work (in Udaipur, Chittor, later in Jaipur), were united in their opinion: Mira was not sung in Rajasthan. Did I not know that a figure such as Mira, rejected by the Sisodiya princely power, could not be publicly acknowledged by others in society? That she could not be revered? Yes, they insisted, it was not just that, as legend avers, Mira was sent a cup of poison by a Sisodiya Rana in order to bring about her death, but the public humiliation that Mira had inflicted on collective Rajput honour meant that her name could not be evoked without rubbing salt on an old wound. Mira was not seen as a saintly figure in the dominant culture of Rajasthan, to be paid homage to, but as a figure to be excoriated, for the erstwhile rulers of Mewar could not tolerate the veneration of a person who had so directly challenged their authority. Did I not know as well that

Mira was a term of abuse levelled at women in Rajasthan, as a charge of promiscuity? (I had not known.)

The starkness of these responses jolted me into re-considering the very basis of Mira bhakti that I had, commonsensically, taken for granted—that she was a revered Krishna bhaktan, an icon and an emblematic figure of piety, after whom renowned figures such as Rabindranath Tagore had named their daughters. These notions sat ill with the sharp denigration of the person of Mira presented to me by scholars in Rajasthan, yet the consistency of these responses by thoughtful researchers who had been born in, who lived in and inter-acted closely within Rajasthani society meant that I was forced to re-analyse and re-think the whole question of Vaishnav, and particularly Mira bhakti.

It became increasingly important to look at the social conflict engendered around the figure of Mira in Rajasthan society. If it was true that the Rajputs continued to revile the memory of Mira, that a silencing, so typical of feudal culture had been affected by the Sisodiyas to the history of Mira (not just in their written records but within their social fabric), how had the legend of Mira gained in power and strength? The same scholars that I posed this question to, averred that Mira was the preserve of the middle classes in Gujarat—that she was a recent and modern phenomenon, resuscitated in Rajasthan post-independence, at the demise of princely political authority. Could it be then that Rajput rule exercised such deep hegemony over the minds of all under its rule, to the extent of exorcising Mira from their consciousness? How then was one to explain the 'Mirabai *mandir*' in Chittorgarh, which was said to have been built for her by the Sisodiya ruler? Even if one were to accept that the middle classes of Gujarat were the strong purveyors of Mira's bhakti, what had existed of Mira prior to the emergence of this class? Neither the rise of Mira, nor the prevalence of Mira bhakti could be attributed solely to the Gandhian nationalist movement. How had Gandhi himself come to her—fortuitously, with no groundswell behind her?

It became crucial to explore Mira within the context of the social tensions which surrounded her within Rajasthan. Since the

Rajputs did not sing Mira—who did? If giving expression to Mira bhajans was a mark of cultural affinity and solidarity with a figure unsung by the Rajputs, then it became important to identify the groups which had granted Mira their cultural and social allegiance. The palpable conflict still present around the memory of Mira demonstrated a need, constantly renewed and under attack, to stamp down on the cultural power that she continued to wield. The attempt by the Rajputs to deny Mira a legitimate space, appeared to point to their weakness rather than strength in gaining the loyalty of those that they had ruled over.

Field-work

Back in Udaipur, I pursued these questions further. I began to make contact with welfare organizations which had strong rural links. They enabled me to establish a relationship with bhajan *mandlis* based in villages. In the city of Udaipur itself, I was introduced to a group of sweeper women who had formed themselves into a bhajan *mandli* called the Mira *mandli*. Not only did the sweeper women sing Mira profusely, they also identified themselves by her name.

I began travelling extensively in the Mewar region, attending bhajan sessions in villages and in towns, within peasant households and in temple precincts. I interviewed bhajniks from all walks of life, as well as Rajputs, to gain an understanding of Mira's place within the different social strata of society. I sat in villages where the night was taken over by the palpable fervour of the bhajniks, and the dawn broke over the gaunt faces of the devotional singers. I visited the bhajniks in their households and at their workplaces, interacting with them in their daily routines. Thus, the experiencing of the Mira bhajans was informed by, indeed was embedded within, the social context of the lives of the bhajniks. I also visited fortified towns and fortresses, temple ruins and sacred groves, noting the absence and presence of Mira within these.

Building upon the field-work experience in the Mewar region, I then travelled around and did field-work in the region of Marwar and Saurashtra. The field-work in Rajasthan was carried out between January 1986-June 1987. The field-work in Saurashtra was conducted in the months of January and February 1988. I sat amidst bhajan singers in gatherings in the villages and towns of Rajasthan and Saurashtra (marked on maps 2, 3 and 4). I attended forty-four bhajan gatherings during the course of this period, and many more in the period outside of this. In Table 1, I delineate the composition of the bhajan gatherings, alphabetically within each region.

The foundation of this work is thus very much evidence gathered, recorded and transcribed from the process of field-work. While attending bhajan gatherings, I ensured that I tape-recorded *all* the bhajans that were sung, thus avoiding unnecesary intrusion into and disruption of the bhajan session, and avoiding also the bias of an early elimination. I left the task of identifying, transcribing and translating the Mira bhajans to a later date.

While the focus of the work was very much the conflictual and differing cultural configurations which had formed around the figure of Mira, and the changing faces of Mira over the different historical periods, this was bound up with and permeated by the prevailing concerns and contemporary anxieties of the bhajniks. Thus, in a particular village (Dechara, Mewar region), the women present there, after singing a Mira bhajan which detailed her rejection of the marital tie, spontaneously turned to a discussion of the social experiences of women within that and the surrounding villages. At another time, a bhajan gathering in the village of Modhvada (Saurashtra) which had been held in the house of a dalit belonging to the Ravi Bhan *sampraday*, and which had begun with an evocation of the figure of Raidas, ended with bitter expressions against the attitudes of the upper castes of the village. There was thus a constant slippage between the messages which flowed out of the Mira bhajans, and the social experience of the various groups which sang these.

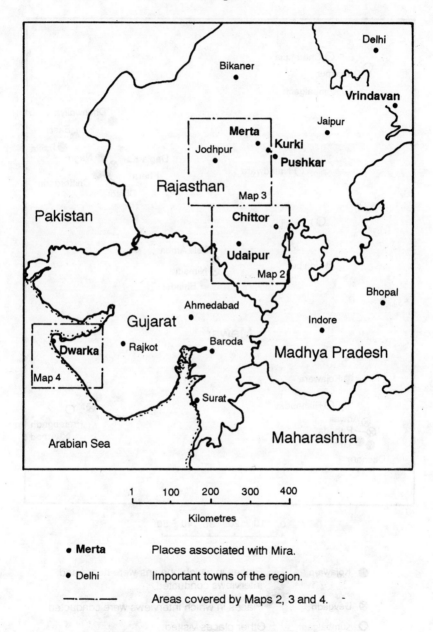

Map 1: Region of research and places associated with Mira

THE COMMUNITY OF MIRABAI

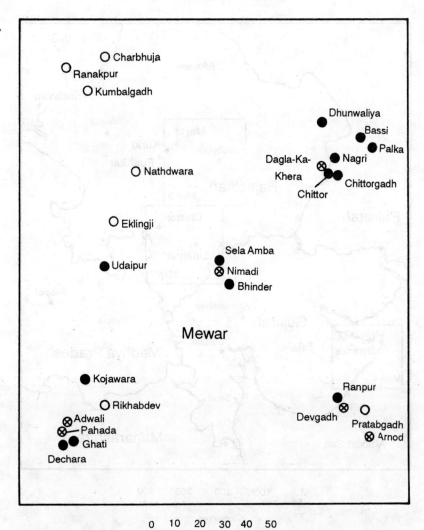

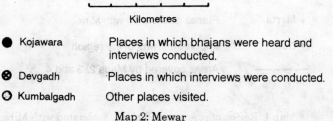

Map 2: Mewar

Prologue 7

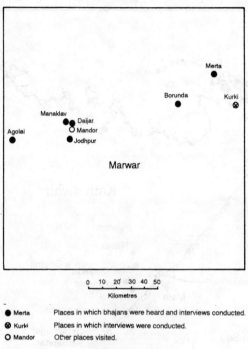

Map 3: Marwar

At the time of the field-work, both Rajasthan and Saurashtra were suffering from the effects of two consecutive years of drought. While the issues of availability of water, minimum wages for relief works, etc. were crucial in the years of this drought, the question of the retention of community life and social networks crystallized very sharply in this time too. Within this, the bhajan gatherings provided one very important focus for a community life, not only as crucial social networks, but as forums where the collective religious expression itself became enlarged and expanded to incorporate the presence, experiences and articulations of the bhajniks.

During the period of field-work, there was massive migration of pastoralists, who moved with their cattle to areas where they could obtain fodder. From Saurasthra, large numbers of Rabaris moved to South Gujarat, to 'Valsad Vapi'. Many Ahirs who had land in villages where there was no water, moved to the coastal

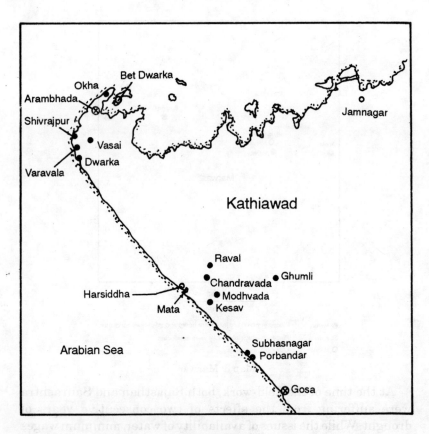

Chandravada — Places in which bhajans were heard and interviews conducted.
Gosa — Places in which interviews were conducted.
Bet Dwarka — Other places visited.

Map 4: Dwarka Region of Kathiawad

TABLE 1

A Places where bhajans were recorded/noted	B Nos. of gatherings attended	C Gatherings within which bhajans were heard
MEWAR		
Bassi	1	Dalits (Salvi). Men only in Ramapir temple.
Bhindar	1	Brahman (Chaubisa). Women only in Vishnu *mandir*.
Chittor (town)	2	a) Brahman women in own house. b) Dalits (men) in Nehru Yuva Kendra.
Chittorgadh	1	Male singer at the 'Mira *mandir*'.
Dechara	1	Mixed gathering of men and women with women leading the singing. Anjania Patel Darji, Suthar etc.
En route to Devgadh (bus)	1	Old women singing together.
Dhunvaliya	1	Dalits, men and women singing.
Ghati	1	Predominantly Patels, in a Patel household. Men and women present, men only singing.
Kojawara	1	Bhil and dalit men singing in a community hall. Women present.
Nagri	1	Kir community. Woman singing to herself.
Palka	1	Mixed community (men only) of Dhakars, Damami Vaishnav *vairagi*, at Vishnu *mandir*.
Ranpur	1	Men from Mina community in the open.
Sela Amba	1	Man and woman, both singing. Kabirpanthis, cultivated land.
Udaipur (city)	4	a) Sweeper women in one of their houses. Men present, but women leading. b) Mixed community, men and women at evening worship in Jagdish *mandir*. Men and women singing. c) Woman singer from Damami community singing to Rajput women in their house. d) Woman singer from Dholi community in Folk Museum.

continued next page

continued previous page

A	B	C
MARWAR		
Agolai	2	a) Men and women singing, outside the house of a Jat family. Kumbhar, Darji, Nai, Sadh. b) Meghwals in courtyard of a Jat house.
Borunda	3	a) Sadh women in house of one. b) Meghwals and Kamad in Ramapir temple. Men only. c) Langas and Manganiyaras in music work shop. Men only.
Daijar	2	a) Dalit women in a Bhil house. b) Dalit women in village square.
Jodhpur	2	a) Kalal women in house of one. b) Langa and Manganiyara men in house of a folk-lorist.
Manaklav	1	Dalit men and women singing in courtyard of a Dalit house.
Merta	2	Women at Charbhuja *mandir*. Mainly Brahman and Baniya. (On two occasions).
SAURASHTRA		
Chandravada	1	Predominantly Mer. Women present, but not leading the singing.
Dwarka (town)	3	a) Vaishnav men in Dwarka *mandir* at evening worship. b) 'Gopi' *mandli*, women from community of Brahmans. c) Satvara and Kharva men in the house of a Satvara. No women present.
Ghumli	1	Koli young men in house of chowkidar of architectural remains.
Kesav	1	Men from the Mer community.
Modhvada	1	Dalit men in house of one of them.
Okha	1	Kharvas and Aboti Brahmans (men) in a Ramdev Pir temple.
Porbander	1	Dalits, men and women singing, in the house of a sweeper woman.
Raval	1	Bharvad and Charan men singing.
Shivrajpur	1	Predominantly Wagher men singing, as well as an Ahir man. Women present, but not singing.

continued next page

Prologue 11

continued previous page

A	B	C
Subhashnagar	1	Men from the Kharva community singing, women present.
Varvada	1	Kharva and Rabari men singing, as well as a sadh. Women present.
Vasai	1	Men from the Wagher community singing.
TOTAL	44	

strip of Okhamandal, and were active participants in the bhajan gatherings held there. While temporarily dislocated from their home environment, the collective singing of bhajans, and the sharing of common world-view and cultural enunciations provided an important forum for a joint identification during a period of dislocation. Many of these migrants were appreciated and valued for the commitment and fervour that they brought to bhajan gatherings. Many agriculturalists were leaving their home villages to share living space with relatives fortunate enough to be in places where there was water available. Although new to a particular village or town, they were pointed out as those who had a fund of Mira bhajans on their lips. In Rajasthan, the issues of deforestation, of programmes for the creation of employment which would tide households reliant solely on agriculture over the times of drought, recurred consistently.

The coming together of Jat women in a programme for the creation of employment in the countryside at a time of severe drought, neighbourhood women providing support to each other at a time of meagre provisions, villagers co-operating on relief works, families offering a roof to others who had to leave their homes as a result of lack of pasture for their cattle, widows gathered at a temple on mornings to sing bhajans—all these and other experiences and solidarities went into the formation of the Mira bhakti.

Attending and listening to bhajan gatherings in various artisanal and peasant surroundings within the region of Mewar and Marwar, what emerged from the Mira bhakti were various forms of identification to Mira. I began to focus on these identifications, detailing their alignments and exploring the communities given voice to by the Mira bhakti.

What emerged over the course of the research process is a historicized and regionally-specific Mira—a Mira taken up by the subordinated classes of Saurasthra and Rajasthan as a vehicle for their opposition to feudal privilege and caste norms, linked in particular to the rise of the weaving communities in the sixteenth century (Part Two, Chapter Three); a Mira who crystallized around her a powerful cultural resistance to socially imposed marital relationships (Part Two, Chapter Four); and Mira as an exile, bereft of caste and family, seeking refuge in Saurashtra amongst mendicants and wayfarers (Part Two, Chapter Six). Section II, which explores the peoples' Mira, is heavily reliant upon the material gathered from the field-work, and in particular from the bhajan sessions.

Part Three of the book moves to different voices. Chapter Seven analyzes the attempted incorporation of Mira within the Sisodiya fold under the aegis of the colonial Political Agent, Colonel James Tod, and carries this forward to the continuing fraught nature of the relationship between Mira and the Rajputs of Mewar in the post-independence era. While Tod's writings granted to Mira a rehabilitated place within a glorified Rajput history, it was not until Gandhi's utilization of Mira in his writings and political speeches from 1915 onwards, that Mira entered into the field of nationalist consciousness as a foremost *satyagrahi*. Gandhi secured for Mira a wide popular base amongst the middle classes of Gujarat, feeding her into a nationalist political culture (Part Three, Chapter Eight). The ramifications of this phenomenon within the recent popular culture, whereby Mira is given a different form in films, on radio and cassettes is explored in Chapter Nine of Part Three.

The book thus traverses the time of Mira (Part One, Chapter Two), through the colonial and nationalist period to the present, showing the diverse social and cultural meanings which have arisen in different epochs around the figure of Mira. It charts the period of increased state control and centralized rule in Mewar (the fifteenth and sixteenth centuries), this being the period which received the Mira challenge. It appears from the evidence that the period of Sisodiya rule demarcated a cleavage in the cultural sphere, with the rejection on the one hand by the Rajputs of Mira—and the enlarging of Mira into a symbol of a social creation. While the nineteenth century marks a turning point in the cultural and political history of Rajasthan, the colonial intervention (in the case of Mira, Colonel Tod's writings) did not succeed in carving out a space for Mira within the ranks of Rajput patriarchy. As Chapter Seven of Part Three shows, the process of the attempted integration of Mira within Rajput social history did not begin till the 1950's, and I ended the discussion of Mira's place within contemporary Rajput society with a bleak description of the acute subjugation of Rajput women within a resurgent Rajput patriarchy, which made the possibility of Rajput women accepting Mira as a symbol of identification very difficult indeed (pages 187-8).

The Rajputization of Mira

Since the writing of these chapters, Lindsey Harlan's book *'Religion and Rajput Women: The Ethic of Protection in Contemporary Narratives'* was published. (Harlan, 1991.) The book analyzes Rajput women's religious practices, in particular the *kuldevi* and *satimata* tradition. Her exploration of Rajput women's belief systems, and the ways in which this buttresses a Rajput patriarchy centered around warfare is of great significance in the context of Mira's own—displaced—space within this system of beliefs. Since Harlan's chapter entitled 'The *Bhakt* Paradigm: Mira Bai' (Harlan, 1991: 205–22) has some bearing on the central contention of this work—that there is a history of opposition and tension between the Rajputs' rejection of Mira and the holding up of Mira by the artisan and peasant communites of Rajasthan—it is important to turn to Harlan's arguments.

Harlan explores contemporary Rajput women's attitudes to Mira, and describes how Rajput women in Udaipur, Jodhpur and Jaipur see Mira as an 'exemplar' in their lives. How are we to interpret Harlan's evidence with the evidence presented in this book? While *'Religion and Rajput Women'* places *kuldevi* and *satimata* worship within a changing historicized tradition, the chapter on Rajput women's relationship to Mira is very much an exploration of contemporary attitudes. Harlan has analyzed with sharp insight the changing traditions of worship, whereby the *kuldevi* has become transmuted from being a protectoress of the clan, king and realm (in times marked by feudal warfare) to being a family deity, relegated to the domestic realm, aiding Rajput women in performing their female duties as protectors of their husband's life and health (Harlan, 1922: 226). I would suggest that Harlan's discussion on Mira could fruitfully be historicized too and placed within the context of a changing political culture within the Rajput communities, whereby the earlier profound rejection of Mira is today being slowly transformed, linking her, contradictorily, to the assertion of a Rajput identity and Rajput valour.

There are ample pointers in Harlan's work on Rajput women's cultural rejection of Mira. Two of her informants stated that Rajput women in Mewar continue to disrespect Mira and that they will not sing her bhajans. One of these respondents, a Jaipur noblewoman, went on to say that only 'common people' sing Mira's songs (Harlan, 1992: footnote 15,214). There is thus a consistency of responses from the field which attests to the radically divergent ways in which the dominant and the dominated relate to Mira. Harlan also goes on to say that Rajput women in Mewar did not by themselves stand out for their hostility to Mira, given that concern over what was perceived to be her 'bad behaviour' was found amongst all Rajput women throughout Rajasthan.

Instructively Harlan describes how the Rajput women acquired their knowledge of Mira bhajans from the radio. Furthermore, few Rajput women were familiar with Mira's story in the villages where she conducted her work—they considered it something only 'educated people' would know (Harlan, 1992: footnote

15,214). This would fit in with the thesis propounded in this work, that through changing social and political circumstances, certain sections of the Rajput aristocracy have begun to pay lip service to the concept of Mira as a 'great bhakt' (interview, Arvind Singh, Udaipur Palace, 7.2.1987), though the lesser Rajputs in Mewar have lagged behind in acquiring the sophisticated composure necessary to overcome an earlier, deep-rooted animosity.

Thus, the evidence presented in *'Religion and Rajput Women'* appears to point to the fact that Rajput women have only recently allowed the memory of Mira to surface within their midst, and that they have been able to do this by Rajputizing Mira, by interpreting her actions and deeds in a way which conforms with notions of heroism and valour prevalent in the Rajput community. Mira is hereby essentialized, to demonstrate palpable Rajput traits and characteristics. Thus, her courage in flouting caste and gender norms is said to spring, precisely, from her caste attributes—from the fact of her being a Rajput.

The Rajput women Harlan interviewed saw Mira's valour as akin to the strength required of a Rajput (man and woman) in facing wars and battles with courage.

The struggle involved in the cultural realm over meanings, beliefs and associative bonds is brought out very clearly by an examination of Mira's history. That it has taken the Rajputs over four hundred years to appropriate the Mira symbol to their own self-image testifies both to the strength of the Mira challenge, and to the rigidity of Rajput patriarchy. While the women Harlan interviewed said that Mira's courage was admirable, none of them saw her as an actual exemplar in the sense that none said that she would follow Mira's example. All were adamant that a Rajput woman should aspire to be a *pativrata* by performing duties and rituals which would enhance her husband's life and standing, rather than aim to be a great bhakt, as renunciation meant abdication of *pativrata* duties. One and all saw Mira's rejection of her husband, and Mira's taking to a life of bhakti, as an action which no Rajput woman could countenance (Harlan, 1992: 209). Since the starting point of my work was an exploration of Mira's bhakti, this brought forth aggressively rejectful responses to Mira from Rajput women in the field, one year after Harlan's fieldwork.

The process of the Rajputization of the Mira figure by Rajput women in Rajasthan as described by Harlan appears to be one in which the respondents attempt to come to terms with the force of Mira external to their community through the layers of their own resistance to her, ultimately redefining her as a person who embodied Rajput characteristics. This redefinition though, is still in the making, and the cracks in the mosaic of a forced pictorial depiction are all too visible.

'Religion and Rajput Women' demonstrates clearly how Rajput women's religion is centered around the upholding of *pativrata* duties. The ultimate end-point of *pativrata* duties is widow immolation—a phenomenon linked to the assertion of Rajput power as was forcefully demonstrated by the burning alive of Roop Kanwar in Deorala on the fourth of September 1987. Within Rajasthan in more recent times, the earlier form of *sati* worship (the worship, within a specific family, of a woman said to have immolated herself) has transmuted into a tradition of living *satis*. These living *satis* are women who are widowed, who are said to live without partaking of food or drink, who live the life of an ideal *pativrata* by her devotion to the memory of her husband and by acting as an example to others of this virtue.

The most telling point about the Rajput women's depiction of Mira is that for them her greatness is vindicated through the manner of her death. When Mira's body is said to merge with the Krishna *murti*, this connotes *sati* immolation to the Rajput women—with the Divine. Mira, rejected for so long by the Rajputs for being unfaithful to the principles of *pativrata*, returns to this fold as the paramount *pativrata* (Harlan 1992: 212).

INTRODUCTION

Chapter One

Introduction: On Community and the Common Life

Hagiography and Historiography

There exist now many written biographical studies of Mira.[1] Despite the fund of written biographies, and accompanying the pool of collective remembrance which is based on the Mira bhajans, there is only one indisputably central association that is known and that is linked with the name of Mira. Namely, that as a woman, Mira spurned her caste and family obligations in order to live out a relationship with Krishna. Within this compressed detail reverberates the social tensions which are a hall mark of a feudal society, but we are nevertheless left with what is only highly condensed detail pertaining to Mira. There is one other known detail associated with the life of Mira—that poison was sent in order to bring a swift end to what her family considered were inglorious actions—but that Mira survived this. All other knowledge of Mira is based upon an influential eighteenth century hagiography, and upon imaginative conjectures derived from this hagiography.

Priyadas' influential writing on Mira emerge in the commentary that he wrote on the much earlier 'Bhaktamal' compiled by Nabhadas (*circa* AD 1600). Priyadas' commentary on the 'Bhaktamal' written in AD 1712 has shaped the historical and contemporary imaginings of the literate classes vis-a-vis Mira. In this 'Introduction', I trace an overview of the ways in which the portrayals of Mira have emerged in the written biographies and histories of the nineteenth and twentieth centuries. I show how the methods of analysis prevalent in these writings have made for a highly individualized and isolated figure of Mira, a curious fact given that bhakti (the life chosen by Mira) is, first and foremost, based on associative bonds.

It is important to remember that the purpose of hagiography (from which much of the written biographies of Mira are derived) was to record the spiritual triumphs of well-known practitioners of bhakti. To attempt to disentangle the 'historical' and 'social' material out of a 'religious' writing is a spurious task, for the last permeates and is the bed-rock of an entire world-view. Nevertheless, it is essential to locate the hagiographical work relating to Mira within its locus of social relationships, both to understand the historical milieu within which it arose, and to criticially appraise the effects that this hagiography has had on subsequent portrayals of Mira.

An association has been sought between hymnody and hagiography, it being suggested that the hagiographers relied upon a corpus of devotional songs to build up a portrayal of revered bhaktas. It is certainly true that the 'Bhaktamal' was fashioned at about the same time that the first anthologies of devotional verses were being put together (Hawley, 1988: 278). While there are obvious difficulties involved in viewing devotional verses created by bhaktas—or attributed to them—as standing in for autobiography (the reduction of spiritual symbolisms, allusions and referant points to literal 'facts' being not the least of these), there has nevertheless been, subsequent to Nabhadas, a consistent tradition of wresting hymnody into a framework of historical realism. This process escalated in the late nineteenth century, whereby the writings on the life of Mira became permeated by, and shot through with, an understanding rooted in positivism. In the first section here, I analyze the ramifications of this understanding derived from positivism and a scientific individualism on the figure of Mira, and I then trace, in the second part of this section, the various kinds of community formations which have coalesced around the figure of Mira.

The 'Bhaktamal'

Nabhadas began the entry on Mira in the 'Bhaktamal' by stating that Mira left her *kul* (unspecified), society and all notions of decorum in order to worship Giridhar. He further went on to say that Mira demonstrated, in an age of Kali, the devotion of a *gopi*, and that she fearlessly expressed in song the glories that she saw *Dushta* (the evil, unnamed and undefined by Nabhadas) saw Mira's actions as a grave fault, and planned for her death. However, said Nabhadas, not a hair on her head was harmed, and the poison sent to her became ambrosia in her throat. Mira beat love's drum, feared nothing, and leaving aside *kul*, society and all notions of decorum, she worshipped Giridhar (Nabhadas, 1801).

It is clear that the description of Mira which emerges from Nabhadas' 'Bhaktamal' does not enable us to locate Mira within a particular time, community or locality. Even the miraculous end which was to be attributed to Mira (of mergence with the Krishna *murti* at Dwarka—a detail surely not to be missed out in a hagiographical work) is absent from the original 'Bhaktamal'.

It is in fact not until the eighteenth century that a much enlarged interpretation of Mira becomes available in the written sources. This came from Priyadas' written commentary on the 'Bhaktamal'. This Priyadas (of Vrndavan) was associated with the Chaitanya *sampraday*, and it appears most likely that the larger renderings of the lives of bhaktas which appear in Priyadas' commentary were distilled out of the oral stories and devotional verses available to him at the time. Since the popular base of the Gaudiya Vaishnav *sampraday* was amongst traders and merchants, with Vrndavan being an important commercial centre, (Sanyal, 1975: 93), it is possible to surmise that these elements linked up with a similar strata within the Braj *mandal*. Certainly if the Mira of Priyadas' extended commentary is a Mira derived from the oral sources available to Priyadas at the time, then she seems to fit into a peculiarly mercantilist framework. Indeed, a culture based firmly on the market-place was being entrenched in Northern India at this time, and one could begin to place Priyadas' writings within this emerging strand (Gupta, 1986; Bayly, 1983).

Priyadas' account of Mira related two essential details pertaining to Mira's history which were missing in Nabhadas. One was the fact that she was born in Merta, and the other was that she was married to a Rana of Chittor (unnamed). Priyadas' account thus contextualized Mira within a particular place, locality, and source of tension. Apart from this though, the other particulars related by Priyadas recounted a story of Mira's life in which she was found to inhabit relationships more common amongst commercial households. Thus, Priyadas related how, just as Mira was about to depart from her natal home (for the marital one), her father and mother, overcome with emotion, asked her to help herself to *'pat abhran'* (clothes and ornaments). Affection here was thus directly linked to granting the daughter further rights to clothing and ornamentation, rather than land with an entourage of servants as would have been common within a princely family. Further in the tale, Priyadas then recounted Mira's refusal to pay obeisance to the Sisodiya *kuldevi*. At this juncture, the mother-in-law went with a complaint to the father-in-law, stating that *'yah bahu nahin kamki'* i.e. that 'this daughter-in-law is of no use/worth'. This is a highly significant phrase where the instrumentality of a transacted commercial relationship is brought out very sharply. The wrathful father-in-law, when he heard of Mira having answered the mother-in-law back, went to attack Mira—but was restrained by his wife (Priyadas, 1801).

A violent father-in-law (and this the valiant feudal hero Sanga!), a vindictive sister-in-law, a jealous husband who heard Mira conversing and laughing behind closed doors and suspected that there was a paramour there (it in fact being Krishna), all these details fit into a construction of Mira which is more in keeping with a mercantilist mentality. It is hardly surprising therefore, to find the orientalist scholar, Hermann Goetz referring to the 'primary' source for Mira (Priyadas' commentary) as a 'collection of silly, sentimental legends' whereby the history of a Mewari princess is 'described in terms and motivations of a lower middle class household' (Goetz, 1966: 2). Latter day biographers and commentators on Mira, who have based themselves uncritically on just this 'primary source', have also repeated and reasserted a portrayal of Mira which is derived from the above social location (Chaturvedi, 1983; Sangari, 1990). While the ideological imputations and cultural configurations attributed to Mira may vary between these writers, nevertheless the *basis* of the Mira history is one that is founded upon an eighteenth century mercantilist milieu. This is in marked contrast to the history of Mira which emerges from contemporary oral sources, but the stage is set here both for the domestication of the Mira figure within the confines of mercantilist family relationships, and for the individualization of Mira.

The Absence of Mira within the Written Traditions of the Sampradays

So if the hagiographies themselves are a construction of a particular conjuncture—what about the Mira verses available in the manuscript tradition, upon which have been built up published anthologies of Mira's work?

Can they take us to the authentic Mira? Mira is known, foremost, by the verses she has created. All those who have sought to gain entry to the oldest—and therefore the most 'authentic'— Mira verses, in order to gain a clear knowledge of Mira have come up against a virtual impasse. There have been grave doubts raised about the two manuscripts which purport to be the oldest Mira manuscripts—one from Dakor which is said to bear the date AD 1585 and the other from Benares said to date 1670 (Hawley and Juergensmeyer, 1988: footnote 9,202). Neither of these manuscripts have been made available for scholars to scrutinize, though an edited collection of these verses was published in 1949 (Sukul, 1949). The task of sifting through and annotating the

Mira verses found in manuscripts in order to record the tradition of deletion, accretion and codification is still in its formative stage. There is thus not an existing corpus of verses which can be identified as being those composed by Mira within her time, the available Mira verses dating most frequently from the nineteenth century.

So why has neither the life of Mira nor her verses been preserved in the growing religious compilations of the sixteenth, seventeenth and eighteenth centuries? There are a number of answers to this. One is that Mira did not align herself to, nor was she taken up by an established or establishing religious *sampraday* as was Surdas for example. In fact there is evidence in the literature of the influential Vallabh *sampraday* of animosity towards Mira.

The story of Krishnadas Adhikari, which appeared in the '*Chauriasi Vaishnavo ki Varta*' described how Krishnadas visited Mira (who had, by then, left the fortress of Chittor) while he was on his was to Dwarka. While other Vaishnav bhaktas were already gathered there, Krishnadas appeared disinclined to stay. Mira pressed him to take some *mohar* (gold) back for Shreenathji, but Krishnadas departed in a huff, stating that as she was not a disciple of 'Acharyaji' (Vallabh) he would not touch any present she thought to send (Barthwal, 1939: 411–6; Shabnam, 1951: 96–8).

The story of Purohit Ramdas which appeared in the '*Chauriasi Vaishnavo ki Varta*' is even more revealing about the attitudes of the Vallabhites to Mira. The story described how Ramdas, who was singing a verse composed by Vallabh in front of the Thakurji *murti*, was asked by Mira to sing an alternative devotional song to Krishna. This infuriated Ramdas, who replied, 'Look, *rand*, since you do not agree with Shree Mahaprabhu [Vallabh], why should I have any reason to call on you?' Ramdas thus left, returning Mira's gift (Barthwal, 1939: 411–6; Shabnam, 1951: 96–8).

It is clear from the above that not only were Mira's attempts to patronize members of the Vallabh *sampraday* spurned, but that she was also subjected to abuse by them. Mira thus did not find favour with the existing Vaishnav *sampradays*. If she had, her works would almost certainly have become incorporated into their devotional traditions, and we would then have some codified version of this. Was Mira so purist about her worship of Krishna that she found it difficult to integrate this with other devotional forms? Did those involved within the Vaishnav *sampradays* find it difficult to incorporate the Mira tradition into theirs? Did Mira's womanhood create dissonance in the world of bhakti, as her encounter with Jiva Gosain suggests (Goetz, 1966: 26). Mira as a Krishna bhakta stands at a distance from both the Vallabh and the Chaitanya *sampraday*. No other established religious traditions appear to have taken Mira up. Mira thus appears as a tremendously isolated and lonely figure within the world of bhakti. This isolation, which has been accentuated by the dearth of material linking her up in cooperative effort with like spirits has had a profound effect on the ways in which Mira has been successively portrayed.

Positivism and Methodological Individualism

Nineteenth century positivism, and scientific rationalism has had a lasting impact on the way Mira has been interpreted in more recent times. The specifically colonial context of the rise of these interpretations has set the parameters to a contradictory and convoluted process, whereby the religious world-view was both rejected and reformulated at one and the same time. I will take up the late nineteenth and early twentieth century interpretations of Mira, and then demonstrate the continuity of these in much more recent times. Contradiction and an involuted implosion continue to mark the response of the Indian literati to religious expression, with which Mira is closely aligned.

A positivism grounded in science attempted to extrapolate salient 'historical' features to Mira's life from the eighteenth century hagiography. This in turn became embroiled within the ideological constructions placed upon the life of a *religieuse*, upon the nature of spiritual expressions and articulations, and upon the relationship of the *religieuse* to the hierarchical values of Hinduism. Within this, the attempt to historicize Mira placed her history within the (various) linear histories which were of concern to the elite literati. The figure of Mira was thus recarved to fit the contours of elite extrapolations and elite projections.

First of all, writers of different ideological persuasions, and with diverse stories to tell, built up a biographical sketch of Mira, utilizing the published anthologies of the Mira verses as evidence.[2] Moreover, rather than concern themselves with the immense power of the Mira symbol, and the meanings put upon this, great concern was shown to unearth exactly which Rana it was that Mira had been tied to, and whether the Rana under scrutiny could be said to fit the role of the '*dushta*' (the evil) of Nabhadas' '*Bhaktamal*'. These writers, while not quite being royal apologists, were taken up with proving whether such a person as Mira could be said to have lived alongside a particular historical prince of Chittor. Thus, the possible date and place of Mira's birth were debated, the 'evidence' of which Sisodiya prince she could have been married to weighed up, and gradually Kumbha, Sanga and Bhoj were eliminated from the ranks of possible Mira persecutors, leaving the socially unpopular Vikramaditya to carry an additional stigma.[3] The tools of analysis derived from positivism which held 'facts' as sacrosanct were utilized upon the figure of Mira, wresting her out of the realm of collective social expression, and providing her with a chronology which is so dear to a linear, bourgeois history.

The writing of temporal, chronological histories has a long tradition in Rajasthan, of course. The *khyat* which concerned itself with the fame and glory of particular Rajput clans, and the *vigat*, which gave details of historical figures in a clan, and contained administrative and political details of a particular state (as in Nainsi's '*Marwar ra Pargana ri Vigat*' written in the seventeenth century) matured under the influence of the Mughal court and the standard set by the Persian chronicles of this period. The *varta* and the *bat* (historical narratives of the Rajputs), as well as the genealogies relied very heavily upon chronological histories (Ziegler, 1976: 226–34). Chronological history is thus not new in the field of Rajasthani studies. The source of this type of history, though, was, firstly, patronage by the Rajput nobility, and, secondly, often first-hand observation of and commentary upon empirical material. Mira does not appear to have patronized a court-related biographer, and neither Rajput chronicles, nor religious hagiography is available for her from the times she is deemed to have inhabited—towards the end of the fifteenth century and early sixteenth century. Mira's history thus has been reconstructed much later by writers and biographers arising from the emergent middle classes.

Apart from providing facticity to the Mira figure, one other main concern of the late nineteenth and twentieth century writers on Mira was to map out and lay claim to an indigenous Romantic tradition, and to a heritage of an elongated artistic creation. Mira, and the other bhaktas like Narasinha, etc. were wrested and made to fit into a history of individual artistic creation. The individualization of these bhaktas, and their removal from the realm of a popular religious expression was thus not only begun, but well entrenched by the late nineteenth century.

Govardhanram Tripathi, famed Gujarati novelist and social reformer of the nineteenth century, gave an important index of the attitude of the literati to the earlier bhaktas. In a work published in 1892, he stated that the bhaktas (now designated 'poets')

> lived among a people who are now dying away (sic), and with whom we, from English schools and colleges, are out of touch when we find them living. (Tripathi, 1892: 55.)

The gulf which existed between the literati noted for their faith in scientific progress and advance, and the mass of the people with a pre-capitalist world-view, who, despite the optimism of those such as Tripathi did not die away, was fully in evidence by this period, and it was to manifest itself in various forms in the analysis of both Marxist and non-Marxist writers of a later date.

Tripathi, while concerned that the 'poetry of the land' (the works of such figures as Mira and Narasinha) confined itself to the theme of religion, was at pains to show that these were creative individuals who were 'unconsciously singing out the poetry of [their] heart.' (Tripathi, 1892: 4). Tripathi's depiction of the 'classical poets of Gujarat' did two things. First of all, it imposed on them an image of isolated lone creators. The notion of individual artistic creativity was, of course very much a product of the mid-nineteenth century (Williams, 1983: 41). And secondly, it presented all of these bhaktas as having evolved out of, and contributing to, the formation of relationships and morals within the trading communities.

Thus have the poets of Gujarat seldom sung about mountains and meadow lands or about patriotism and war. They have neither seen nor praised any living king or courtier, for they have never been in touch with them. Industrious and peaceful, they were usually a home-keeping people with homely wits. They generally knew no more; but this much is certain that they were conscious of the intense charm and beauty that spread a network of magic over their little homes and dear families. (Tripathi, 1892: 4.)

Tripathi's placing of bhakti within the strata of society which was industrious and peaceful had the effect of *domesticating* the bhaktas into the cosy depiction of their 'little homes and dear families'. As far as Mira was concerned, the domestication of her bhakti assumed a highly feminized form.

In one thousand sweet and homely songs has the broken heart of Mira sung itself out, and the love that the Rana had claimed in vain, was poured upon the divine and invisible ideal of her soul, and her little songs live to this day and have survived four hundred years. Pious women in Gujarat sing them in the presence of the same ideal and feel that they are nearer to heaven than to earth when Mira's music is on their tongues. Young women sing them at home and in public choruses, for Mira's ideal is held to be an ideal for all women, and the heart of Mira was as pure and innocent and sweet and God-loving as the heart of woman should be. (Tripathi, 1892: 16.)

One can begin to trace from Tripathi's writings the process whereby the figure of Mira was placed within a subordinated feminized domestic sphere, and Mira's lauded skill in turn was aligned to feminine creativity. This was reduced to one which lacked sophistication or craft, and which was an uncomplicated outpouring of the heart. While the later nineteenth century depiction of Mira was to be given a political turn by Gandhi in the 1920's, the alignment of Mira with the qualities of purity, of feminine creativity, and of an artless charm was to continue well into the 1970's. So for K.M. Munshi, Mira's language was 'simple and appealing'. He was also to state that

But passion, grace, delicacy, melody—Mira has all these gifts. Her longing is exquisite; it seizes all hearts, penetrates all souls. Her poetic skill possesses the supreme art of being artless. (Munshi, 1967: 183, first published in 1935)

And for Kalinikar Datta, Mira's

odes and hymns are so rich, sweet and inspiring not because of any high rhetoric or dexterity of language, but because they are characterized by a tenderness and simplicity of feeling as genuine outpourings of a heart dedicated to God. (Datta, 1953: 329.)

The nineteenth century thus set a tradition where the history of Mira was feminized and placed within a history of the growth of vernacular literature, establishing for Mira a place within the long line of 'poets' who 'considerably influenced the literature of succeeding periods' (Munshi, 1967: 184). Thus was Mira's history again put in the development of a linear history, this time of literature. One of the earliest of these histories of Gujarati literature, first published in 1914, by K.M. Jhaveri, shifted from calling Mira a 'singer' to a 'poet', neither term truly capturing the nature of bhakti articulation (Jhaveri, 1938: 34,42). The wresting of bhaktas into a history of 'poets' has caused a dissonance in the way that these figures have been received in the contemporary period (through textbooks on Hindi literature etc.), out of their context of a devotional gathering.

The emphasis on Mira as a woman possessed of a pure and simple heart, and the emphasis on a linear progression in history, at one and the same time individualized the figure of Mira, by placing her in the tradition of lone creators—and it granted Mira a constituency only among women confined to a domestic sphere. It is clear that these writers did not place credence upon the experiences and expressions of those classes which lay outside their own milieu.

While one of the ramifications of the writings on Mira was to confine Mira to an elite view as to the growth of vernacular literature, a second important conjuncture which arose was the positioning of Mira either within a high Hinduism, or within the newer forms of Hinduism popular amongst the alienated urban middle classes.

The various articles in *'Mira Smriti Granth'* (Sukul, 1949), an influential collection of verses with commentaries, were full of allusions which lay claims to the Mira expression being a reflection of the Absolute, the Parabhrahma (Bahuguna, Kaushik, etc. in Sukul, 1949). Not only was the Mira figure moulded within the parameters of a high Hinduism, but the Mira worship was conjoined to the figure of Krishna in which the pastoral deity became the very 'embodiment of triumphant manhood' (Munshi, 1967: 174). Thus Mira became embroiled within the differing processes which took shape in the late nineteenth and early twentieth century, namely the creation of and emphasis put upon a separate domestic sphere, the emergence of a purified and revivalist Hinduism, and the emergence of the ideology of a feminized, middle class womanhood.

An example of the peculiar manner in which a high Hinduism blended with mysticism and hokum came from the Aurobindo Ashram in Pondicherry. D.K. Roy, who lived at the Aurobindo Ashram, first published a play entitled 'Mira' in the nationalist journal, *'Mother India'* (Feb.-Aug. 1952). He had in part based this version of Mira on the notes of Indira Devi, Aurobindo's foreign disciple. Aurobindo, a terrorist-turned Vedantic philosopher, admitted that it was possible for Indira Devi to receive Mira's verses when she went into a trance.

There is nothing impossible in Mira Bai manifesting in this way through the agency of Indira's trance, provided she (Mira) is still sufficiently in touch with this world to accompany Krishna where He manifests. (Roy, 1979: 85.)

This particular brand of religion received its support from members of an English speaking class of urban India who surrendered scientific rationality in particular spheres of their life. In D.K. Roy's play, Mira appeared as a philosophical proponent of Vedantic principles.

The conjoining of the figure of Mira to the histories of an elite literary tradition, to a high Hinduism, and to a high cultural form, were all processes initiated by nineteenth and twentieth century interpreters of Mira. Within all these, the Mira of the people, the Mira who lived as a symbol of social emancipation for various classes in Rajasthan and Saurashtra, remained mute. Mira and bhakti itself, underwent a contradictory transformation within which they were raised—and devalued.

Milton Singer, in an influential and important article which traces the different trajectories of bhakti and its impact on the different social classes in Madras, describes how, for the classical critics, there is a definite hierarchy of cultural forms. As one ascends the hierarchy, the values of bhakti become less and less, and the values of a 'pure art'—which he says 'is not completely secularized'—become more important. Singer points out that this espousal of a high art represents a distinctive path to release and the Absolute, and a kind of sublimation of ritual observance and of knowledge. Singer maintains that for the classicists of Madras, frequenting bhajans is not a regular occurence, as they regard this as too emotional and 'uncontrolled' a form of religious expression, suitable for less cultivated people. (Singer, 1959: 155).

The more recent writers on Mira have taken twentieth century collections of Mira verses available in textual form, and have tried to arrive at both a biographical picture of Mira, and more fundamentally, have attempted to arrive at what she stood for. Again though, Mira exists as an individual, who stands—or falls—by her own personal strengths or weaknesses. The deriving of 'facts' from the available text verses is sometimes carried to a dispropotionate extent. So for example, the Mira verses which articulate separation from a *'jogi'* are held to mirror an *actual* relationship Mira is deemed to have had with a Nathpanthi (Shabnam, 1951: 127). The symbolisms, the imagery, the philosophic allusions within which Mira's verses are steeped which formed part of the common sense world of bhakti, within which there were fluid transitions and borrowings from *sagun* to *nirgun*, and *nirgun* to Nathpanthi (Hawley, 1987. Dwivedi, 1985) are, in the positivist readings, reduced to sexual liaisons.

The elitism of all these analyses are clear: an elitism which seeks to merge Mira's history into the history of a high philosophy, an elitism which seeks to merge Mira's religious expression to the creation of a high art—and an elitism whereby the *individual* subject—in this case Mira—is held to be the repository of philosophical and intellectual social trends, and who, as an individual, fails to match up to our more modern yard-sticks, always falling short of these. Thus for Kum Kum Sangari, Mira's Krishna worship is an act of—personally chosen—'willed servitude' (Sangari, July 7, 1990: 1472)—and all religious belief is analyzed as stemming from the *smritis*, the *puranas*, the *dharmashastras*, and the all pervasive concept of *maya*. Both Kabir and Mira's work is set in the context of these texts rather than in the context of an expression which had a popular base and which does not bear a direct linear correspondence to the classical texts (Sangari, July 7, and July 14, 1990). Sangari, like literateurs before her, utilizes latter day twentieth century published anthologies from which to draw a critique of Mira, and like her earlier forebears (such as Tripathi) finds Mira's 'obsessive religiosity' (Sangari, July 7, 1990: 1467) an obstacle in the drawing up of a progressive tradition. Needless to say, this progressivism is itself premised on a linear model of the making of history.

Mira lived within a society, and within a cultural milieu, where people's consciousness was suffused by religion. To take Mira to task for failing to develop a social critique which fell outside the purview of a religious sensibility, is to impose anachronistic expectations on the figure of Mira, particularly given the fact that bhakti was the cornerstone of Mira's life. The anachronism inherent in such a view (Sangari, 7.7.1990: 1468) comes very close to viewing religious expression as stemming from a mentality designated by certain post-Enlightenment writers as 'primitive', as flowing from amongst the people who 'are now dying away, and with whom we, from English schools and colleges, are out of touch when we find them living.' (Tripathi, 1892: 55.)

This strand of thought is today underpinned in India by the knowledge that religious belief is *not* limited to a small section of society, and that it is not a phenomenon which will fade away. And this lends to the unease of the Indian intelligentsia, who from the time of Tripathi onward, have viewed a fervent religious expression like bhakti with deep suspicion. A more engaged and informed attitude by the intelligentsia to the phenomenon of bhakti might well have had some effect in altering the social processes of the twentieth century.

The Accretion of Mira Verses

We have seen how difficult it is to authenticate any of the Mira verses as being those that were created by Mira. This makes the endeavours of those who have relied on textually available twentieth century material to build up their versions of Mira extremely problematic. There has of course been a recognition by all these interpreters that there is a long accretion of Mira verses but rather than pursue the evidently popular base of the Mira verses, they have remained confined to the available published texts. All however, acknowledge, the additions to popular Mira verses.

And there is also no doubt that many a clever little woman has composed her own sweet song in the name of Mira—and has enjoyed the interest taken in it by her circle of friends and admirers. (Tripathi, 1892: 61)

Jhaveri in 'Milestones in Gujarati Literature' says:

Mira Bai's great popularity especially with the fair sex, has produced a crowd of imitators, who have passed off their own verses under her name (Jhaveri, 1938: 41).

Hawley too talks of 'bardic groups and female singers, who were not literate' who would have sung the Mira verses and suggests that the large quantity of verses now bearing Mira's signature, grew as a response to her well-known legend. (Hawley and Juergensmeyer, 1988: 123).

Whether it is that these songs are said to be the creations of 'many a clever little woman', or as belonging more to the 'folk idiom' (Hawley and Juergensmeyer, 1988: 123) it remains true that they have not received the attention of serious scholars. Mira has thus hung in a peculiar limbo, as belonging in a very generalized way to the 'folk idiom' or to the articulations of a 'clever, little woman'. This work thus attempts to return Mira to recognizable communities and solidarities and it attempts to place Mira's history within the history of a collective cultural revolt, and within the context of a collective struggle for social emancipation, thus divesting Mira of the isolation imposed upon her by a large number of writers, from Priyadas' time to today.

Bhakti and Mira

We have seen how the existing depictions of Mira have located her within the sphere of domesticity, feminized creativity, and within the expressions of house-bound women. Mira has certainly not been linked to the imaginings of the subordinated, nor has she been seen as an emblem of women's assertion. The most recent work on Mira (that of K. Sangari's) asks questions of the person of Mira which no individual subject can be said to bear (such as 'did she turn to mendicancy only because she was rejected by her natal and marital family? Did she then have to 'fit' into a sanctioned model of sainthood simply as a vulnerable woman seeking a form of security? Were her bhakti and the reputation of celibacy maintained as defensive shields in the absence of patriarchal protection?' etc. Sangari, 7.7.1990: 1468). The search for clues which will make explicable the actions of figures in periods far removed from one's own requires finer tools, and finer questioning.

The majority of the articles in the *Manushi* tenth anniversary issue on 'Women Bhakta Poets' (*Manushi*, Nos. 50, 51, 52—1989) concentrate on the lives of the individual women bhaktas

(Bahinabai, Muktabai, Toral, Amarbai) and their teachings. While it is of great importance to retrieve and bring to light the grave hardships faced by individual women bhaktas, and to pay homage to their lives, there still remains the task of meticulously documenting the transmission of their legacy, the nature of silencing and appropriation that each has been subject to, and the social configurations surrounding the potential and limits of their rebellion.

So, *can* the life of Mira be extrapolated from existing published verses, utilizing the framework of methodological individualism? *Can* Mira be analyzed in terms of what she exemplifies—or does not—as an individual? Mira as a renouncer of her *kul*, Mira as a woman bhakta who did not lend to the formation of a *sampraday*, fits easily, too easily, within the framework of a methodological individualism, and into an uneasy relationship with a body of renouncers and ascetics. I would argue though, that it is a grave misreading of Mira and the Mira phenomenon. It fails on three major counts: firstly, it fails to account for the very specific conditions, the specific social and historical conditions which contributed to the rise of the Mira figure—the 'bhakti momentum' being of very little help in enabling us to understand Mira's place either within the Rajput community which she rejected, or the lower class communities she has inhabited. Secondly, and related, it fails to explain the social force which has led to the Mira figure acquiring such a sharp oppositional force in the Rajput-dominated states of Rajasthan. Thirdly, it fails essentially in seeing Mira as a product of nothing more than her personal convictions and faith. Certainly the power of these convictions and faith should not be underplayed, and should certainly not be reduced to a mere 'product' of the larger religious ferment. If one accepts that someone very akin to the Mira legend existed as an actual social being, the power of her convictions broke the brutal feudal relationships which existed at the time. But for Mira to have survived in social memory in the way that she has done, there must be more than the respect earned through personal faith and conviction.

H.H. Wilson is one of the few writers who granted Mira a collective formation. He referred to a group of 'Mirabais' (in the plural) who he considered formed a sub-division of the Vallabh Vaishnavites, and who he said worshipped Krishna as Ranchhor, adopting Mira as a 'leader' (Wilson, 1862: 136–7.) Wilson's description of the sect of 'Mirabais' is far from satisfactory, especially as there is no supportive evidence for the existence of such a sect in W. India. It seems likely that he was referring to the widows belonging to the Vallabh *sampraday*, who would be looked upon by others, significantly, as having a particular kind of relationship to Mira through the fact of their widowhood, and through their devotion to Krishna. This is certainly the sense in which G.N. Sharma describes the

small sect called Mirabais composed of Brahmans and other caste widows, acknowledging the leadership of the Rajput princess, wearing dress in the manner of Mira and professing the same attachment to Krishna (which) is still in existence in Mewar. These Mirabais maintain themselves on public charity... (Sharma, 1968: 235)

There are a constellation of factors here which lead to the women referred to above as 'Mirabais'. One is that they are widowed, in the main from higher castes, secondly that they are Krishna worshippers, and, probably most significantly, that they are destitute women reliant on charity. There are large numbers of widows who are bereft of family sustenance, who earn their living by a pitiful existence at major pilgrim centres such as Vrndavan, Mathura or Nathdwara, receiving a meagre meal after an enforced period of chanting of prayers (Badhwar *et al.*, November 15, 1987: 139–45). The destitute widows, here dressed in white, are reduced to a conformist life of a degrading and enforced worship and are dubbed 'Mirabais' by a piously repressive society. Both H.H. Wilson and G.N. Sharma have failed to distinguish between those victims who are condemned and lauded at one and the same time by respectable society who dub them as 'Mirabais'—and those who would necessarily have to associate themselves positively as belonging to a distinct sect of Mirabai.

In this work, I give shape, form, and content to Mira, not through an analysis of verses derived from textual collections— but through the place Mira holds within the articulations of very specific peasant and artisan communities in Rajasthan and Gujarat today. The methodology used here has two immediate and palpable results. One is that Mira is *unfrozen* from a textual biography, and emerges very much as a person to whom very specific social and historical relationships have been established. Mira hereby emerges not as a lone bhakta, an isolated creator of verses, or a renouncer, but as living within, and contributing to the formation of a community of Mirabai. Let us now turn to this community.

The Community of Mirabai

The delineation of those who have 'coloured [Mira] with their own colour' (Chaturvedi 1983: 28), raises the question of *communitas* in the Mira bhakti. *Communitas* in the sense of community of relations or feelings (Raymond Williams, 1983: 75) is what emerges so startlingly from the Mira *bhajans*—not the facts of Mira's biography, not a history of a figure whose life is charted in a linear sense, but the processes and relationships involved in Mira spurning the princely community and forging other solidarities.

This *communitas* which emerges out of the bhajans validates Mira's existence, provides her with the acceptance needed to keep her alive in social memory, and provides the emotional nurturance so essential to retain her in a social tradition within which a symbol becomes much more than a sum total of her parts. This community of Mirabai provides first and foremost the support, the network, the embedded social acceptance necessary to have kept her memory alive—all qualities denied to her by the Rajput community, and to a lesser extent, denied to her by the established religious *sampradays*. It is *this* community of Mira which historically has been responsible for providing a powerful social base to the Mira bhakti—upon which other figures of Mira were built upon in the course of time.

Since the community of Mirabai is one based around *communitas*, around a community of *feelings*, (Raymond Williams, 1983: 75) then this community emerges out of the contours of the feelings of those groups whose social experience provides a continuing depth and force to Mira's own experience as this is articulated in the bhajans.

It is rare indeed to gain access to very complex structures of feeling which describe privation, want, humiliation, pain—and the subordinated communities in Rajasthan and Gujarat are able to do this through the medium of the Mira bhajans. Bhajans thus form a crucial medium in the enunciation of a community of feelings.

In India since the medieval times, there has been a long tradition whereby active fellowship of believers have gathered together in an associative life of bhajan singing and in *kirtan*, drawn around the figure of individual bhaktas and the teaching of these bhaktas. The major sustaining element of bhakti which has gone into binding together this fellowship has, precisely, been congregational bhajan singing. No work on bhakti can ignore the vitality and differing permutations that arise from this form of worship. While bhakti has, over the centuries, engendered strong philosophical and scholarly traditions (Ramanuja, Ramanand, the Vrndavan *gosains*), it has also, conversely, given rise to religious fervour and passion which, by emphasizing religious experience as the truth, places the conscience of the believer and the spiritual experience of the devotee over and above both the claims of religious authorities and existing social ties. For women bhaktas, the rejection of the power of male figures whom they were tied to in subordinate relationships became the terrain for struggle, self-assertion and alternative seekings (*Manushi*, tenth anniversary issue, 1989). In this, Mira is in company with Lal Ded, Akka Mahadevi, and other women bhaktas.

While individual bhaktas, both men and women, have gifted to the present, wonderful verses and sayings, socially, it becomes important to locate the various ways in which different groups coalesced around the symbols that these bhaktas became. It is therefore essential to trace the contours of the community that forms around the figure of individual bhaktas. While kinship and caste structures have provided the bedrock of community formation in India, bhakti has on the other hand led to a radically different form of community association—one that is not (at least not initially) based on social prescriptions of birth, caste status, and defined sexual roles, but one that is based on an active will and a choice of belief. This community engendered by bhakti has, at various times, given rise to and nurtured within it figures of rebelliousness (such as Mira) as well as provided shelter to those outside the pale of respectable society. For example, in Bengal, the 'Bostoms', Vaishnavs of a low social status, were of three categories—those who had lost all their relations, widows who had children, and prostitutes who had given up this profession (Chakravarti, 1985: 299). This community has thus, immutably, given refuge over time to both dissenters and those rejected by dominant society.

Namdev a tailor (1270-1350), is credited with the beginning of *kirtan* sessions in Maharashtra, utilizing the songs created by himself as well as others. Namdev was joined in singing and in the worship of Vithoba by people from all walks of life, and from all castes. Namdev considered Chokhamela, an untouchable Mahar, a true bhakta. Janabai, Namdev's serving maid, wrote *abhangs* and was thought to be a bhakta of true devotion. Namdev had around him Gora the potter, Narahari the goldsmith, and Sena the barber. He knew Kanhoptra, a dancing girl too (Zelliot, 1987: 93). Narsinha Mehta, a Saurashtrian bhakta, is said to have danced and sung bhajans with *kartal* in hand amongst the untouchables in their quarters, leading to his being outcasted by the Nagar Brahman community. The gathering of people across the caste barrier and across the sexual divide, is a crucial factor in the formation of a community which is based on like spirits. In the early part of the sixteenth century in Navadvip, the town that Chaitanya was born in, seven separate *kirtan* groups were organized. Each of these groups was led by one of Chaitanya's disciples, and was equipped with cymbals, drums etc. The people of Navadvip, breaking out of the strong control imposed by the Brahmans of the town, were greatly attracted by the songs, processions, and ceremonies organized by Chaitanya and his followers. *Kirtan* singers violated rules of untouchability with impunity (Chakravarti, 1985: 56–7). Women bhaktas like Lal Ded and Akka Mahadevi flouted sexual norms by abandoning their clothes and wandering around naked (*Manushi* tenth anniversary issue, 1989). Congregational devotional singing thus provided a major ground for the growth of both structured, religious communities and congregations and for *communitas*.

There are three different, but interelated meanings attached to the term the 'community of Mirabai' in this work. The obviously recognizable community of Mirabai is that composed of the Mira bhajniks who are identifiable by their knowledge of and commitment to the singing of Mira bhajans. The second crucial meaning attached to the term 'community of Mirabai' are those members, past and present, who may not be active adherents in the evocation of this community, but whose experiences are articulated by the Mira bhajans, these feeding into and giving social depth to the force of the Mira bhajans. These are those who have subjectively experienced the rule of the Rana, those who have experienced the tying of an unwanted marital knot, those who have been widowed, those who have experienced untouchability, and those who have felt the penury of alms seekers. This is the *communitas* that emerges from the Mira bhajans.

The third way in which the term 'community of Mirabai' is used here denotes both the reality of a common life as this emerges from a class configuration and an active class affiliation around the Mira bhakti, and a projection of an imaginative community, a community of affinity, a community of solidarity which nurtures, heals and strengthens the community of the oppressed through the power of a religious expression.

The contours of this community assume a different relational aspect as it shifts its geographical and social location. In Mewar, the locale which bore the blows struck by Mira's acts of rebellion, the community of Mirabai takes a fierce stand against patriarchal political authority and caste arrogance. It flaunts the powerlessness of the Rana, declares itself against untouchability, and vindicates relationships based on one's heart. The community in

Marwar bears a striking resemblance to the Mewar one, and is at one with it in the stands it takes. Mira the rebel emerges most strongly within Mewar and Marwar, and she gives voice to the community standing up against feudal oppression.

It is difficult to disaggregate the three main strands which emerge out of the community of Mirabai—the attack on Rajput political authority, the defiance of patriarchal norms of marriage, and the attack on the caste system. All three co-exist within this community, and in fact co-exist within each articulation of the community, through each bhajan. However, the further Mira travels away from her seat of rebellion, and the closer she gets to Dwarka, the place in which she sought her own particular fulfillment, the more the depth of tension and the complexities of emotions of Mira the woman mendicant emerge. In Saurashtra, in the villages and towns around Dwarka, Mira's suffering under the rule of the Rana is acknowledged, and her challenge to it is vindicated—but the central feature of the Saurashtrian bhajans is an exploration of the position of Mira the mendicant, Mira the exile. The community that emerges in Saurashtra is a community of mendicant singers and alm-seekers, a community of exiles facing harsh privation.

It is significant that it is within Rajasthan and Saurashtra, areas directly linked to the history of Mira, that a moral, political community of Mirabai emerges. There are other versions of Mira, for example in Bengal, which do not bear the stamp of Mira's historical struggle. In Bengal, in one of the *sahajiya* texts written in the middle of the seventeenth century, the *'Vivarata-vilas'* of Akincanadasa, it is claimed that 'Srirupa performed *sadhna* with Mira' (Dimock, 1966: 216.) The linking of Mira to Rupa, one of the main *gosain* who developed Vaishnav canonical literature, and who died between 1556 and 1558, is an attempt to give to the *Vrndavan gosain* a partner of equal spiritual status. The *sadhna* referred to is the sexual ritual undertaken in tantric influenced religions, whereby the man has intercourse with a woman without a seminal discharge (Dimock, 1966: 157.) Despite the approval bestowed on these rituals by writers such as Dimock who claim that it emphasizes the *sahajiyas* 'contempt for the Vedic and

Brahmanical tradition' (Dimock, 1966: 217) the women made use of in this ritual (a ritual to assist the male practitioner to achieve a higher spiritual state) were women from the lowest castes, often untouchables, whose social inferiority was at one and the same time lauded and taken advantage of. The fact that the women are mere instruments in this ritual is made clear in the writings. Yugaldas, in *'Premvilas'* said.

The honeybees... gather honey from many flowers, but afterwards have no further use for the flowers. (Dimock, 1966: 163)

In the *Sahajiya* text, the 'Vivartavilas', Mira is noteworthy simply for being the medium through whom Rupa performed *sadhna*, her history of persecution in Mewar being made secondary if indeed it is not blotted out.

This is not the Mira one is familiar with in the area that this study is concerned with. It is the historical and social grounding of different groups of people in Rajasthan and Saurashtra to Mira's life of struggle that gives the special character to the community of Mirabai.

Here it becomes of critical importance to theorize the centrality of song (and in particular of collective singing) in the formation of community consciousness, community solidarity and in the acquisition of community identity. In this particular instance, the community consciousness and community identity evolved in a continuing process of struggle and sharp class antagonisms—between the Rajput rulers and the ruled, and later, overlaying this, the antagonism between the proponents of a high aesthetic culture, and those committed to giving voice to a collective suffering. The antagonisms surface over both the content of devotional songs—and over the form of worship adopted, articulated and affirmed. It is therefore essential to delineate the way in which bhajans have given an audible public form to the existing class tensions.

The identification of bhajan singing with the 'common people' (Harlan, 1992: footnote 15, 214), the alignment of a common devotional expression with intense emotionality and an 'uncontrolled' fervour (Singer, 1959: 155) has lead to an elite concern with a disruptive and passionate articulation. While the dominant have reacted to this mode of religious expression with some fear and misapprehension, the dominated have sought to give voice to their opposition through it.

The consciousness, emotional sensibility and aesthetic which arises out of the Mira bhajans is one of intense sorrow. This aesthetic is shared by large numbers of oppressed groups who seek to give voice to their experiences and suffering in song and music. The religion of the slaves provides a powerful example of the way in which devotional singing leads to the formation of an acute community and class consciousness.

The religious expression, from the late eighteenth century onwards, of the slaves in the southern states of America are termed 'sorrow songs' by W.E.B. Du Bois (Du Bois, 1961: 181). Frederick Douglass says of these sorrow songs

> Every tone was a testimony against slavery, and a prayer to God for deliverance from chains.... To these songs I trace my first glimmering conception of the dehumanizing character of slavery. (Douglass, 1960: 37–8)

Eugene Genovese has discussed with acute insight the shaping of a slave religion, separate and apart from the masters and one can trace many parallels between this and the bhajan singing of the dominated groups in Rajasthan and Gujarat. The slaves' religion enabled them to stress the values of freedom, and enabled a community of love for one's brothers and sisters, which contributed immensely to their preservation of dignity and self-worth (Genovese, 1974: 246).

The slaves, though, were much more circumscribed by the power and the presence of the white slave holders in their lives than were the subordinate groups in W. India. Despite this, the slaves continued to sing of emancipation, equality and brotherhood. We know that the slave owner and his overseer attempted to control the very character of the songs that the slaves sang, insisting on happy rather than sad ones.

> I have heard that many masters and overseers on these plantations prohibit melancholy tunes or words and encourage nothing but cheerful

music, deprecating the effect of sadder strains upon the slaves whose peculiar musical sensibilities might be expected to make them especially excitable by any songs of a plaintive character, and having reference to their particular hardships

reported Frances Anne Kemble in her *'Journal of a Residence on a Georgian Plantation* 1838–9' (quoted in Katz, 1969: xiv–v).

A black preacher might be rebuked and even run the risk of lynching if he harped too loudly upon the liberation of the Hebrews from Egyptian bondage, the parallels with slavery being too obvious (Katz, 1969: xv.) The 'sadder strains' objected to by the slave owners did not only affect the work pattern of the slaves (crucial in the calculation of a slave holder) but more importantly, songs which were evocative of anguish caused by the institution of slavery were likely to cause disaffection amongst the slaves. One sees here the profoundly subversive power of the combination of religion and musical expression to move a whole community to acquire a cognizance of itself.

The singing of Mira bhajans has faced a similar history of repression too. The fear of losing the patronage of the Sisodiya ruler, the real possibility of being stripped of status and privilege led those who were in the direct employ of the Sisodiya state to disavow any knolwedge of, or commitment to the Mira bhajans (page 69). Those itinerant groups which were not so intrinsically tied to the Rajput hierarchy but who were reliant on their livelihood as popular singers and entertainers on a wider support base, found that they came up against the wrath of the lesser-Sisodiyas in villages when they attempted to evoke Mira in song (pages 178–9). Thus, the Sisodiya Rajputs wielded enormous power over those whom they had authority and the Mira bhajans evolved outside of the boundaries of Rajput rule, amidst the dalit quarters and peasant dwellings.

These Mira bhajans mark both a relationship of conflict between the feudal princely domain and the domain of the subordinated, and they mark too a process of community affirmation whereby the articulation of common experiences and solidarities engendered the validation of an alternative moral framework to the dominant one.

However, a social history of Mira and the Mira bhajans does not simply celebrate the features of oppositional culture, and subjective expressions found in the space unclaimed by the ruling classes. Neither does it demonstrate a simple affirmation of self-respect and sublimated aspirations. It lives, rather, as a tense but purposeful possibility, poised on the brink of a potentially liberationary moment, but shackled by its lack of engagement with political movements, and hemmed in by a usurping mass culture.

Gramsci, in his cultural writings has pointed to the existence of a 'morality of the people' which is distinct from and in opposition to 'official' morality, the former containing imperatives which are

much stronger, more tenacious and more effective than those of official 'morality'. (Gramsci, 1985: 190.)

Gramsci has argued that this 'morality of the people' is un-elaborated, unsystematized, and by its very nature lacking in a centralized political articulation (Gramsci, 1985: 188–9). While Gramsci's distinction between the morality of the people and official morality is extremely important, I will show in this work that the people's morality, as this arises from the Mira bhakti, rather than being a confused agglomerate of fragments, is systematic and coherent, containing within it an alternative set of social relationships[4]. The task of this work is to detail the people's morality embedded around the figure of Mira, as this relates, inter-acts with, and responds to other social moralities over time. One must enter the vale of tears to grasp the conditions of the people's morality. Mira enables us to enter this vale.[5]

PART ONE

PART ONE

Chapter Two

Opposing Loyalties: Mira's Bhakti and Rajput Dharma

Mira's history is inextricably linked to the two ruling families of Rajasthan, the Mertiya Rathors who established and held sway over the region of Merta for less than a hundred years, and the Sisodiyas of Mewar state, who have come down in Indian history as the valorous protectors of Hindu polity against Muslim invasions. The most bitter invective levelled at Mira by the Rajputs themselves, which retains its venom even today, is that she was a *'kul-nasi'*, a destructress of the clan. In order to understand what it was in Mira's deeds and being which elicited the wrath of the Rajput ruling families one must understand the centrality of the *kul* in Rajput polity, and understand the nature of Rajput *dharma* to which Mira's bhakti articulated an antithesis. I will first analyze the meaning of the term Rajput, second, delineate the main features of the *bhaiyad*, the brotherhood, and then go on to examine the nature of Rajput *dharma*, as enunciated in the ideal projected. It is precisely the illusions of an epoch one is seeking to unravel, for it is in these that are embodied the ideals that every Rajput is deemed to strive for.

Much is imputed in the term 'Rajput', a term for the warrior class which clashed fiercely amongst itself and other groups to retain territory based on conquest. In the sixteenth century, apart from the state of Mewar, the other Rajput states of what later came to be called Rajasthan, accepted the domination of Mughal rule. However, though the majority of the Rajput states did not retain their territorial integrity, they retained the much vaunted legends of glorified militarism and chivalrous self-sacrifice. Tod's writings, *'Annals and Antiquities of Rajasthan'* in three volumes (Tod, 1971) best exemplifies this. Tod, the British political agent of Mewar from 1818 to 1822, did much to keep alive the glories of dominant Rajput values.

In the face of British colonial onslaught, nationalist historiography turned to the examples of Rana Sanga and Rana Pratap of Mewar as freedom fighters of yore. Sober post independence historians such as Rajat K. Ray, too portray the state of Mewar as one which

exhibited the ancient and uncorrupted condition of Hindu polity practically unchanged by Mughal interference,

and as being the only dynasty which

outlived six centuries of Turkish domination in the same ancestral lands where their forefathers had staked out a claim before the coming of the Muslims

who

proudly maintained the purity of their stock by refusing to follow the other princes of Rajputana who gave their daughters in marriage to the Mughals. (Ray, 1978: 206.)

In this, and similar portrayals, the rulers of Mewar are depicted as being notable for their pristine stands against Mughal rule. What has been missing is a serious and sustained critique of medieval Rajput polity, both in terms of the coercion entailed in the rule of the Ranas, and, more deeply, the values and beliefs inscribed within their systems of power. It is here that Mira makes a dramatic entry, with her spurning of the power of the Rana, and her repudiation of loyalty to a rule based on the principle of force. Mira's history does not give sustenance to a brutal feudal order, but rather, challenges it from deep within.

Mira emerged at a time when the term *'Rajput'*, as denoting a *jati*, was consolidating, and at a time when the states of Marwar and Mewar were establishing greater state control over their dominions. Rajasthani sources portray the earlier founding fathers of these states as being no more than herders of cattle, or as agriculturalists (Ziegler, 1973: 17). The term *'Rajput'* before the fifteenth century meant 'horse soldier', 'trooper', 'headman of a village' or 'subordinate chief'. Moreover, individuals with whom the word was associated were generally considered to be products of *varna-samkara*, of mixed caste origin, and thus inferior in rank to Kshatriyas (Ziegler, 1976, 242–3.)

The Rajput clans which ensued, occupied Rajasthan between the seventh and the twelfth century. By the fifteenth century they occupied practically the whole of Rajasthan. The change from *varna* to *jati* went hand in hand with colonization of new areas within which the process of the expansion of agrarian economy went. It is then that the term 'Rajput', began to be employed (Chattopadhyay, 1976: 62). Epigraphic evidence from the Sisodiya dynasty points to the fifteenth century as being the defining period when this change occurred (Ziegler, 1976: 242). It is important to note that Muslims were included in the definition of the term 'Rajput', that they were deemed to be part of this *jati*. The Muslims included in this term were those who were warriors of power. The *jati* was the Rajput: within this, were those warriors from Hindu and Muslim background (Ziegler, 1973: 59).

Varna was then replaced by numerous and more particularistic *jatis*, which followed separate occupations and livelihoods, and which were scattered over a large territory (Ziegler, 1973: 173). Subordinate *jatis* arose to those which were dominant ones, and it is these subordinated *jatis* that took to Mira when she broke from the ruling Rajput families.

Mira's life is bound up with the Rathors, who held power in the state of Marwar. Rao Jodha laid the foundation of a fort and city of Jodhpur (the Rathor Capital) in AD 1459. The Rathors of Marwar had subjugated the Mers of this area, and, by the fourteenth century, ruled over Pali, Khed, Bhadrajun, Kodra, Mahewa, Barmer and some area of Bikaner (Sharma, 1977: 3). At the time of Jodha's death in AD 1488, Rathor power extended over a larger domain than any of his predecessors. Jodha had fourteen sons, who apportioned to themselves the best lands of the area (Tod, 1971: 949) under the system of *bhai-bant*, in which the male members of a clan had right of access to territory over which they held control. Duda was the fourth son of Jodha and he established his rule over Merta in AD 1462 (Bhatti, 1986, 20). The Mertiya Rathors were said to be small but independent rulers till they were brought under the suzerainty of the parent Jodhpur state by Maldeo in AD 1556. Mira would thus have been born in an independent state of Merta, which would, however, have been inferior in status and power to the state of Mewar into which she was married.

Merta, though not as powerful a state as Mewar, was nevertheless of importance, its capital lying on the main trade route to Delhi. Duda had established sway over Merta by AD 1468. The Rathor *sardars* and princes of newly founded *thikanas* settled in their respective territories other Rajputs and Jats by inviting them from neighbouring areas, to extend the area under cultivation and increase the number of people loyal to them (Sharma, 1977: 6). Muhnot Nainsi[1] in his *'Marwar ra Pargana ri Vigat'*, written in the seventeenth century, provides important detail for Merta in this period. The *pargana* of Merta was agriculturally well developed in the seventeenth century, compared to adjoining areas, being well irrigated and growing wheat in 165 out of 334 villages. The Jats formed the largest group within the peasantry. Apart from wheat, gram, opium, and musk melon were grown. Two other important crops grown were cotton and indigo, making Merta an important textile producing centre. At this time, the peasants had half of their produce extracted from them as *bhog* from the *rabi* crop, and they had to give a third of their *kharif* crop to the state (Bhidwani, 1975: 217–21). In Mughal India generally, the rates would not have been much dissimilar, which though varying from tract to tract, meant that the conditions of the peasant generally approximated to the lowest possible levels of subsistence (Habib, 1963: 191).

Merta emerges as a flourishing trading centre from the sixteenth to the nineteenth centuries. There were a large number of *mahajans* and *multanis* in the town of Merta (2,638 out of a total of 5,860) which shows that in the seventeenth century, Merta was an important financial centre. It was on the main route connecting Gujarat to Agra. Markets were held every week in the town of Merta where indigo, cotton wool, yarn and cotton cloth were sold (Bhidwani, 1975: 224). It is significant that textiles and shoes (entailing the labour of weavers and leather-workers) were the main exports from the town of Merta (Sharma, 1981: 76). The state and town within which Mira was brought up (Merta), thus had growing numbers of artisans engaged in the production of textiles and leather goods, who were considered to be untouchable. It is likely that these groups would have taken to the message of Mira quickly. Together with other urban, financial centres of Rajasthan, Merta declined in the nineteenth century under British rule, especially with the break-up of the earlier trade routes and the shifting of the centre of trade to Bombay. From the early twentieth century onwards, Merta declined drastically, it being proportionately much larger in AD 1663 than in 1921, and larger in 1921 than in 1961 (Bhidwani, 1975: 225).

In the sixteenth century, the Mertiya Rathors underwent many political vicissitudes. Caught between the expansionism of the state of Marwar (Jodhpur) and the growing threat to their power posed by the Mughals, the Mertiya Rathors increasingly combined their forces with those of Mewar, to oppose the invasion of the Mughals from Turkistan. In the battle against Babur in AD 1527 the Rathors of Marwar made a combined stand with the Sisodiya ruler against the Mughal onslaught. It ended in defeat, with Rana Sanga of Mewar seriously wounded, and the death of Ratan Singh (who is said to be the father of Mira).

Maldeo intensified the process of centralization of state power in Marwar. Viramdeo, Rao Duda's eldest son, ruled over Merta in AD 1536. Maldeo, claiming rule over members of his clan, wrote to Viramdeo

Merta is yours, but in the house, I am the *tikayat*, you are my *bhai-bandh chakar*.

i.e. that Viramdeo could continue holding Merta, but only as a subordinate servant of the ruler of Jodhpur (Sharma, 1977: 10). Merta ceased to exist as an independent state in 1556 when Maldeo wrested it from Jaimal, building a fort and wall around the town. Jaimal then sought to give of his services to Rana Sanga who made a grant of Badnor, with its 360 townships to Jaimal and the Mertiya Rathors. Tod describes the Mertiya Rathors as one of the 'great vassals' of Mewar, who in return for obtaining the grant of the territory of Badnor, gave their lives in fidelity to the ruler of Mewar whose salt they had eaten (Tod, 1971: 955). The history of the Mertiya Rathors, within whom Mira was born, ended in their subordination and incorporation within the state of Mewar. Jaimal Rathor died in the defence of Chittorgarh against Akbar in AD 1567, and a hero stone commemorates this at the entrance of the fort. The very fort Mira left, never to see again, was defended by close members of her family, and the land she swore never to set foot on again, having faced persecution there from the Sisodiya family, succoured her kin in the 360 townships. Mira's history is remembered as embodying a life of sustained rejection of the ruler of the state of Mewar, while the Mertiya Rathors gave their loyalty and their allegiance to the rulers of Mewar.

Sisodiya rule in Mewar is traced back to Bappa Rawal who came to Nagda from Idar about AD 728 (Tod, 1971: 281). Bappa Rawal rendered subject the Bhils in the area and took Chittor from the Mori princes, the then sovereigns in this land (Tod, 1971: 265). Rahup then came to the throne of Chittor in AD 1201 and he defeated the Rathor Rana Mokal of Mandore, the capital of the Rathor state then being shifted to Jodhpur by Jodha in AD 1459. Rahup made Mokal renounce the title of Rana in his favour. The constant struggle for power between the two clans in this region, the Rathors and the Sisodiyas is a discernible theme throughout this period, with the Sisodiyas retaining the upper hand, both ideologically and politically. However, it was not till the reign of Rana Kumbha that the area under the rule of the Sisodiyas was expanded, strengthened and consolidated. Kumbha had 32 fortresses built in his life. The most important of these was

Kumbhalgadh overlooking the plains of Marwar. Kumbha erected a citadel at the peak of Abu, fortified the passes between the western frontier and Abu, built the fort of Vasanti near Sirohi, and established the fort of Machin to defend Deogarh against the Mers of Aravalli. He re-established, too, Ahor and other smaller forts to overawe the Bhils of Jharol and Panarwa (Tod, 1971: 336). Kumbha's reign (1433–68) laid the foundation for strong, centralized rule. In AD 1440. Kumbha defeated Mahmud Khalji, sovereign of Malwa, and held him captive in Chittor. The Tower of Victory (the Kirti Stambha) was erected in Chittor to commemorate this victory in battle. There is no doubt that there was fierce strife with the expansionist Muslim dynasties, but it is clear that this was not seen as a fight between two competing religions. This communal colouring was not given to the history of this period till the nineteenth century (Ziegler, 1976: 239). An essential part of the design at Kirti Stambha is the name of Allah repeated in bands on the third and eighth storeys which is coeval with the building of the pillar, and not a later addition (Garrick, 1887: 116).

Rana Sanga succeeded to the throne of Chittor in AD 1508. His reign was noteworthy for the formidable confederacy he was able to organize in the war against Babur. The 1527 battle at Kanauj saw the death of not only Ratan Singh of Merta, but also of Rawal Udai Singh of Dungarpur with two hundred of his clan; Ratna of Salumbar with three hundred of his Chundawat kin; Raimal Rathor, son of the ruler of Marwar; two Chauhan chiefs of the first rank in Mewar and many more. Sanga was an astute tactician, an able administrator and he displayed at his death all the gory marks of a Rajput hero: an eye lost in the dispute over succession with his brother, an arm lost in battle with the Lodi king of Delhi, and eighty marks of wounds on various parts of his body (Tod, 1971: 358).

The fortress of Chittorgadh occupies a symbolic position for the ruling clan of Mewar. Tod gives it great weight in his writings: 'There is sanctity in the very name of Chitor' (Tod, 1971: 362.)

Forming the centre of Sisodiya rule, displaying its military might, and standing as the embodiment of the height of Sisodiya rule, Chittorgadh still dominates the consciousness of the people of Mewar today. It was thrice sacked—in 1303, in 1534 and lastly by Akbar in 1567. Thirteen hundred women are deemed to have burned themselves alive in 1534, rather than be taken captive. A *johar* took place in 1567 too, in which nine queens, five princesses with two infant sons, and the families of chiefs who were not at their estates, are said to have died in the flames (Tod, 1971: 363,381). If Mira had been living in Chittor at one of these times, as a prominent woman of the ruling clan, the *johar kund* would have stared her in her face. Mira had sundered herself from the fortunes of the Rajputs though, and her fate was not dependant on the political victory or defeat of the Sisodiya princes.

Lok Devta and Rajput Hegemony

The imposition of rule in the area of Mewar and Marwar was arrayed in a cloak of religious sanctity. It was believed that the foundation of the state of Jodhpur was foretold by a *jogi* (Tod, 1971: 948). The founder of Mewar state was also initiated into Shiv worship by a Nath *jogi*. It was said that Bappa Rawal gained a shield and sword through the worship of Shiv, thereby acquiring a spiritual legitimacy to his predatory power (Briggs, 1973: 245). Bappa Rawal had a temple built to Shiv at Eklingji, which remained the centre of worship for the rulers of Mewar. Tod gives a graphic picture of the religion of the Rajput which as a Shaivite system of beliefs stands in contradiction to Krishna worship.

The Rajput he said, 'worships his horse, his sword and the sun', he 'delights in blood', and glories in warfare (Tod, 1971: 81–2). Although Kumbha wrote a commentary on the *Gitagovinda*, and Jaimal Rathor is said to be a Vaishnav, the Sisodiyas were by and large staunch Shiva (and Mahakali) worshippers. The antagonism of the Sisodiyas to Mira was not merely a sectarian one of Shaivites against a Vaishnav worshipper. It was, rather, a wider battle between an individual holding on to the principle of love through Krishna—and the political authority of the Ranas based on force and might.

Apart from the sanctity conferred on the rulers of Mewar and Jodhpur states by the Naths, Rajput rule and norms penetrated deep into society through the deification of certain warriors who died in battle. The glorification of the symbols of war—the sword, the horse, the skull—is symptomatic of the glorification of death in battle. Not only were male warriors who died in battle worshipped, but Rajput women were crucial lynch-pins in upholding the value of dying for one's allegiance and honour. Rajput history is replete with examples of women who goaded and sent forth their men into battle with words celebrating victory or glorious death. Mothers railed at their sons for not having

the heart of a true Rajput [which] dances with joy at the mere name of strife... some carl must have stolen to my embrace, and from such ye must be sprung. (Tod, 1971: 718.)

Women renowned for their attachment to a particular lord, sent him into battle in the foreknowledge of ultimate defeat (Tod, 1971: 726). The example of a newly wed queen, who doubted that her lord would be able to do fierce battle because he was enamoured of her, and who thus beheaded herself, asking that her head be sent to him on a platter before the commencement of battle in order to renew his vigour for war, is today repeated and retold by those who continue to hark back to feudal values.

Certain Rajput warriors who died in battle between the eleventh and the fifteenth centuries, began to be deified in a serious way in the sixteenth and seventeenth centuries, again at a time that state power was being consolidated. It was Maldeo of Jodhpur who granted villages to Mithu Mehta, the first writer to put down on paper the stories of Goga, Pabu etc., thus consolidating the worship of these war heroes (Maheshvari, 1980: 59). These Rajput deified heroes subsequently became *lok devtas*, worshipped by large sections of the peasantry and artisanal classes. Of these Ramdev Pir has had the most profound influence, not only in Rajasthan but in Gujarat and parts of Madhya Pradesh too.

The support given to Meghvals by Ramdev Pir, the shelter given to Thoris, a small subordinate group who are said to be like

Bhils, by Pabu (M.R.M. 1891: 564) and the widespread worship of these figures drew into the Rajput fold large sections of society. What was upheld through these Rajput deities was valour in battle, a life glorifying blood and gore, and death through a fierce protection of land and property. A highly virulent patriarchal system was created, in which the theft of cattle was represented in ritual terms of symbolic castration of the men whose herds had been stolen (Ziegler, 1973: 81). Those threatened by this symbolic castration responded by proving their valour in battle.

Though it is correct that these *lok devtas* sanctified Rajput rule, it is important to note that different communities have interpreted these Rajput deities in their own particular way and have made these figures accord more with their own lives. Ramdevji is the best example of this. From being a Rajput hero, he has been transformed into a champion of the dalits. Ramdev Pir is now a symbol of the assertion of dalits in western India. This is recognized by the upper castes who affirm that '*Ramdevji ko mile so Dhed hi Dhed*', i.e. that only the Dheds are found with Ramdevji. In Saurashtra, the worship of Ramdev pir is derogatorily referred to as the '*Dhediya panth*'.

Pabu is similarly revered by the Thoris for granting them a respectable position, and the Raikas of Rajasthan, a nomadic community, associate Pabu with the cure of camels rather than being a warrior of power. A number of stories and beliefs link the *lok devtas* to the theme of snake bites. The worship of Goga and Teja is said to cure snake bites, and both these figures are depicted through the symbol of a snake in village shrines (Pema Ram, 1977: 34). Thus what had initially symbolized militaristic valour became transformed as it reached the other classes. The process of establishing hegemony was by no means axiomatic.

The Kul and Bhaiyad

In order to understand Mira's rejection of Rajput authority, it is necessary to delineate its internal structure. The structure of the *kul* and the *bhaiyad* (brotherhood) were closely linked to the systems of land ownership, and to the system of political power and sovereignty in the states of Rajasthan. The *kul* included all those related to a common ancestor by ties of male blood. The *bhaiyad* was the brotherhood composed of the sons and brothers of the ruler who held power over land conquered by them. At its simplest, the chief of the *kul*, the clan was the hereditary head. The rule of primogeniture held although this was not always adhered to in practice. The territory was divided off and inherited amongst the various branches of the dominant clan. While the sovereignty of the chief was accepted, he was at the same time treated as the first among equals (Sharma, 1977: 5).

The *bhaiyad* was held together not just by a common material interest in wielding power over a particular region, but by close-knit bonds of loyalty and fidelity to each other and to the continuity of their own rule. The two entities, brotherhood and land, were felt to be inseparably linked and mutually supportive. Other brotherhoods of the same clan were comprised of more distantly related 'brothers', occupying territories of their own (Ziegler, 1978: 223–4).

Rajput honour, both collective and individual, and the concern with its preservation form an integral part of the overall concern with the maintenance of power and rank of the brotherhood. Two rules which bring this out most clearly were first, the emphasis on the avenging of the murder of kinsmen, and second, the rule enjoining that no killing take place within the same group of kin. Both these rules laid stress on solidarity, and the expectation was that individuals whose social existence was defined with reference to the brotherhood, would render support, particularly against outsiders (Ziegler, 1978: 232).

Highly complex notions of fidelity to the brotherhood ensured the continuity of an ideal notion of living in service to this structure of power. While solidarity to the brotherhood was often broken, most frequently through internecine struggle by sons and brothers aiming to wrest control of the throne, it is not likely that the brotherhood could have brooked a challenge by an individual woman such as Mira. The term *kul nasi*, destructress of the clan, which was levelled at Mira shows starkly that Mira's actions within her life-time were interpreted as striking a blow against the whole corporate clan of Sisodiyas. Within Rajput society, a woman who was seen to actively engage in destroying the foundation of the clan's existence, which was based on loyalty, would not have been tolerated.

The *bhaiyads*, the brotherhoods, did not remain egalitarian and undifferentiated structures. Indeed, it was during the period of the sixteenth century that increasing differentiation was taking place, with the chief increasingly asserting his power over the rest of the brotherhood and the clan, setting himself up as more than the first among equals. The institutions of rulership and clientship developed greatly during the sixteenth and seventeenth centuries at the expense of kinship as a basis of organization. As rulers gained wider control over land which representatives of their own clans had traditionally dominated, they sought to transform relationships on these lands from those based on kinship and customary access by birthright, into relationships based on service and exchange (Ziegler, 1978: 226). Thus, loyalty demanded was not based just on patriarchal concepts of kin and devotion to the head of the clan (although these values still continued), but also on the notion of the ruler as a dominant head of a highly stratified state system. Mira's challenge to the Rana of Mewar, as ruler, head of clan and husband, meant that she did not cede allegiance to any of the structures of political and patriarchal power. Mira was thus seen as a *kul nasi*, as a person who spurned the basis of Rajput hierarchy. Mira then had no choice but to leave Chittor in pursuance of her own goals. That she survived to lead a life outside of this ruling sphere would suggest that she had a powerful following which offered her some protection. Medieval Rajput state systems are notorious for their brutal elimination of individuals who stand in their way. The stories of the Rana sending Mira a cup of poison, and a venomous snake, are stylized means of pointing to a deep-rooted hatred borne towards Mira by the ruling Sisodiya family.

Today, in the villages of Mewar, and most tragically in the villages around Chittor, poorer Rajput cultivators revile the memory of Mira. The hostility to Mira is not limited to the Rajputs of the royal house-hold, but it permeates right down, to humbler Rajputs who have not seized upon Mira as a symbol of liberation. Writing in the early years of the nineteenth century, Tod reported:

> The poorest Rajput of this day retains all the pride of ancestry, often his sole inheritance. (Tod, 1971: 162.)

Lyall similarly observed that,

> the tradition of common ancestry has preserved among them the feeling which encourages a poor Rajput yeoman to hold himself as good a *gentilhomme* as his Chief and immeasurably superior to a high official of the professional class. (Lyall, 1899: 248.)

Though the ruler of the state was consolidating his own power against that of the clan, the clan did not take to a figure like Mira who emerged at this time to spurn the authority of the Rana. The term *kul-nasi* shows that Mira was seen as a threat to the prestige of the whole clan.

Rajput Dharma

Mathai sut bandho cho. Hathe hathiyar jhalo cho. Rajputro kholiyo dhariyo chai. Marano ekarsum chai. (You tie a turban round the head. You hold a weapon in your hand. You have assumed the body of a Rajput. The opportunity to die comes only once). (Ziegler, 1973: 67.)

The above crystallizes what constituted the moral being of a Rajput. It is important to understand what bound one Rajput to another and to society around him or her in order to contrast the bonds articulated by Mira. The process of differentiation which intensified in the sixteenth century within the Rajput clans, brought into being the ideology of *samm dharma*, or duty to one's lord. There were two grades within the Rajput *jati*—the *chote* Rajputs and the *rajvi* Rajputs. The distinction here was between ordinary (*chote*) Rajputs and royal (*rajvi*) ones. The former included the *gimvara*, the Rajputs who were peasants. In contrast to the brotherhood there developed the form of organization of the master and his servants. Beneath the sovereign but outside the circle of the royal family was a category of servants called *chakar*. The term *chakar* was restricted to mean someone who performed military or administrative service for the ruler, in return for which he was granted access to land. All Rajputs would be familiar with the hierarchy which denoted who was a *chakar* of whom.

Being a *chakar* entailed giving one's life in the service of one's master. This was the main axiom of Rajput *dharma*. The terms *samm, swami* and *dhani* were used for one's master. In addition to master, these terms are also used to refer to God and one's husband. The system of service was elaborated so that there was service to the ruler, service to those who wielded power at the local level (who in turn were *chakars* of the ruler) and so on down the hierarchy until one entered the family, where the *dhani*, the husband, was the master. Acceptance of the power of the *dhani* was crucial to the maintenance of one's own position within this system.

Mira did not accept the Rajput *dharma* of service to one's *dhani*. She spurned the power of the ruler and husband over her, and refused to grant him her allegiance. She declared that she was the *chakar* of Krishna and would serve no-one else. Mira's bhakti tore aside every vestige of social and political allegiance to the ruling family of Mewar. It marked the inability of a newly consolidating nobility to draw forth from an individual in its very midst the required loyalty.

Mira's stand was in stark contrast to *samm dharma*. Service to the master required sacrifice through brave and valorous acts in battle. This included support for the group to which the ruler belonged, to all the enmities and prejudices of the ruler, and entailed the taking on of all allegiances forged by the ruler.[2] As far as women were concerned, it entailed that they reproduce through their actions the system based on loyalty, obedience and giving of one's life for the master.

Women formed an important bulwark in the perpetuation of Rajput *dharma*. Not only did many of them support Rajput power, which was based on the exercise of militaristic strength, but women were used through the institution of marriage to wipe out previously held vendettas and forge new alliances.

Vair (vendetta), and the acceptance of the obligation for vengeance of the death of a father or a member of the brotherhood, was a principle of Rajput *dharma*. It was deemed that such a death reduced the strength of the brotherhood. It could be settled only by an act of equalization, either by killing the person responsible for the deed, or a close male relative. Otherwise it would have to be avenged by subordinating the foe in battle. (Ziegler, 1973: 71-2).

Vair was an essential element in the Rajput code of conduct. What is important to note here is that the system of marriage within the Rajputs was embedded in a history and working of *vair*. If the *vair* was between two different clans, then short of battle, the murder could only be avenged if the defeated side gave a daughter in marriage (Ziegler, 1973: 71-2). Through the act of giving a daughter, the male members would in effect be announcing their subordination publicly. Instead of being bitter foes, the two sides would then become *saga*, or related through marriage. So a marriage involved within it a history of war, of hatred, of revenge. At the very least it involved the forging of an alliance between two lineages of very unequal power.

A part of the ethic of war among Rajputs was the acceptance of daughters in marriage from the conquered group while not giving a daughter to a group of Rajputs which had been subordinated. A hypergamous system of marriage thus developed whereby women were always married into a family of superior status than the one they had been born into (Karve, 1965: 168-9). One must remember that the state of Merta (let alone the small domain held by Mira's father) was puny in comparison to the might of the Chittor state. A marriage of a Mertni to a Sisodiya prince entailed her subjection to a stronger political power.

At the time of the marriage ceremony itself, the woman ceased to belong to her paternal family, and became a member of her husband's. Among Rajputs, though, she continued to retain the name of her paternal clan, thus the reference is always to Rathori Mira.

The marriage of Bappa Rawal is described in great and laudatory terms by Tod who freely admits to being the apologist for the Rajput cause (Tod, 1971: 858). Bappa Rawal, from whom the Sisodiyas trace their ancestory, is said to have 'froliced' with the daughter of the Solanki chief as well as other village 'maidens'. 'One frolic was as good as another'. This resulted in a 'heterogenous issue' for whom Bappa Rawal bore no responsibility, having fled into the mountains (Tod, 1971: 261-2).

This same apologist has a bizarre tale to tell about Mira. Having described how Kumbha married Mira who was noted for her beauty and piety, Tod then goes on to describe, within the same paragraph and in the next line, how:

Kumbha mixed gallantry with his war like pursuits. He carried off the daughter of the chief of Jhalawar, who had been betrothed to the prince of Mandor: this renewed the old feud, and the Rathor made many attempts to redeem his affianced bride. (Tod, 1971: 338.)

It is clear that the humiliation of an opponent through the capture of women from the opposite camp, and the flaunting of military might and virility were embedded within the practices of the Rajput ruling class.

At the murder of Kumbha's father, Rana Mokal, in 1433 Mokal's maternal uncle Rao Ran Mal Rathod had come to Chittor to avenge his death. Ran Mal, having killed Chacha and Maira, two military officers responsible for Mokal's death, married Chacha's daughter himself, using Chacha's body as a *bajot* to sit on during the wedding ceremony (Sarda, 1932: 40).

There were two alternatives to the dominant man-woman relationship. One was the emergence of romantic love, which formed the theme for legends and epics such as *'Dhola Maru ra Duha'*, which expressed the yearning between two people who loved each other but who were thwarted in realizing it. The other alternative was the world of bhakti. This had an intense emotional thrust. This would have been attractive to a woman of sensitivity who sought to escape the hatred and domination which underlay the Rajput system of marriage. Mira's bhakti must be seen essentially as enunciating the principle of love in an age and a society marked by war, vendetta and the rising power of the state.

Bhakti enabled Mira to uphold a life based on love. Bhakti enabled her to establish a relationship which was of her choosing and which was self-directive. The power to express and bestow a love was of her own volition. Krishna was a potent figure in northern India at this time, and Krishna worship was a powerful force. Krishna appeared in various forms and was worshipped in multifarious ways. Jaydev's Krishna as portrayed in the *Gitagovinda* was a highly sexualized figure. Narsinha Mehta's Krishna was the amorous lover of *gopis* and Chaitanya's bhakti embodied the *rasik ras*. Mira's Krishna on the other hand, symbolized divine love as a guiding principle in life in a milieu which upheld its opposite.

The Challenge of Mira Bhakti

Mira's challenge to Rajput *dharma* lay not simply in her enunciation of Krishna bhakti, but in the stands that she took in the pursuance of her love for Krishna. She posited the power of her relationship with Krishna against her relationship to the Rana, her lord and husband. This earthly master meant nothing to her. She refused to consummate the relationship. At his death, she refused to immolate herself with him, declaring that the tie with her beloved was an immortal one, and that she did not accept the status of a widow. Mira accepted the supremacy and mediation of none save Krishna. At a time when the ruling family was consolidating its political power, Mira's challenge marked the impotence of the Rana to elicit a devotion from a woman that his self image was so intrinsically linked to.

Mira brought into question the authority of a prince, a husband, a patriarch all at the same time. If she had upheld her love of Krishna quietly in her heart, or within the precincts of a temple, this would have been tolerated. What was not tolerated was her *public* affirmation of this. Even before she left the fortress of Chittor, she is said to have kept company with itinerant bhaktas and danced and sung in their company. Mira thus did not keep to the code of conduct expected of a woman from a Rajput ruling family.

It is precisely this antagonism—the conflict between the demands of a warring state power and the dictates of one's heart—that lies central to the Mira bhakti. And it is this conflict that resonates in the bhajans today. Her breaking of loyalty then resonated with those who were ground down by the power of the Rana. Mira broke the loyalty to *kul*, to prince and husband and created a new life based on love.

PART TWO

PART TWO

Chapter Three

A Community Forged: The Birth of a Song

Bhattnagarji belongs to a family of *killedars*, (fortkeepers) in the fortress of Chittor. The Bhattnagars were brought from Gaya in 1299, and they continued as *killedars* throughout the period of princely rule in Mewar, being given *jagirs* by the ruling family. Today, Bhattnagarji lives within the fortress of Chittor, and his experience is an important indicator of the way Mira's name was obliterated within the state of Mewar. He works in the Finance Department of the Collectors Office in the town of Chittor, and when I met him he began by laughing about the irony of discussing the history of Mira within a state office. Bhattnagarji was emphatic that this would not have been permissible if he had been working for the princely state, as his father had done. He stated that no one with any link to the state of Mewar would have dared to utter the name of Mira.

No, it was not that we were ordered to never mention the name of Mira. We knew not to. Mira was not just part discarded by the princely family. She was hated completely. Those who gave us *jagirs*, those we were in service to, remained silent on the history of Mira. I know that if anyone had dared to talk about her, he would have been thrown out of state service.

Sing Mira's bhajans? How can one sing or hear the bhajans of someone whose name is not to be uttered. You do not know the strength of feeling against Mira. This carried on right till my time. Today, the old terror still exists in the rural areas, and people are still not free to express themselves. But things are changing. I have always admired and loved Mira. Now, I am free to express this, sitting in this office, talking to you. I am now free to participate in the singing of Mira bhajans. Come up to the fortress where I live. You will meet an old, blind Teli there who sings Mira bhajans beautifully.[1]

The bhajniks of Mewar are aware that they, and only they, have retained the history of Mira. Huki Kodra Patel (photo VIII), a fifty year old widow who comes from the Anjania Patel community, and who lives on her own in the village Dechra in Udaipur district tilling her unirrigated nine *vighas* of land, said in the quiet that followed a Mira bhajan sung during a bhajan gathering.

They only sing about their warriors and their battles, pointing in the general direction of Udaipur. *We* sing Mira.

On the bus to Deogarh, a group of Od women, who were brick kiln workers in Udaipur travelling to Pratapgarh in order to accompany someone recently widowed back to her parental home, on being told of my work, sang a number of Mira bhajans with great zest, swaying with the bus and clapping for emphasis. Pratapi Modhu Od said,

Mira made Rohidas, a Chamar, her guru.

She smiled in appreciation.

Obviously the Rajputs could not tolerate this.

In the village of Basi near Chittor, when I asked a group of dalits in a bhajan gathering whether Dhakars (a cultivating caste,) sing Mira, Devaram Salvi, who had woven cotton till ten years previously, but then had been granted land by the government, and was at the time employed in relief works replied:

No, the Thakurs will never sing. Mira.

(He had misheard Thakur for Dhakar.)

They tried to kill her for having brought shame on their name. Why should they sing of her?

The chowkidar of Hava Mahal in the fort of Kumbhalgadh asked me what I thought of the palace. I replied that I had come there as I was studying Mira's history. His face lit up, and he said simply:

Mira to Mira hi thhi. (Mira was Mira i.e. there is no one like her.)

However, no Rajput in Mewar will bestow the name of Mira on his daughter. To ask this, and thereby concede this possibility, is to him an insult. And yet large sections of people in Rajasthan identify with Mira, value her life and hold her close in their everyday existence. Dalits on pilgrimage to Ranuja for the Ramapir *mela* from Mewar, when asked where it is that they come from, will answer:

Mirabai ke desh se. (From the land of Mira).

It is an answer which resonates with the other pilgrims. Mira is a living presence in Mewar, both as a continuing threat to the Rajputs, and as a source of inspiration and identification for the lower classes.

The Past Behind the Present

How then does one grapple with the presence of Mira within the lower classes? What are the historical and social processes which make explicable why certain identifiable groups took to Mira? Can one begin to identify the processes that led to the formation of the Mira bhajniks? Since the evidence at hand is through the contemporary oral sources, it becomes essential to look at the possibilities of expanding and broadening the insights derived from these sources, and to place them within wider social processes. Let us then begin to examine the nature of the Mira bhajan tradition as an expression not just of contemporary woes and community affirmation, but as a medium which contains a strong historical record.

The Mira bhajan tradition contains within itself, and in its articulation, strong traces of the past, and traces of the way in which this particular tradition came into being. Since it is not an elite articulation, well chronicled in the written texts and enfolded within the structures of power, it has left traces of its existence in a sphere of life which is separate and apart from the dominant one. It is a form of bhakti which is not ritualized and displayed in temples and *havelis,* but is expressed in the arena where people recreate themselves in intimate family and community. This space is not intruded into by those who are not involved in the recreating of this community, but who reap the labour thereof. The Mira bhakti has emerged and come down to us through the affirmation of a life upheld by bhajniks gathered together under a common compound, or under the roof of a cultivator or artisan.

Traces of the past *can* be grasped from the oral tradition. Gramsci suggests that:

> every real historical phase leaves traces of itself in succeeding phases, which then become in a sense the best document of its existence. The process of historical development is a unity in time through which the present contains the whole of the past and in the present is realized that part of the past which is 'essential'—with no residue of an 'unknowable' representing the true 'essence'. The part which is lost, i.e. not transmitted dialectically in the historical process, was in itself of no import, casual and contingent 'dross', *chronicle and not history,* a superficial and negligible episode in the last anlaysis. (Gramsci, 1976: 409, emphasis mine).

There can be no more powerful argument for the seeking of a record of the past within the present.

It is a tremendous task attempting to draw out from the people's articulation of Mira the past that lies behind and informs the present. Anyone attempting this task has to approach it with a respect to its continuity, and a hardiness of knowing that that which survives has done so in the face of severe injury.

I have, in attempting to understand the Mira bhakti, grappled with the traces left in the present. It would be useful to be able to trace the exact emergence of this bhakti, to be able to see the manner in which the various communities coalesced around Mira, to be able to feel the lives of the bhajniks and understand how the

Mira bhakti spoke to them and they to Mira. It would be wonderful to know who it was that Mira journeyed with, who it was that provided nurture and active community when she broke with the ruling families which had been hers. It would be enlightening to be able to move with the ebb and flow of the Mira bhakti prior to the twentieth century, for it could not have remained static—to know the depth of its fierce clash with dominant culture and how it survived this battle, and to know when it was that this bhakti reached a stubborn maturity of self recognition.

However, it is not in the nature of the Mira bhakti to provide us with the detail which would make the past leap before our eyes. What has been retained though, speaks of a process of association which I will come to after drawing a scene from the past-present.

Today, in the villages and significantly in the towns in Rajasthan, the strongest force of the Mira bhakti lies within the dalit communities, within the weavers, the leather workers and the sweepers. Again and again one comes across the very specific association of Mira with the leather working communities in particular. The process whereby this specific association was/is created is rendered sharply and poignantly by the bhajniks today. This does not mean that Mira is exclusive to these groups. But there is a specificity to this relation which must be sought in the formation of this across the period of the Mira bhakti, from her time to the present. The link forging this relationship is Rohidas, the fifteenth century Chamar bhakta, a leather worker, whom Mira is said to have accepted as guru. More significantly, Mira is seen to have borne the fury of the Sisodiya rulers in order to maintain this relationship. What is created and recreated in the bhajans is the tension involved in the formation of this relationship between a woman from the ruling family and a bhakta from a despised community. What is expressed in the singing though, is not the relationship between these two individuals but the societal force that lies behind each of these, the breaking of a dominant, repressive power by Mira and the creation of a more egalitarian one.

I will, first, detail the history that lies behind this articulation and offer an interpretation of this. It is an interpretation derived from a close listening to the only available documents and traces left of Mira's past, the bhajans. I attempt to extrapolate from the present to the past because I do not consider the expression of Mira bhakti to have been accidentally derived and reproduced, in a social and historical sense, nor do I consider it to be limited to the recent past. The strength and force of this bhakti today, after a period of a sustained attack by the incipient bourgeoisie in search of a sentimentality to mask its colonized degradation, must make us pause and ask what kind of salience it must have held in times when the ruling classes wielded extra economic force exultantly.

A committed writing of the history of the leather workers, the weavers as indeed of the peasant communites of Rajasthan and Gujarat is still awaited. I have utilized existing sources to build up a historical picture which seeks to understand the rise of Mira within the artisanal groups. I will then proceed to a description of the other groups within whom Mira is prevalent today and their histories—the cultivating groups of Anjania Patels, Kolis, Dangis, Dhakars, Jats, etc in Rajasthan and, in Saurasthra, the Satvaras, Kolis, Mers and Waghers, as well as other groups such as the pastoralists (Raikas, Bharwads, Ahirs, etc). Today, Mira spans a large section of the agrarian order.

For the moment, I ask the reader to bear three things in mind while reading the historical account. First, to read this keeping in mind the Mira story, central to which is her rejection of the Rana and the privileges and wealth that flowed from this. Secondly, to be sensitive to the acute social differentiation in the feudal social hierarchy, within which distinctions of clothing, ornaments, modes of travel, and differences inscribed by the stigma of poverty (such as the kind of food one ate), symbolized a demonstration of power or lack thereof. Lastly, to realize that the existence of each social being was integrally bound up with the existence of the social community, and any deviation or break from this entailed a sharp challenge to the social order.

The Rise of Mira and the Consolidation of the Artisanal Classes

It is not coincidental that the period which saw the rise of Mira also saw the increased expansion of the weaving and leather working communities in Rajasthan and Gujarat. The fifteenth and sixteenth century saw a growing class differentiation in society, with an expansion in trade and commerce resulting from the opening of the sea routes to Europe. The arrival of the Portuguese in India in the late fifteenth century saw the beginning of the rapid expansion in maritime trade, leading to the massive rise in the numbers of weavers engaged in textile production. The foundation of the English East India Company in 1600, together with the coming of the Dutch, led to rivalry within the European powers to capture this profitable trade. Cotton textiles and the clothing material produced by the handloom weavers in India provided an essential barter commodity in the expansion of Europe's first imperial age (Chaudhury, 1984: 386–7).

This expansion had a profound influence on the communities one is concerned with in this work, the Chamars and the weavers, drawing them into the vortex of world commodity production, while leaving their social standing in the caste hierarchy unchanged. While the sixteenth century saw an enormous increase in the numbers of skinners, dyers, leather workers, spinners and weavers, by the seventeenth century the artisans formed a highly significant section of society.

Muhnot Nainsi, the seventeenth century Marwari chronicler, provides us with evidence from the *pargana* of Merta, on the importance of the artisanal groups. The Julahas (among whom Nainsi includes the Bunkars) formed 24.67 and 23.30 per cent of the artisans in the towns of Jaitaran and Merta. In Sojat, the Julaha population was second only to that of shoe-makers, the Mochis, forming 6.88 per cent of the artisan population, with the shoe-makers forming 14 per cent. The shoe-makers themselves formed the second largest group of artisans in the towns of Jaitaran and Merta (Sharma, 1981: 75).

These town-based skills and labour would not have been possible without the associated labour from villages, of groups such as the Bambhis and Regars in Rajasthan, who were closely linked to leather working and weaving and who also acted as agricultural labourers. Though the leather industry was based in the towns, the hide was supplied from the rural areas. Accounts from Udaipur and Jaipur states show that in the seventeenth and eighteenth centuries, saddles, bridles, scabbards of swords, and covers of books and bindings formed important items of expenditure for the rulers. This leather was supplied by Chamars in the villages and then worked upon by the craftsmen in towns. By the eighteenth century, these skilled craftsmen, the Shikligars and Myangars had taken over the skills of reworking and refining leather (Sharma, 1968: 309). The village Bambhis and Chamars would have been the first links in the production of leather goods, and they would not have been the most advantaged link.

The division of labour involved in these crafts created several skilled groups which assumed the status of separate *jatis* named after these skills (Sharma, 1981: 76). This happened particularly in the textile and leather making crafts. B.L. Bhadani gives information on these groups based on the writings of Muhnot Nainsi. In the town of Merta in the seventeenth century there were 203 families of Julahas (weavers), 75 families of Balai Bangar and Jatiya Bangar who were also weavers, 57 families of Pinjara (cotton carders), 51 of calico printer (Chhinpa), 26 of dyers and 114 of tailors (Darji). Well over half of the artisans were dependent on the manufacture of cotton textiles (Bhadani, 1986: 125).

It is important to look at the communities of leather workers and weavers whose growing strength and assertion went hand in hand with the emergence and assertion of Mira. Rohidas, who is considered to be Mira's guru, was a Chamar. And yet, Mira's affiliation is found not only in the Chamar community, but amongst the weavers too. How has this come about?

The answer lies in the very close links between these two communities, not simply in the sharing of the experience of untouchability, but in the labour they performed, and the position they occupied in rural society. Till quite recently, it was difficult to know under which occupational category to classify a Bambhi. The 1901 Rajputana census states that Bambhis were leather workers as well as weavers, and that they were also widely employed as field labourers. It describes the Bambhis as performing the general work of the village (this means they performed unpaid services of a menial sort) in return for which they obtained the skins of all unclaimed animals. The Chamars are described as tanners and leather workers, who also worked as field labourers and were forced to give of their labour in village service (Rajputana Census, 1901: 139,147).

The richest description of these communities is contained in the vernacular census of Marwar (1891), the 'Mardumshumari Raj Marwar' (M.R.M.). Here, it is clear that the term *bambh* refers to forced labour so that a Bambhi is one who performs all the menial duties of a village. Bambhis are also called Dheds, as they carry off dead animals in the village for skinning and dyeing. In 1891, for skinning and dyeing the leather, the Bambhis received from the owner either half the hide or the value of this. For skinning the hide, they received four per cent of the value of the hide, as well as the right o keep the meat (M.R.M., 1891: 527). The *gaun Bambhi* (the village watchman) was always from amongst the Meghwals, an untouchable community, another reason for them being called Bambhi. He was tied to the village, keeping a stick in his hand, and although he was exempted from the payment of cesses, his degrading position is evocatively articulated in one of Eknath's *bharuds*.

Eknath, the sixteenth century Maharashtrian bhakta, was a Sanskrit scholar, who produced a Marathi version of the Valmiki Ramayan. Eknath wrote a large numbr of *bharuds* in the persona of prostitutes, travelling acrobats, and a Mahar *veskar*, a gate keeper. It is surprising that Eknath, a Brahmanic scholar, could have written with such verve about the experience of people who were socially degraded. Zelliot comments that Eknath was able to do this through 'empathy' with the oppressed (Zelliot, 1987: 92), but it seems more likely that they were composed by people who came from these socially ostracized communities, who appended

Eknath's name at the end of the verses. There are fourty *bharuds* which Eknath is thought to have composed in which the speaker is an untouchable Mahar. There is a similarity and continuity to the social base of bhakti in this period which I will return to.

I do more than my routine work,
I answer to anyone who comes or goes,
I guard the houses of all the villagers.
Is this hard life such a small thing,
O my masters?

I must get firewood for so many people,
It's me who supplies the bones and the horns,
I suffer the yoke of the dirtiest of work.
Is all this such a small thing.
O my masters?

My fate is tethering pegs, hobbles, feed bags.
Soul weary is this forced labour,
I roam eighty-four hundred thousand villages!
Is this sorrow such a small thing,
O my masters? (Zelliot, 1987: 105).

The humiliation and degradation of forced labour was expressed precisely at the time that these groups were increasing in number and strength.

The stories of the origins of both the groups of Bambhis and Regars in Rajasthan, though they are probably of recent origin and though they seek to trace a Brahmanic ancestry, have one thing in common. The story of the origin of Bambhis or Meghwals is that one day, a cow died in heaven. God then created a figure from the dirt of his body, gave it life and the name Meghchand, and Meghchand brought the dead cow to this world. From thence forth, he earned his living from the hides of animals (M.R.M., 1891: 527).

Of the Chamars or Regars, it is said that a family of Brahmins were cooking in a particular place in Delhi when a calf died. After much discussion, it was agreed that one of the family members should take the dead animal away. He did so, and on his return, found out that he was not allowed back into his family and caste, so he left, earning his living from skinning and dyeing. (M.R.M., 1891: 540).

It is said of the Garudas, the priests of the Bambhis that Brahma had two sons, Megh Rishi and Garg Rishi. One day, the son of Megh Rishi picked up a dead cow in order to throw it further away, and was outcasted for this. Brahma, though, allowed the son of Garg Rishi to go and conduct the marriage of the son of Megh Rishi on condition that he accepted nothing in return for this. However, he brought back a ball of cotton hidden in his *paghri* (turban), and was thus outcasted, Brahma stating that he could from thenceforth earn his living by conducting the marriages of this group (M.R.M., 1891: 545–6). The essential point here is to see the link of social ostracism between these occupational groups.

Thus, the growing numbers of weavers, and leather-workers, arising at the same time as the challenge of Mira, bore the stigma of social exclusion, and fretted against it.

Irfan Habib too has identified the emergence of Kabir, the weaver bhakta and Rohidas, the Chamar and linked this up with the growing strength of the artisanal classes and their search for a religious expression which would enable them a self dignity (Habib, 1965).

Though the 'historical' claim to the relationship between Mira and Rohidas is open to question there are strong indications that on the ground, Mira was widely revered as the disciple of Rohidas. So much so that by AD 1693 the linking of Mira's name to Rohidas had spread to the Punjab, and had been accepted in the hagiographical literature there, (namely, in the *Pothi Prembodha*). There was thus, clearly, prior to the writing of the *Pothi Prembodha* a ground swell of public opinion which acknowledged a very strong tie between Mira and Rohidas (Singh, 1981: 15–16). It is difficult to find further written evidence of the linking of Mira's name with Rohidas and hence with the untouchable communities from the seventeenth to the twentieth century but it would be erroneous to deduce from this that there was not a continuity. It appears extremely likely that Mira was taken up by the rising artisanal classes who did not see a change in their social status commensurate with their strength in the economy, and who sought to give voice to their discontent through the Mira bhajans. The continuity of the imagery of weaving in the Mira bhajans is extremely striking, particularly as, unlike Kabir, it is at odds with Mira's social position. The reference to Mira being a subservient woman weaver is particularly telling (see page 114).

Unfortunately, we know very little about the conditions of women who undertook particular tasks in the production of textiles. The formation of the cloth on the loom, preparation for winding or rewinding, the carding of yarn, were all operations performed separately. The increase in the volume of textile production brought into existence a group of professional spinners, too, who were exclusively engaged in producing yarn for the full-time weavers (Gopal, 1975: 219). A large section of these spinners are likely to have been women. It appears, however, that the artisans took to Mira as a whole class. Whether there were any differences in the way that Mira was taken up by women from the artisanal classes, separately from the male artisans, does not emerge from the oral record. The one strong bhajan which links Mira to the condition of a woman weaver (page 114) could as well have been composed by male artisans who see a woman weaving cloth for her husband as a subservient being.

The condition of weavers, whose labour was in great demand at this time, yet who were unable to improve their social standing, would have led to their giving support to the Mira bhakti. The weavers and leather-workers, who suffered from the imputation of untouchability, would have sought in Mira not just a figure of rebellion, but a figure through whom they could gain in dignity and self-respect. Mira, a woman from a privileged background, would be seen to have expressed a promise of more egalitarian relationships through her association with Rohidas, a Chamar bhakta, thereby refuting the caste system.

The experience of untouchability has preceded the sixteenth century (D. Sharma, 1966: 429–33). The foundations of the Rajput states in Rajasthan and Gujarat are bloodied with the sacrificing of human lives, almost invariably the lives of dalits. In the tenth century, the ruler of Mandore (the capital of Marwar which then moved to Jodhpur) Nahad Rao, had leprosy. He was told that if he dug at a particular place and found water there, he would be cured of leprosy by this water. Though he dug deep, no water was to be found. The pundits of Kashi advised him to perform a human sacrifice. This was Mahachandra Meghwal.

Chittor's Rana Khetsingh's son, Rana Lakha came to the throne in AD 1382. He had many reservoirs, lakes and dams built (Tod, 1971: 322) and in order to make the water rise in a particular lake, a human sacrifice was demanded. Manna Meghwal, a weaver and his first wife were both killed. His second wife, being pregnant, escaped death (Gokuldas, no date: 148).

In Patan too, in the reign of Sidhraj Solanki in the twelfth century, Mayo the Dhed was sacrificed to help raise water in a well—but it is said that Mayo managed to wrest from the ruler certain concessions for his community, namely that they would no longer have to wear the degrading marks of servitude—a brush at the back which swept their footsteps away, a bell to announce their presence to passers-by, and a spitoon so that none other might be polluted (Forbes, 1973: 86).

In the Ekalinga inscription of AD 1488 Ekalinga, the main deity of the ruling family of Mewar, stated that no upper caste person should show any kind of favour or generosity to 'Chandals', nor give them any charity (Sharma, 1968: 99). Forced labour in the form of *begar* continued.

As late as 1918, the Bambhis of Dangawas and Sojawas of the Merta *pargana* were forced to sign a document by the Jats of this area, stating that they would not wear *phools* (medallions) round their necks. The Jats had made it clear to the Bambhis that unless they agreed to live by this agreement, their services would not be used, thus depriving them of their livelihood. The Bambhis took this matter up with the state, complaining that they were beaten by the Jats and prevented from wearing the *phool* of Ramdev Pir (B.A. 7.7.1925). The Jats had earlier submitted a petition to the state asserting that the low castes should not be allowed to establish customs and usages in their community which were equal to those of other classes (B.A. 28.4.1923).

The degradation of the lowest castes has remained remarkably constant, despite major structural changes in the economy and polity. The Nathdwara temple came into conflict with organized groups of dalits when it refused to open its doors to the dalits of the town (Times of India, 11.8.1988 and 13.8.1988). Thus while the dalit communities have continued to bear the stigma of social exclusion, large sections have sought to voice their commitment to the breaking of hierarchical caste relationships through the medium of the Mira bhajans.

Indeed, in the literature of the Ravidasis in Uttar Pradesh, Mira is given a central role in nurturing and validating Rohidas as a preceptor. In the stories which have become prevalent amongst the Ravidasis of Uttar Pradesh (one of the heartlands of Chamar assertion), the stories of the meeting between Mira and Rohidas have multiplied and assumed many hues. The *'Ravidas Ramayan'*, written by a Bakshidas from Uttar Pradesh, was published in the early twentieth century. Bakshidas described Rohidas as being on pilgrimage. Reaching Multanpuri (presumably in the Punjab) Rohidas is said to be alone and in need of food and shelter. Both Mira and Kamali (Kabir's daughter) are said to have taken the pilgrim wayfarer home, and to have fed him. Mira's sojourn to Punjab, and her being in the company of Kabir's daughter are significant additions to the Mira stories, this time aligning Mira not just to Rohidas, but to the daughter of a weaver bhakta (Bakshidas, n.p.d. 67–9). The *'Sant Ravidas Mahatmay'*, published by Shree Ravidas Sant Ashram in Uttar Pradesh attempted to counter the arguments of those that disputed the veracity of the claim that Mira was Rohidas' *param shishya*, foremost disciple (Singh, 1979: 216). The organized sections of the Raidasi movement have thus actively sought to subordinate Mira, a woman from a higher social group, to the spiritual authority of Rohidas the Chamar.

Rohidas became an important symbol in the twentieth century movement for Chamar self-assertion in Punjab and Uttar Pradesh. Both Mira and Rohidas became enmeshed within this assertion, but the main point to note is that the Ad Dharm movement in the Punjab, and the Raidasi movement in Uttar

Pradesh took up existing symbols in the regenerative culture of the dalits and gave these a new form (M. Juergensmeyer, 1982. B. Cohn, 1987: 296). M. Juergensmeyer's sympathetic study of the Ad Dharm movement makes clear that the newer political movement was built upon older forms of worship. Juergensmeyer states that:

Ad Dharma did much to highlight the oppression of Untouchables in the Punjab and to accelerate their growing self-consciousness and transform it into an effective political force; it made their common identity more visible than it had ever been before. But it did not create that identity. That had been expressed long before in the veneration of Ravi Das and in other, more general features of the religion of the lower castes. The Ad Dharm might win the allegiance of a small coterie of leaders... but what mattered to the masses was the continuity between the Ad Dharm and these old and familiar realities.

When the Ad Dharm appropriated the figure of Ravi Das, the sixteenth-century poet-saint (*sant*), and used his picture as their emblem, his sayings as their sacred texts, and stories about his life as illustrations of lower caste pride and power, it was touching the heart of the cultural tradition of lower caste Punjab. (Juergensmeyer, 1982: 83).

The allegiance given to Mira by the dalit communities, today, evident in the bhajans sung profusely within them, has the nature of the same continuity as that of Rohidas. Unlike Rohidas, though, who has a direct organic link to the Chamars, and who was later taken up within a political movement, Mira remained (and continues to remain), enmeshed within the sphere of religious expression articulated through the bhajans. The Mira bhakti can perhaps best be seen to be one among many different strands which has kept alive the quest for altered, and more egalitarian relationships amongt the dalits.

Mira within the Peasant Communities

While Mira has achieved a tangible link with the dalit communities through her association with Rohidas, Mira bhakti is not confined solely to this section. It is very strong amongst the peasant communities too. The Anjania Patels, the Kunbis and the

Minas around Deogarh were the first to introduce me to a version of Mira which was very different from the middle class one I had been familiar with. Whilst bhakti amongst the *adivasi* communities of Minas, Bhils, etc., is of recent origin, spanning no more than sixty years in this area, it is fair to assume that amongst the settled peasant communities it is of long standing.

These peasant communities appear to have taken to Mira precisely because she appeared as an antithetical figure to Rajput feudal power. The Mira bhajans as sung amongst the agrarian classes today mock, deride, and pour scorn on the figure of the Rana, and place great emphasis on the humiliation heaped by Mira upon the throne of Chittor. It is difficult to overestimate the dominance of the Rana in holding the peasantry subject to his rule. It is also difficult to map out all the strands of material deprivation and social humiliation that entered and coalesced into an acknowledgement of resistance to the Rana in the form of the Mira bhajans. The very basis of the power and pomp associated with the Rana of Mewar was based upon exactions from the peasants. It is highly significant that the Mira bhajans do not flout the authority of a particular historical Rana by name, but seek to revel in the shame incurred by a feudal power who symbolizes the authority of kingship. Mira thus emerges from the bhajans not as a figure of rebellion against one particular Rana, but as someone who despised and condemned the essential embodiment of Rajput kinghood.

The cultivators were well aware of each minutiae of the Rana's living and extravagance that was dependent on their labour. The terms used for the revenue paid to the state was called *bhog* or *hasil* which was either taken in *kankut* or *batai*. *Batai* was a tax levied on sugar cane, poppy, oil, hemp, tobacco, cotton, indigo as well as garden stuffs. The *kankut* was a conjectural assessment of the standing crop, made by the state's or the *jagirdar's* agent. In the *batai* system, the share of the state varied from a third to a two fifths of the spring harvest, such as wheat and barley, and sometimes it went up to as much as half, which was the proportion of the autumn crops (Tod, 1971: 582).

Over and above, the *bhog* or *hasil* was the war tax, *ghanim barar*, *ghar ginti barar* which was the house tax, *hal barar* a tax on the plough, etc. (Tod, 1971: 169). On top of all these, extra cesses were levied upon the peasantry, called *lag bag*, to sustain royalty in its various public ceremonials and pomp. It was these that made the peasantry acutely aware of the differences in their own living and that of the princes. They were extremely burdensome cesses. Their specificity enabled the peasants to realize what exactly it was that they were contributing to. On the marriage of a prince, of his daughter or son, it was incumbent on the *bhomias* and the *jagirdars* to ensure that these were glittering occasions. However, these levies were not

solely from the coffers of the rich; by the chiefs [they were] exacted of their tenantry of all classes, who, of course, wish[ed] such subjects of rejoicing to be of as rare occurrence as possible. (Tod, 1971: 188.)

While evidence for the state of Mewar is scanty, that from other areas points to an increasingly oppressive system of taxation in the nineteenth century. In neighbouring Dungarpur state, a cess was paid towards the maintenance of the Rawal's wardrobe, and a cess was charged for the buying of a '*sir putora*', a silken covering for the *rani*. The peasants paid these various cesses in cash, the Patels often extracting more than the Rawal had ordered.

The list of *lags*, cesses imposed on the peasantry, is revealing as it shows that the lifestyle of the rulers as well as the *jagirdars*, and their maintenance of splendour was systematically and deliberately founded on the backs of the peasants. The rulers used every life occasion to extract some amount from the peasants. These *lags* were imposed by households in a particular area. A *kamtha lag* was imposed for the construction of a fort, and for its maintenance. A *danti jawari* was levied to meet the Holi and Diwali expenses of the *thikana*. When the *thakurani* purchased a new ivory bangle, the cultivators had to pay towards its cost. At a marriage within the *jagirdar's* hosuehold, a *neota lag* was imposed. This was greatly resented. When a son was born to a *jagirdar*, a *kanwar janma lag* was imposed. When he came of age and became old enough to ride a horse, the cultivators had to pay a cess towards the buying of a horse. A *jharoola lag* was paid at the time his hair was shaven. When the son acceeded to the throne, a *lag bag* was paid. There was no respite even at the death of the *jagirdar*. A *mausar* or *khand bara lag* was then paid, and a *Gangaji ki lag* was paid when his ashes were thrown in the Ganga. A *tilak lag* was paid when the new Thakur ascended to power. There was even a *garaj lag*, a flattery tax which was paid when a *jagirdar* visited his villages (Pema Ram, 1986: 314–6).

It is true that the above were cesses levied by the *jagirdars* in their own area of control, but it is also true that these petty rulers modelled themselves, in their structure and their administration, on the Ranas and Raos. The *jagirdars* could certainly not have functioned in the manner that they did without the sanction of the ruler, and the peasants were aware of the close ties that existed between these two authorities.

It would indeed be mistaken to assume that the brunt of taxation borne by the peasantry was their prime grievance against the Rana and his underlings. Though the medieval period saw acute resistance to the appropriation of surplus value in the form of land tax (Habib, 1963: 330–51), and although the grievances surrounding land and land tax featured prominently in the peasant struggles of the early twentieth century in Rajasthan (Pema Ram, 1986), it was also the reproduction of a hierarchical culture with its myriad marks of social differentiation and cultural exclusiveness which imposed strains. In their endeavour to preserve a superior social standing the princely class excluded those subordinate to them from exercising social privileges. The struggle in the cultural sphere over values, beliefs, and meanings attached to the life of Mira, shows that within the exercising of hierarchical rule, the Ranas wielded a contested hegemony. The subordinated resisted, flouted and mocked the social, moral and political power of the Ranas within their own self-chosen associations. The peasants then found in Mira a symbol through which they have voiced their rejection of the authority of the Rana.

On Becoming

It is in the collective singing, in the voices of those long degraded and long humiliated that Mira becomes more than an isolated being fighting her own specific oppression as a woman wanting a different life from the socially ordained one. Mira becomes the voice of the oppressed people just as the bhaktas become Mira through their singing.

The male bhaktas sing in the *stri vachya* (feminine gender), as and in the being of Mira. This is not an abstract becoming, for although there may exist abstract notions of womanhood to which women are expected to conform, the living of a woman is marked by an active will and an active struggle to grasp the world as she constructs it, and renders it meaningful. That society finds it more fit to imprison this within abstracted and rigid walls of thought makes it even more imperative that we allow her her own unique meaning. When men of a society in which the male consciousness and male constructs are used as yard sticks for the whole of the human experience begin to sing in the *stri vachya*, then a radical shift occurs in the moral order. It requires a break from and a transcendence of the world as created and upheld by men. It requires the recreation of humanity in the female image. The world has to become *strimay* i.e. the world has to become female. This requires more, much more than an empathy with the female subject. Within the Mira bhakti, the process of becoming Mira and thereby entering the mind and heart of a woman comes out most strongly in the bhajans which evoke Mira's rejection of the Rana as husband. These bhajans will be detailed later. Here I am concerned to attempt to describe this process of becoming.

It can be argued that Mira herself becomes the Mira of the people, a specific figure with a complex structure of feeling, by being given this shape by those who have sung of her. However, there is a strength in the person and history of Mira which stops a complete appropriation of her image by varied and different social classes. Mira cures no disease, she showers no blessings. The miracles in her life are not miracles performed *by* Mira to daze those around her and thus elevate herself above them.

Rather, Mira exists as a potent symbol of spiritual strength, who was also able to forge and comment on human, political bonds.

There is a kernel to the Mira story which stops her from becoming just another folk heroine. Mira, the people's Mira, is neither a romantic heroine nor a deified goddess. The core of her life is nothing more and nothing less than her rejection of princely society, and her establishment of a life of affinity with pilgrims and wayfarers in her pursuit of a relationship with Krishna. Around this kernel have crystallized voices which have given birth to a powerful person of Mira in which she is more than herself. Mira's reality is the reality of a common creation. It is the intellectual and emotional domain of bhakti that has given this creation its own specific impetus and historical continuity.

There is a tradition amongst the medieval bhaktas, in places where their own identity is proclaimed, to refer to themselves in the third person. It is as if the bhakta is addressing himself as a separate person, looking out at self from within. Crucial within this process of the bhakta naming himself is the connoting of collective humanity within this. The bhakta becomes the embodiment of collective endeavour and collective humanity, to whom truths are addressed and to whom a critical solution is posed. This is the reason why a lot of the sayings of the bhaktas have attained the form of proverbs (Schomer, 1987: 89) used in the daily lives of people to point to some well known truths. Culturally, in hearing these sayings etc. one knows that it is not Kabir or Dadu who is being addressed, or whose particular experience is being expressed, but that it is being addressed to the collective, to the singers and listeners gathered there. No division exists between the 'historical' bhakta, the named bhakta, and the present day singer-listener. But there is a crucial difference between Kabir and Mira. Kabir's *dohas* are about the general human condition and are not specific to Kabir alone. It is significant that the very sayings which are broader and more socially encompassing are the ones which are the most popular. Within the Mira bhajans though, we have a different phenomenon. Here we have a two way interaction, a mutual affiliation, in which Mira does not become an abstracted humanity striving for wisdom, but rather we have a very specific process of affiliation in which Mira voices the anguish of facing an imposed marriage, widowhood and having links with an untouchable.

Within this process of identification and merging, there are different kinds of becoming in the sphere of bhakti. When Eknath becomes a Mahar *veskar* or a spurned woman, he ceases to be a Brahmanic scholar, an idealist philosopher, and he enters into the marrow of an untouchable or of a woman despised. This becoming entails an experiencing, an expressing of the social relationships contained within these lives. It entails an earthing, a bonding, a becoming of the bhakta in which he becomes a particular kind of person. However when Dasi Jeevan, the Saurashtrian bhakta who came from a dalit family sings in *gopi bhav*, becoming a *gopi* to Krishna, he is unbonding himself from his community and his social relationships. He transcended these to become someone who holds a particular relationship to Krishna and Krishna alone. In looking at the tradition of the peoples' Mira one is looking at the process whereby a bond was forged between the person of Mira and the people. Each process of becoming and of transformation needs to be located in it own sphere of expression.

However, the relational aspect of bhakti enables the taking on of identities of others. Rather than a 'taking on', it is a mergence, an entering into the other's nature and it entails living the presence of the subject of the bhajan. In an age and a society where the notion of an individuated subjecthood has not yet achieved hegemony, the becoming and transforming is intense. There is a wholeness to this experience (the wholeness broken and disjunctured once one leaves the sphere of bhajans and bhakti and one enters the socially ordained life) in which being is not dismembered into separate analytical categories, whereby one lives, experiences and forms an indissoluble part of the life upheld, and is not detached from it.

Constraints of a linear historicity do not bind the Mira tradition. It is true that this tradition itself has been a continuously changing one, and the disjunctures in the song of Mira allow us entry into a changing social process. On the ground though, where Mira remains organically linked to the mass of the people, no sharp division exists between the past and the present. The past is evoked and born anew and it returns to form a real part of the present. It is a deepening of time rather than a mere lengthening of it. The past and present stretch around in a mutual clarification of each other, a phenomenon common in medieval society (Gurevich, 1985: 26-38, 94-151). It is, at one and the same time, a leap into the past and a widening of the present of all those who uphold Mira. This is the only way that the Mira tradition can be grasped in its fullness. This tradition, this presence, this becoming is not so much apprehended as experienced, and what is articulated is not the history of Mira the individual, but the experience of the community of bhaktas. Let us turn to this experience.

The Rana and the Lok: Rejection and Alignment

In Mewar today, the most commonly sung bhajan is, *'Mira sadha ro sang chhodo ai, chhodo ai, laje tharo Merto, Mewar laje ho'* (Mira, leave the company of the saints. Your Merto is covered with shame, Mewar is covered with shame.) The word *sadha* here, in the plural, refers not to wandering *sadhus* and *sanyasis*, but more generally to the large and agglomerate mass of bhajniks who are identifiable particularly within a bhajan session.

Embodied in the notion of *sant* is one who does not hold a privileged position in life, who does not have access to material gain (nor chooses this) and one who consciously rejects a life based on accumulation. Many writers on the *sant parampara* have pointed out that the word *sant* embodies within it an ethical meaning. It must be recognized though, that within the Mira bhakti the terms *sadha* and *sant* acquire a political meaning, incorporating within it all those believers who suffered under the rule of the Ranas. K. Schomer has pointed out that the word *sant* comes from *sat* meaning 'one who knows the truth', but that in more recent times it has come to mean a 'good person' whose life is a spiritual example (Schomer, 1987: 2-3). Charlotte Vaudeville states that a *sant* is not a renunciator, but a lay person, a *shudra* who delights in the Name, and that the *sants* are not the learned but the 'just' who emphasize the company of *sants, sat-sang* (Vaudeville, 1987: 22-36). John Stratton Hawley has stated that for Kabir, the *sant* was not the ascetic of the world, but the good (Hawley, 1987: 202). The Varkari *panth* based in Maharashtra is known as the '*santasajjananci mandi*' or the society of saints, past and present. The word *sant* is used for any pilgrim on the way to Pandharpur (Deleury, 1960: 3,75).

The *sadha* or *sants* thus form a group of the under-privileged, who are tied to each other by a distinct set of values that affirm a simple life uncorrupted by wealth and privilege. It is a group which deems that the good, the just, cannot flow from those exercising power and force. The members of this group are tied to each other by a system of morality and a system of values which uphold a community of like minds and hearts, held together by a sharing of common conditions, and a common purpose. In the Mira bhakti, the tension and the power of these values is provided by the fact that Mira had to fight hard to retain her affiliation to a life of simplicity. In the following discussion, I will take each bhajan as a whole expression, and then describe the relationships embedded within this. Within a bhajan, there are often different voices speaking, in combat or in consonance with each other. It must be remembered that in the context where this expression takes place, within a gathering of bhajniks, the story of Mira would be familiar to all, none would find it difficult to identify whose voice is being enunciated, nor with which voice the assembled identification lay.

(This bhajan is sung much too widely for me to be able to cite a particular source. I heard it first sung by a group of Minas, peasant cultivators, in Deogarh, later in the city of Udaipur by a group of dalit women who worked as sweepers, then by a group of Kunbi Patels in the village of Ghanti near Kherwara, and it continued to appear in every single bhajan gathering that I attended in the region of Mewar.)

Mira, leave the company of the *sadha*. Your Merto is covered with shame, Mewar is covered with shame. The Sisodiyas are feeling a deep shame, the Mewada are covered with shame. Mira, leave the company of the *sadha*.

What can the Mewadiyo do to me? The Sisodiyo, what can he do? What can the Mewadiyo do to me? The Sisodiyo, what can he do?

Mira, leave the company of the *sadha*. Your Merto is covered with shame, Mewar is covered with shame...

Mira came down from the fortress with a *tilak* on her forehead. She by-passed Merto on her left, and went straight to Pushkar.

Mira, leave the company of the *sadha*. Your Merto is covered with shame, Mewar is covered with shame...

What can the Mewadiyo do to me? The Sisodiyo, what can he do? What can the Mewadiyo do to me? The Sisodiyo, what can he do?

The Rano sent Mira a cup of poison.
She drank it after making an offering to Krishna.
Raghunath is my protector.

Mira, leave the company of the *sadha*. Your Merto is covered with shame, Mewar is covered with shame...

The Rano sent Mira a venomous snake, covered in a basket.
She wore it around her neck, it turned into a necklace.

Mira, leave the company of the *sadha*. Your Merto is covered with shame, Mewar is covered with shame...

Years passed and she walked a *kos* and a hundred *kos*.
Rana, I vow never to drink the water of your land again.

Mira, leave the company of the *sadha*. Your Merto is covered with shame, Mewar is covered with shame.

In a feudal society where the public demonstration of one's wealth and prestige were the hallmarks of status and power which commanded respect, Mira associated herself with the humble, lower caste *sadha*—with those whom the Rana held in derision, and over whom he wielded his rule. Mira left the rule of the Rana, and removed herself from the domain of his influence

I. 'Mirabai' in *Darshano ki Kitaab*, Udaipur Palace Library.

II. Kabir at the loom, the bhaktas Raidas, Namdev and Pipa surrounding him.

III. Village Chandravada, district Jamnagar. Singing bhajans at the local temple after a day spent on relief works.

IV. Returning from a day at the relief works, the women carrying utensils for food and water as well as their work tools.

V. Dahyabhai Satvara, Dwarka, singing bhajans within a group of male casual labourers.

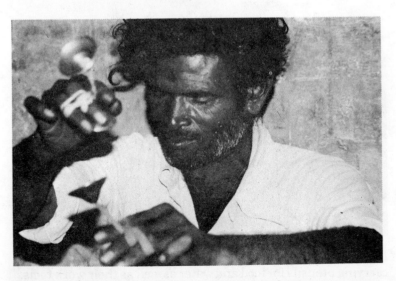

VI. Playing the *manjira* within a bhajan gathering amongst a group of Kharva fishermen, Kharva neighbourhood, Subhashnagar, Porbandar.

VII. A Brahman widow (foreground) leads a group of housewives in bhajan singing in the Merta *mandir*.

VIII. Neighbours congregated at the house of Huki Kodra Patel (top middle), village Dechra, Udaipur district. The women are having a laugh about how to make ends meet on meagre resources. Author at back.

Ravishankar Rawal and Kanu Desai, Gujarati painters influenced by Gandhi and the nationalist movement, were instrumental in paving the way for an embourgoisement of the figure of Mira.

IX. Rawal's 'Mira' (c. 1924) was used by the Government of Gujarat as a calendar-photo after independence. It shows a Mira more akin to the figure of a chaste housewife-widow, who is immersed in *murti-puja* within the household.

X. Titled 'In Quest', this is part of a series of portraits of Mira by Kanu Desai, published in 1943. It shows a woman gazing out to sea romantically, her hair blowing in the wind, the Dwarka temple in the background.

XI. 'Mira in Ecstacy' by Kanu Desai.

XII. 'Mira Dancing' by Kanu Desai.

A middle-class sensibility which emphasized the purity of woman and the sublime heights of bhakti found space within this to demonstrate its opposite—an objectification of woman as a sexually-charged bhakta. Both notions exist, contradictorily, side by side. In the two paintings here Mira is at once a sexually flamboyant and supplicating figure.

XIII. The cover of an L.P. record containing Mira bhajans: Mira bowed low over the *tanpura*, clad completely in white, the badge of widowhood. The bhajans contained in this collection are in Hindi, catering to the taste of urban dwellers in north India.

XIV. The cover of another L.P. record: this aimed at a regional (Gujarati) middle-class, shows a figure who hovers between popular depictions of a princess/folk-heroine.

The uneven development of cultural notions and sensibilities are even today held under tension in Indian society.

XV. While the notion of Mira as a figure of purity continues to be widely propagated nationally, she has, inadvertently, become linked to a recent fascistic upsurge. Bhakti amongst the lower middle classes is more and more channelled into Hindu revivalism; for instance, by groups such as the Shiv Sena in Maharashtra. This thrives on utilizing historical figures for its own virulent divisiveness.

This photograph shows models of figures—'religious' and otherwise—(Mira, Krishna, Shivaji) being sold on a street stall outside the main temple in Trimbak, Maharashtra, in 1987.

XVI. Hema Malini in the title role of the film 'Meera'. As the figure of Mira becomes more distanced from the folds of the oral tradition, as the visual arts continued to depict her in a refracted manner, so the Mira born out of the imagination of the film media took over. Today, amongst the lower middle and middle classes, the story of Mira is familiar through the film directed by Gulzaar, replacing the earlier means of singing, story-telling and communication.

XVII. Page from the strip-cartoon story of 'Mirabai', part of the 'Amar Chitra Katha' series for children, published in 1988. Children removed from an oral tradition are presented with a droopy-eyed Mira who faints at the sight of Krishna.

In this version of the Mira story, after Mira had left Chittorgadh, her husband Bhojraj repents of his actions. When Mira recognizes her husband in front of her in Vrindavan, she falls at his feet and says: 'Has Mira ever gone against the wishes of her husband? Yes, I will come to Chittor!' The comic version continues: 'So Mira, led by her husband, and followed by her devotees, returned to Chittor. (*Mirabai*, Amar Chitra Katha series, India Book House, Bombay, 1988.)

XVIII. Exterior of 'Mirabai' temple at Chittor. Consecrated as such by Lalsinha Shaktawat in May 1955.

XIX. Interior of the same temple in Chittor—a cardboard cut-out figure of Mira in worship of Krishna.

Despite—and because of—the presence of Mira on calendars, postcards, cassettes, L.P.'s, and within a temple designated the 'Mirabai mandir', the Mira who challenged feudal Rajput values and who showed a clear alternative to this, remains unassimilated within the heart of Rajput-dominant society.

and power. However, her name continued to be associated with the ruling families of Merta and Mewar and hence her affiliation to the socially marginalized groups in society brought shame upon the Rajput ruling families. The bowing down of the pride of Mewar is a recurrent theme in the bhajans. Mira's survival, after the cowardly acts of violence on her life behind the strong-holds of the fortress, her active and public living of a life outside these walls, humiliated the might of the Chittor rulers. Humiliation and shaming were, in a feudal society, worse than death.

There is a fluidity to the bhajans, a constant historical slippage, a shifting of time, and a changing of voices and being. At no point, in the quality of singing and expressing is the identity of the Rana or the critics of Mira assumed. The chorus, the recurring repetition of 'Mira, leave the company of the *sadha*' is sung with great fervour and great pathos, in the knowledge that the much despised *sadha* are themselves, the bhajniks who have held Mira close. There is suffering entailed in the knowledge that attempts were made to sever the relationship between Mira and the common bhajniks. There is strength in knowing that these attempts failed, and that this community won through. There is solidarity in the singing of this bhajan, a collective taunting of the Rana, and a collective knowledge that they are all engaged in the humiliating of the Mewadiyo. The Rana is not referred to in the respectful noun, but rather he is '*tu-toied*', as the Mewadiyo and the Sisodiyo. This is a complete denigration of the ruler.

All these understandings overlay the singing, and in the structure of the bhajan too, there is a constant slipping back and forth of events. It begins with Mira leaving the fortress of Chittor, embarking as a lowly pilgrim to Pushkar, having severed her link with her paternal family in Merta. It returns to the enmity faced by Mira while living within the fortress, and it ends with a declaration of contempt for the Rana and his land, whereby Mira swears never to drink the water of his land. It is the subjects of the Rana's land who have maintained the song of Mira, and who sing in the first person Mira's vow of disaffiliation. Mira left the land of the Rana. but the people of this land continue to evoke her power.

(The following bhajan was sung in village Ghanti, district Udaipur, amidst a community of Kunbi Patels. There was a bhajan *mandli* in the village which was often invited to sing in other villages, having travelled outside of Rajasthan as well. Those in the bhajan *mandli* were Kabirpanthis, but they sang Mira too.)

Mira was born and kept company with the *sadha*.
She was tied to the name of Hari.
Mewada Rana, Hindupat Rana, Sisodiya Rana, I have become a *vairagin*.

I have covered my body in sandal paste, Rana, I have become a *vairagin*.

Mira was married to and worshipped Hari.
She was tied to the name of Hari.

Mirabai, come and take up your abode in the new palace.
I will sit in the company of the *sadha* and thus go to heaven
Mewada Rana, Hindupat Rana, Sisodiya Rana, I have become a *vairagin*.

Mirabai, sway, sway in the abode of *sadha*
Heaven will be reached through the company of *sants*.
Mewada Rana, Hindupat Rana, Sisodiya Rana, I have become a *vairagin*.

Mirabai, come, come and live in the kingdom of Udaipur.
Come and sit on the throne of Chittorgadh.
Mewara Rana, Hindupat Rana, Sisodiya Rana, I have become a *vairagin*.

Ranaji, burn the kingdom of Udaipur, burn it.
Burn the throne of Chittorgadh.
I have to go to Ram's house.
Mewara Rana, Hindupat Rana, Sisodiya Rana, I have become a *vairagin*.

There are three voices which emerge out of this bhajan. There can be no doubt though, about which voice engages our sympathy and holds power. The voice of the bhakta introduces Mira, sustains and upholds her, thereby sustaining and legitimizing Mira's stand in relation to the Rana. The power of the most important line of the Rajput rulers is annulled and rendered impotent by Mira and the bhaktas.

Mira's declaration of *vairag* did not, in its outcome, symbolize what Romila Thapar has described as

death to society. (Thapar, 1978: 81.)

Romila Thapar, in her description of the alternative and parallel system of renouncers (who differentiated themselves from the *grahasta* by the dress they wore, the food they ate, the name they adopted, and by their flouting of caste and other social conventions) concentrates very much on the history of Jainism and Buddhism. These two ascetical sects gradually became powerful landed bodies, which nevertheless continued to allow the entry of individual renouncers within it.

With Mira though, we have a very different phenomenon, essentially differing from and qualitatively departing from the above. We do not know how Mira actually lived in her life—what she wore, what she ate, who she associated with. But in the rendering of bhajniks from peasant and artisanal communities, Mira returns to the very society she left, not embalmed within the folds of a wealthy *sampraday*, but as indelibly linked and aligned to the lives of the subordinate classes there. Mira returns to this society and is alive within it not as a renouncer, and not simply as a bhakta either, but as one who lived a life close to the people. It is an affiliation which is strong and which is unexclusive, in that she is not retained by any sectarian order, but by many and varied bhajniks who hold an emotional and political affiliation to her. Mira herself enunciates this:

I will not go to my marital home, mother,
My heart lies in *fakiri*.
In *fakiri*, in *garibi*. In *fakiri*, in *amiri*.

My heart cannot rest in high palaces, mother,
my heart lies in a broken hut,

I am bound to a life of *fakiri*.
My heart lies in *fakiri*...

Beautiful clothes do not suit me, mother,
Tattered rags and saffron take my heart.
Mira's heart is bound to *fakiri*.
In *fakiri*, in *garibi*, in *fakiri*, in *amiri*.

Golden necklaces do not suit me, mother,
my heart lies in a *tulsi mala*.
My heart lies in *fakiri*...

Delicacies do not suit me, mother,
my heart accepts dry and stale pieces.
Mira's heart lies in *fakiri*.
In *fakiri*, in *garibi*, in *fakiri*, in *amiri*.

(Sung in village Dechra, Udaipur district, in the house of Huki Kodra Patel, from the Anjania Patel community. The gathering was attended by a wide variety of people—from the community of Darji, Suthar, etc. but the majority were Patel cultivators. A *'saathi mandli'* has been going in the house of Huki Kodra Patel for the past ten years, whereby she herself incurred the expenditure of purchasing an *ektara*, *dholak* and *manjira*. The *mandli* meets every eleventh day of the lunar calendar, and sings mainly of the worship of Ramdev Pir.)

In the bhajans, a constant theme is Mira responding to the Rana's allurements and to his taunts.

Mertni Mira, Rathodi Mira, leave the company of the *sants*.
Come and live in the palace.
Who is this Giridhari of yours?

I cannot leave the company of the *sants*, Rana Mewada, Rana Sisodiya,
I will not live in a palace.
My Giridhari is the true one.

Discard your covering of saffron, Mira Mertni, Mira Rathodi,
wear a shawl and two shawls.
Who is this Giridhari of yours?

I cannot discard the saffron coverings, Rana Mewada, Rana Sisodiya,
I will not cover myself in two shawls.
My Giridhari is the true one.

Stop eating the leavings of alms, Mira Mertni, Mira Rathodi,
feast on grapes and pomegranates.

I will not stop eating the leavings of alms, Rana Mewada, Rana Sisodiya,
I will not feast on pomegranates.
My Giridhari is the true one.

(Sung in the city of Udaipur, in the house of Chandabai Chavan. Phulibai Chavan, a seventy year old widow who lived in the locality, had started a bhajan *mandli* named the 'Mira mandli' fifteen years previously. The *mandli* met regularly, with different members playing different instruments. Chandabai played the *ektara*, while Phulibai played *manjiras*, and an old woman called Gulabbai Ganvri danced to the bhajans. All the women in the locality were employed as sweepers by the municipality.)

In a different version of this bhajan, Mira declares that she will not stop eating the *'tadha tukda'* and the *'khati chhas'*, that these are like *'amrit'* to her. The 'broken hut' that her heart is in peace in is referred to as the *'tooti tapri'*. All these indices tie her to the living conditions of the poor. It takes place of course within a context of her bhakti for Krishna. But one must remember the context within which these bhajans are sung. They are sung in the evenings, after a day's labour, by poor peasants or by workers who occupy the lowest rung in the urban economy, by people who are gathered together to share in the unburdening of toil. It is a collective articulation whereby one voice leads, and others follow, a second voice takes the refrain a note higher while other voices lend it weight. What has brought people together in that particular relationship of bhajnik to bhajnik is a joint evaluation of a moral life. The evocation of a life which is based around the *'tooti tapri'*, around the eating of *'tadha tukda'* and *'khati chhas'*, is an evocation of a common life, which is inhabited by all those who are shut out of a privileged existence. It is a common life in which the shared indices of existence—food, clothing, dwelling—and the social being that flows from this, marks them off from the richer strata of society. It is a common life which is held in contempt by others, but which is here upheld as one which brings them all together in a common framework of reference. These bhajans are not sung by ascetics, renouncers, who bear only a tangential relationship to social life, but by people to whom poverty is a condition of everyday living. The evocation of this life within a bhajan gathering binds people in solidarity to each other.

It is Mira's relationship to poverty, and to the living of an ordinary, common life that the bhajans uphold, for the people see in the actions of Mira her affinity with them. The stark indicators of poverty and of the common condition which are evoked in the singing of the bhajans describe a historical badge of subordination and solidarity between all those who have experienced it.

Within the lives of ordinary people, differentiation of clothing, of ornaments worn or not worn, were very clearly marks of their ascribed status in life. This was an imposed status because if they attempted to transgress these boundaries, they faced severe repression. One could tell the difference between a Jatni and a Bambhni because a Bambhni woman wore bangles made of lac while a Jatni wore ivory bangles. The women from the family of the *gaum* Bambhi were sometimes, as a special privilege, allowed to wear silver ornaments on their feet, and to wear gold ornaments on their neck. Certainly the other Bambhi women could not (M.R.M. 1891: 529). As we have seen earlier, right up to the 1940's the Bambhis were denied the right to wear gold *phools*. The Jats in Sikar faced extreme punishment for attempting to construct *pukka* houses—so the *'tooti tapri'* was the norm for peasants and artisans.

In terms of food, there was a saying that *'ghoda ghans aur Chamar pani'* i.e. that as a horse ate grass all day, so a Chamar drank water all day long, pointing to their extreme poverty (M.R.M., 1891: 540). The Chamars and the Bambhis were held in disdain for eating *'mui mati'*, the flesh of the dead cows etc. that they were responsible for removing out of the village (M.R.M., 1891: 540).

Within the midst of this degradation and poverty, though, the poorer classes had strong community bonds and social responsibilities which gave them the strength to survive. These strengths derived from ties of community, in which the harshest aspects of life were made bearable. At the death of a member of the Bambhi family, it was usual to hold a death feast. This involved a lot of expense as the whole caste had to be fed. However, none who attended the death feast left without contributing. The contributions added up to a substantial amount, although individually they were small sums. This was a source of considerable help to the family in which the death had taken place. This custom is expressed, tragically, in the saying that a living Bambhi was worth only one *taka* while a dead Bambhi was worth a hundred *taka* (M.R.M., 1891: 533). When Bambhis went to a different village for a *maukhan*, they took a bag of flour with them in order not to burden fellow members with the cost of feeding them (M.R.M., 1891: 533). If a Bambhi could not afford to hold a death feast, then he would fill twelve pots of water and carry them to the house of their priest, the Garuda, and this was held equivalent to holding a death feast (M.R.M., 1891: 533).

It is in everyday social living that deprivation can be glimpsed. In the late nineteenth century it was usual at the time of a marriage ceremony, (which was held at the house of bride's father), for the bridegroom's father to present the other side with a contribution of rupees thirty to forty, in order to help with the cost of the occasion. If the bridegroom's father was unable to contribute towards this, he would publicly acknowledge this by not attending the wedding, and suffer in silence this humiliation (M.R.M., 1891: 532).

It is in the context of the lives of poor people who are bound to each other by bonds of mutual co-operation that the Mira bhakti must be understood. The articulation of the Mira bhakti takes place precisely in the domain where the relations of co-operation and community exist. In this articulation, Mira does not emerge as a lone, isolated voice, but as the voice of the community gathered around, which is not just confined to one's immediate caste community. The community embraced through the bhajans stretches beyond the confines of the gathering, to take in all those who are known to share a common life: a common life of labour, a common life of deprivation and a common life of suffering. It is a class expression, which cuts across the divisions of caste, and in fact levels down the minute and complex differences which mark out one caste community from one another. The poor are all brought together in the evocation of a common life.

Mira is seen to have actively cast off her privileges by assuming *bhes*, and by taking to a life of poverty. She is seen to have tied her life to that of the poor and the lowly who were subjected to indignities under the rule of the Rana. The poor and the lowly have thereby declared an allegiance to her. Crucial within this structure of feeling, which forms the main emotional force to the people taking to Mira, is the suffering and humilation Mira endured in forging the links to the common life.

The humiliation Mira suffered was not small. She spurned not only the might and the privileges of the Rana, but she spurned too the norms of conduct and decorum entailed in being a member of the princely family. By taking *bhes*, she cut the cord that tied her to her *kul*, to her family, and to her worldly social relations. The rules which governed her as a woman, as a member of the Rajput caste, ceased then to hold any meaning for her. Mira does not belong to that category of renouncers who by assuming *bhes*, had their name, caste and previous life obliterated. Rather, what we have through the bhajans is the tension involved in Mira rejecting her social ties and her creation of alternative ones.

(Sung in village Borunda, near Merta, by a Kamadia, a priest of the Bambhis, within a Ramdev Pir temple.)

In your *desh*, Rana, there is no *sant*. All those who live there make up unjust lies. I do not like your *desh*.
I am dyed in a different colour.
I do not like your *desh*.

Rana, this *kajal*, this *tiki*, I will give them all up.
And I will give up braiding my hair.
I do not like your *desh*.

I am dyed in a different colour.
I do not like your *desh*.

All these fineries, Rana, I will give them all up.
And I will give up wearing bangles on my arms.
I do not like your *desh*.
I am dyed in a different colour.
I do not like your *desh*.

Bai Mira sings the glory of Giridhar.
I have found the true guru.
I do not like your *desh*.
I am dyed in a different colour.
I do not like your *desh*.

The structure of feeling here is Mira's own. There is no other intrusive voice. The bhajan contains Mira's opposition to the Rana, and to the people of his land. She declares that his land is full of slanderers, that there are no *sants* there. The bhajan carries an indictment of the land and the rule of the Rana in which Mira sings again and again of her rejection of his *desh*. She sings of the breaking of all ties which bind her in marriage to the Rana—she refuses to put on her forehead the *tika*, the sign of a married woman, and she declares that she is going to give up wearing bangles. The subversion inherent in the song of Mira in flouting the sanctioned man-woman relationship is very strong. I will describe this in greater detail in the next chapter. Here, it is important to note that Mira holds the complete space in this bhajan. Neither the voice of the supporting bhakta, nor the mocking voice of the Rana is present. It is Mira's voice which is unambiguously and irrevocably declaring her stand. It is a mature stand. Mira knows the repercussions flowing from her challenge, having experienced some of the reprisals. Yet Mira sings of rising above the enmity of the Rana.

(Sung in village Agolai near Jodhpur in the house of Gogadevi Chaudhri. The cultivators in the village are mainly Jat peasants. The bhajan gathering was attended by a number of Jat families, but the Mira bhajans were sung in the main by Kanharam Nair and Jwalaram Kumbhar. The latter sang the bhajan below, although he was joined in this by others.)

This ill fame is sweet to me, Rana, this ill fame is sweet to me. Your slanders are sweet to me.

In your land, Rana, there is no *sant*.
All make up lies to you, Mewadi Rana,
this ill fame is sweet to me.

The mother-in-law, the sister-in-law all make up vicious stories
Mewadi Rana, this ill fame is sweet to me.

Mira, show me your Ram in person
or you will be shown up as a charlatan.

Rana, my Ram is visible within each heart.
Only you are unable to see him
as the foundation of your heart is rotten.

I have found my *satguru* in the alleyways of love.
I am not now able to turn back.
Mewadi Rana, this ill fame is sweet to me.

Bai Mira sings the glory of Giridhar.
My bangles are dyed a deep red,
Mewadi Rana, this ill fame is sweet to me.

Behind this 'ill fame is sweet to me' lies a whole history of social ostracism and repressive social sanctions. At a time and in a society where to lose one's good name and honour was to go beyond the pale, Mira subverted this notion and insisted that it was her slanderers who lacked any moral basis, who did not even feel the presence of God within them because their hearts were rotten.

In the society of Rajputs even today, to utter the name of Mira is to evoke a woman who is best forgotten, whose very name is associated with loose morals. If one considers this, one can begin to understand some of what Mira must have actually endured in her lifetime.

There is tension between the bhajans, where in one Mira declares that she is not going to wear bangles, and in the other she says that her bangles are 'dyed a deep red'. Those singing the bhajans and those listening to these understand that these are two separate phases of Mira's life. One is where she is rejecting the Rana as husband, and the second is where Mira refuses absolutely to accept the status of a widow. In the latter, her wearing of bangles of a 'deep red' is a defiance of prevalent norms as to how a the widow should dress.

(Sung in village Agolai by Kanharam Nair. This particular bhajan has been made well known by various professional Rajasthani singers, and is available on cassettes.)

You appear to me, Rana, like the bitter *kair* fruit in a garden.
Mewadi Rana, why have you kept up a vendetta against me?

Ranaji, I have left your norms of shame,
and the false decorum of the princely life.
I have left your town.
And yet, Rana, why have you kept up a vendetta against me?

Rana, you gave me a cup of poison.
I drank it, laughing.
Udyapur Rana, why have you kept up a vendetta against me?

Rana, I will not be destroyed by you.
The grace of the guru is upon me.
Udyapur Rana, why have you kept up a vendetta against me?

The repression that Mira endured was no small one. And yet Mira is able to declare herself stronger and inviolate under the hatred and the vendetta of the Rana. Mira pays no respect to the authority of the Rana, to his political authority, his patriarchal authority and even more his moral authority. She immobilizes the power of the Rana and empties it of its force.

Even if I incur the Rana's displeasure, what can he do to me?
If he is angry, he can keep his *nagri*.
There will be no place for me to go to
if I incur Hari's displeasure.

I will sing the glory of Govind.
Even if I incur the Rana's displeasure, what can he do to me?

I will dance and clink my anklets.
If I incur the Rana's displeasure, what can he do to me?
If I incur the Rana's displeasure, what can he do to me?

(Sung within a group of Manganiyaras at a workshop in village Borunda, Jodhpur district. This Mira bhajan is well known and very widespread within Rajasthan.)

The authority of the Rana is ripped to shreds in the above. And again in the following:

Rana, I was standing in the bazaar
and saw the king elephant walk majestically past
taking no notice of the barking of the dog.

(Sung in the village of Keshav, district Junagadh by Bachudas Premdas Dudhrejiya. The whole village is inhabited by Mer cultivators. Bachudas Dudhrejiya conducts the worship of Ramdev Pir and also cultivates.)

In the above, a common proverb is turned against the Rana to throw a barb at him. It is clear that Mira faced slander (the 'barking of the dog') and social ostracism. It is equally clear that she demonstrated her truth over this tide of repressive norms, and that her history is sung by the very people who derive strength from her life and living.

The tie forged between Mira and the people was forged through a sharing of a common suffering and a common humiliation. The bhajans contain an acute intensity, which is marked not by values of aesthetic enjoyment, or musical appreciation, but by a jagged and unfulfilled promise of a dignity denied in everyday social relations. It is those who endure daily social humiliation who understand what Mira went through in her discarding of riches and leading a life of poverty. This is held up and painfully exposed in song. This is the central force and the central thrust of the Mira bhakti.

The bhajniks, through the voice of Mira, crystallize the humiliation faced by the people, and demonstrate a solidarity based around the experiencing of this. It is an affirmation of a community in open antagonism to the ruling one, and within which lies the seeds of a new social order. The community of Mirabai is essentially the community of bhajniks who, over the centuries, have provided a voice to the struggle for dignity, and hope of a better life. The community forged includes within it the community of all sufferers.

Breaking Caste: Pollution and Grace

In the above discusson, I have concentrated on the expression of the poorer groups (including the dalit groups) as a *class* in their upholding of Mira. However, the retention of Mira within the artisan class, within the leather workers, weavers and, at the bottom, the sweepers, all of whom continue to be harrowed by the imputation of untouchability, is very specific to them. Mira broke from her caste not just by assuming *bhes*, but more actively and significantly by choosing Rohidas as a guru. The bhajans mark a tremendous struggle in the formation of this relationship, a relationship which subverts and overthrows the socially dominant norms of pollution and untouchability.

Rohidas was born in or around Benaras and he was a contemporary of Kabir (Pema Ram, 1977: 70). Rohidas travelled widely and his followers are found throughout northern India, in Uttar Pradesh, Punjab and Rajasthan (Singh, 1981: 40). Rohidas is known to have visited Rajasthan and to have influenced the bhaktas Pippa and Dhanna there (Pema Ram, 1977: 71). The *Rohidas ki parchi* (life of Rohidas) has the information that the Jhali Rani of Chittor (Sanga's wife) invited Rohidas to Chittor and that he made many disciples there (Pema Ram, 1977: 71). Whether Mira ever met him and accepted him as her guru (or indeed whether the Jhali Rani did) is not certain. Goetz has a convoluted account of how the child Mira was given a Krishna *murti* by Rohidas, which he himself had obtained from the Jhali

Rani, and how this served as a talisman for Mira in Chittor, granting her protection (Goetz, 1966: 7,11). Be that as it may, it is clear that by AD 1693 the linking of Mira's name with that of Rohidas had spread to Punjab, and been accepted in the hagiographical literature. This is mentioned in the *paricayi* of the bhaktas, called *'Pothi Premabodha'*, in which Mira is represented as a disciple of Rohidas (Singh, 1981: 15–16).

Attempts have been made to Brahmanize Rohidas, and provide him with a pure ancestry, so that his power as a bhakta becomes linked to Brahmanic hegemony. In one story, Rohidas is said to have peeled off his outer skin to all those assembled in Chittor, and showed them the identifying mark of a Brahman, the golden sacred thread (Khare, 1984: 45). Despite this, it is in the moral assertion of the Chamar caste *as a community* that the power of Rohidas lies. Like Kabir, in whom the dalits have sought an egalitarian ideology and a vision of an alternative, Rohidas promises dignity to the dalits of northern India. This is not a *sampradayika* relationshp though i.e. it is not limited to the disciples of Rohidas. Rohidas is a symbol of social and political worth amongst the leather workers. The Chamars of Uttar Pradesh (Rohidas came from the region of Benares) have taken to calling themselves 'Raidasis' (Cohn, 1987: 264). In Punjab too, a similar assertion took place (Singh, 1981: xi).

In Rajasthan, the person of Rohidas is crucial in enabling the Regars (leather workers who dye the leather) a self pride and worth. The Regars also worship Luna, Rohidas' wife. Amongst the Regars it is said that Rohidas' daughter was very beautiful. The story continues that the Rana of Mewar heard of her beauty and sent the *fauj* of Mewar to capture her. However, the river Ganga was the protectoress of Rohidas. At the approach of the Rana's army, the Ganga rose up in anger and swept away the *fauj* of Chittorgadh (M.R.M. 1891: 540–1). It is significant that the direct exploiter in this story is the Rana of Mewar. It provides a further link with the Regars' holding Mira close to them, and sympathizing with her fight against the Rana.

The story of social exploitation of lower caste women is symptomatic of a very real exploitation that takes place commonly, not withstanding the concept of 'pollution'. Bernard Cohn, in his monograph on the village of Madhopur in Uttar Pradesh, has shown how in the 1940's, it was commonplace for the Rajput landholders, the Thakurs, to exploit Chamar women sexually (Cohn, 1987: 273). The story of the Rana of Chittor sending his army to capture Rohidas' daughter for sexual gratification is a crystallization of a demeaning humiliation that took place commonly, which was projected on the ruler of Mewar. Mira's refusal to recognize her relationship with the Rana would thus have resonated with these communities.

For Mira to accept Rohidas as guru was to deal a blow to the established caste relationships. The people's Mira is a struggling being, struggling to forge relationships which break through the barriers of caste, and class and which break through the barrier of a forced marriage relationship. This struggle has been held in the bhajans over the years, and it has been articulated and re-articulated through them.

This tension stems from the fact that Rohidas was a leather worker. This fact is brought to the fore again and again. There is no artifice in any of these bhajans to make Rohidas other than a Chamar, to Brahmanize him. Even the recognized status of a revered bhakta is overlain by the overwhelming mark of his untouchability.

In accepting Rohidas as her guru, Mira is herself, in the peoples' version, seeking his grace. She is the maker of this relationship. Rohidas is timid and hesitant, seeing himself not as a spiritual preceptor, but as a lowly leather worker whose hands are tainted by the work he performs. The message in the bhajans is fraught with tension, there is a terrible pathos in it, although one listens to the bhajans knowing that the relationship won through. One is pulled into the struggle to establish this relationship, between a woman of rank and a bhakta of low status, through the expression of the bhajan but much more by the presence of the dalit community surrounding one within a bhajan gathering, for whom one knows and in whose presence one experiences that this struggle is a historically continuous one.

(Sung by Jamkhubai Meghwal in village Manaklav, district Jodhpur. Jamkhubai's mother and grandfather had been weavers, though she herself was an agricultural labourer. Those attending this bhajan gathering were all Meghwals.)

Mirabai, seek the help of someone in the east.
Give up the company of *nugras*.

Mirabai went to the Jatiya *vas*, to the Regar *vas*,
Someone tell me where I can find Hari.

Bai, they say that Rivdas is a *das* of Hari.
Go and see this guru.

Garusa, lay, lay your pure hands on me as a blessing.
It will purify my body.

Bai, my hands are dirty, they are very dirty.
How can I lay them on an unblemished soul like you?

Garusa, I have sought the company of a *sant* in the east, and found it.
My body will thus become pure. My body will become pure gold.

Garusa, I have found a guru in Rivdas. I have found Rivdas.
I have held the hand of the *sant* in the east.

The voice in the dream had advised her to travel to the east. Yet, it is the Jatiya *vas* that Mira goes to. The Jatiyas are a branch of Regars, leather dyers, and closely allied to Rohidas. In the above bhajan, one can see the overturning of polluting relationships, and the acceptance of purification from the hands of a Chamar, whereby the touch becomes 'gold'.

Within the closed Tantric worship still prevalent in large parts of Rajasthan and Saurashtra today, there has been a tradition for a member of the untouchable community to act as an initiator, to lead a new disciple into a ritual which involves the flouting of commensal regulations, and which involves sexual, ritual practices. In one of the Saurasthra bhajans, there is a faint echo of Mira being linked to this Tantric ritual through the linking of her name to Khimdio Kotwal, an untouchable initiator and guardian of this sect. I cannot say whether this is a throwback to an earlier, stronger appropriation of Mira within this sect, or whether it is an inadvertent linking of Mira's name to Khimdio Kotwal through her association with Rohidas. I have attempted to probe this within the Saurashtra tradition, where the 'closed' worship is opening up remarkably, with bhajans being broadcast across whole villages over large loud speakers, amplifying the content of the gathering. Apart from the one particular bhajan in which Mira speaks of having received advice from Khimdio Kotwal I was not able to find any clear evidence as to whether Mira is differently represented within this sect. However, it is unmistakably the case that Mira is linked to the dalit communities of Mewar, Marwar and Saurashtra, and that they declare an affiliation to her today.

Nagpur, in Maharasthra, is a strong dalit base, being the city in which Dr Ambedkar had publicly converted to Buddhism as a mark of his opposition to dominant Hinduism. On 6 December 1987, a group of dalits, poor peasants and agricultural workers, forcibly entered the Bombay Express train, in order to be able to make their way to Bombay to celebrate Ambedkar's anniversary. I was on this train and witnessed the episode (Mukta, 19.12.1987: 2199). It was an anniversary which was particularly significant, as right wing Hindu organizations were demanding censorship of passages from Ambedkar's *'Riddles of Hinduism'* which had offered a critique of the Hindu pantheon of gods.

The passengers who held reserved seats on this train had colluded with the police in locking all entries into this train, in order to stop the dalits exercising their right to travel to Bombay in time for the celebration of Ambedkar's anniversary. The dalits asserted force in gaining entry, causing anger amongst passengers who held reserved seats. One of them, a Marwari business man, mocked an older dalit woman, addressing himself to the middle class passengers:

They carry their *rotla* with them, he taunted, they'll sleep on the pavements or in Shivaji Park the night before their anniversary! Ha! They'll soon go running back to their villages the next day, as their *rotla* will run out! *They* can't afford to buy restaurant food!

At this point, the older dalit woman broke into a Mira song, in Marathi, about the dignity of eating stale and dry pieces of *roti*, nullifying in song the grotesque class arrogance of the Marwari businessman. The effect of this song on the other passengers was remarkable. It evoked a laugh that the businessman had been bested by a poor woman, and it created respect for the dalit woman who travelled the rest of the journey without harassment.

In Saurasthra, the most commonly sung Mira bhajan is on the person of Rohidas, in which he pleads with Mira to return to her family. This song emerged in every single bhajan gathering that I attended, and it was sung by non-dalits too (by the peasant communities of Mers, Waghers, Kolis, etc.) The two most poignant renderings were in the village of Modhvada, Junagadh district, by two young dalit schoolboys, and, in the city of Porbander, amongst a community of sweepers. In the latter case the bhajan was sung by Jagdishbhai Patnish who worked as a peon in the municipality.

Mirabai, you are my faithful devotee.
Mirabai, please return home.

Mirabai, you know you are a princess, a Rathori princess.
Rohidas is a Chamar by caste.
Mirabai, please return home.

Mirabai, the Rana will be wrathful.
He will kill me. And he will revile you.
Mirabai, I ask you to return home.

Mirabai, your maternal home will be covered with shame.
The fortress of Chittor is covered with shame.
Mirabai, please return home.

Mirabai, you can hear people are slandering you.
And they are slandering me.
Mira answers, my God will see to them all.
Mirabai, please return home.

Rohidas at the feet of Ramanand says,
Mirabai, remain true to your beloved.

This bhajan marks a fine process, from an anxiety as to the wisdom of the action, the punitive measures that could flow from this, of which the social repercussions are visible ('you can hear the people are slandering you')—to a calmer, stronger acceptance of the relationship, within which Rohidas supports Mira in her love for Krishna. The full historical struggle is enacted within this bhajan, allowing us to have a glimpse of it, but not providing any more detail.

When this bhajan is sung amongst a group of dalits, there is an intense pain voiced here, the pain inherent in trying to form a relationship sharpened by the knowledge that Mira remained true to her relationship despite social sanctions.

As has been said earlier, it is not simply the dalits who sing the above bhajan in Saurashtra. Apart from the dalits and peasant communities, the fishing community of Kharvas, the agricultural labouring community of Satvaras do so too. When non-dalits sing this bhajan, they interiorize within themselves the experience of untouchability, and feel it intensely. Through this, they are able to cross the caste boundary which divides the bhajniks in their everyday lives. The experience that emeges out of this bhajan, and their own knowledge of the historical weight of untouchability enables the non-dalit bhajniks to enter this condition of degradation, and feel the corrosive force of it. This is experienced at a deeper level than an understanding derived solely from an intellectual understanding, or from an over-arching political commitment. The singing of this bhajan enables the singers to experience a particular structure of feeling of dalits. By its depth of force, it can provide the emotional passion necessary for the over-throwing of this condition.

The spiritual force of Rohidas in strengthening Mira, and showing her the worth of her own actions is indubitable within the bhajans. The most subversive are the Saurashtrian bhajans, in which it is Rohidas, an untouchable and a man who enables Mira to have the conviction to reject the Rana as husband. I will come to this in the next chapter. Here, I am concerned with delineating the caste-class configuration. One particular bhajan that makes explicit Mira's relationship to Rohidas also subverts the socially degrading act of skinning and dyeing.

(Sung by Kamladasi, in a place called Sela Amba, near Bhindar. Kamladasi is a Kabirpanthi, and lives by cultivating land, together with her guru Shantilalji. They are both called upon at religious gatherings to sing bhajans. She plays the *ektara*, he the harmonium.)

Mira's Giridhar, come to the *desh* of the Mertni.
To the Mertni's *desh*, to the *garibdi's* desh.
Mira's Mohan, come to the Mertni's *desh*.

Mira found a guru in Rohidas.
She bowed at his feet, and asked his blessings.
Mira's Mohan, come to the *desh* of the Mertni.

I have nothing to do with caste or other divisions.
Let the world do what it will,
I offer you my body, mind and soul.
Mira's Mohan, come to the Mertni's *desh*.

I skin animals, and dye the skins.
My work is to dye.

This dyeing is dear to me, this dyeing is dear to me,
Dye my soul in it.
Mira's Mohan, come to the Mertni's *desh*.

Bai Mira found a guru in Rohidas.
She touched his feet—take me to the other side.
Mira's Mohan, come to the Mertni's *desh*.

In her accepting of Rohidas, in her granting worth to his labour (dye my soul in it), Mira, the outcaste from her own society, has become indissolubly bound to the outcastes of society at large.

Mira's Janma Patri

There is an epic to Mira, anonymously composed, which is not sung much by ordinary bhajniks today, being a long and specialized song. I am grateful to the Institute of Folklore in Borunda for making this song available to me. Their recording of the

'*Janma Patri*' was done in the early nineteen seventies from a Bauri singer. The Bauris are a socially ostracized community, who live apart from the other communities within a village. In colonial times, they were branded a 'criminal tribe', with restrictions imposed on their movements. Earlier, they had earned their living by trapping animals, and are now often employed as *chowkidars*, or guards in the villages. The Bauris have a language which is specific to them, which perpetuates the stereotype of them being lurking, shifting thieves.

The '*Janma Patri*' (see appendix A) is rich in social detail. It differs from other bhajans not just in form and structure—but essentially in the fact that it makes Mira act and speak in the voice of a woman weaver. In no other bhajan is there such an explicit appropriation of Mira. The experience of the weaving community is interlinked to, and imposed on the life of Mira. It is therefore very likely that this song is a creation which arose out of this community. Being a lengthy song, it is impossible to say whether there was an initial core to which verses were added, and if so what this core was. The creativity of the weaving community is well known. The Kamads are a group tied to the Bambhis, who earn their living through singing. They sing Mira profusely, as do the Bambhis as a whole. The '*Lok Mahabharat*' which is different in content from the dominant '*Mahabharat*', is also sung by the Kamads (Gupta, 1974: 28).

The '*Janma Patri*' starts with an enumeration of the months of the Rani's pregnancy (who is to give birth to Mira). At the birth of the child, the aunt goes round to various people announcing the birth, and ordering that preparations for a celebration take place.

Mira grows up. She goes to the outskirts of Duda's town, and asks to be made the disciple of 'Rivdas'. He refuses, and asks her to keep a distance from his hands. He tells her he cannot be her guru because she is from a prestigious family (*mota gharan*), and that he is afraid of the wrath of Dudo Mertiyo. At last, at Mira's insistence, she is accepted as a disciple by Rohidas.

Mira is married against her will—physically hurting the maids who come to dress her in wedding attire. Mira arrives in Chittor, and the Rana comes upon her in worship. He asks her who it is she is worshipping, and she replies that her guru is Rohidas and that she is doing the *puja* of *Shaligram*.

The Rana orders her to leave the palace immediately, saying that she has brought pollution to his beautiful palace. At this point, Mira asks him not to throw her out of his life, and says that she will build a small hut at the foot of the fortress of Chittorgadh for herself, where she will spend her time spinning cotton, and making *dhotis* for him.

The song ends with Mira being in a forest on her own—Rohidas divines this—and he appears in front of her, showering her with blessings.

The structure of feeling within one particular section of this long epic, the section where Mira declares that she will spend her life in spinning cotton and pleasing the Rana by making *dhotis* for him, is very different from the other songs of Mira. The other bhajans give Mira her own space, in which she continues to act and be within her own history and specificity, through which she forges links to form an alternative community. It is an equal relationship on the side of Mira and on the side of the bhajniks, where both come together from very different bases and social experiences, and each shares deeply in the other's struggle and pain. The *'Janma-Patri'* though is an active appropriation of Mira where she is made, at one crucial point, to speak and act as a subservient woman weaver. While it provides an added link to Mira being a creation of the weaving classes, it does sit at odds with the other bhajans in which there is a forging of solidarity with a woman of a high social status—and a lower class community.

A Dream Validated

One of the most remarkable features of the Mira bhakti as enunciated by the subordinated groups in Rajasthan and Saurasthra, is its sustained challenge to norms governing the marital tie and the marital life. Yet the twentieth century interpreters of Mira coming from within the literati (including Gandhi) have been unable to accept Mira's forging of a relationship with Krishna as being one in absolute negation of the Sisodiya prince, the Rana. Attempts have been made by these interpreters, again and again, to reconcile the socially ordained relationship (the Rana as husband) with the spiritual relationship so integral to Mira's life (with Krishna as the beloved).

These attempts at imposing a reconciliation do a grave injustice to the power of the symbol Mira subsequently became, and to the force of values embodied in this symbol in challenging the dominant man-woman relationship. They fail to understand that for a woman who has the courage and self-dignity to search for a fulfilling relationship, there is no separation possible between the mind and the body—between the giving of heart and the giving of self. That the body and spirit do not occupy different spaces but are housed together, bearing a fine relationship with each other.

Mira's creation of a relationship with Krishna encompassed her whole being and truth, in which the non-phenomenal became phenomenal, yet which was constantly eluding her, providing the deepest tragedy to her life. It is this aspect of her life which provides her the innermost conflict—and yet it is this aspect of her life which enabled her to stand up against the world. Within the sphere of bhakti, Mira stands out as a woman claiming a right to her own spiritual relationship, hitherto long granted to male bhaktas.

Tuka Ram, the seventeenth century Maharashtrian bhakta, was a grain dealer. He is said to have paid no attention to his trade and domestic affairs, being immersed in the name of God. His wife starved to death, there being no food in the house. When there was some criticism of Tuka Ram for not looking after the needs of his family, he took refuge in philosophy and replied calmly,

What is to happen can never be avoided. (Abbot, 1930: 79)

Chaitanya's first wife died young and he accepted without protest his mother's arrangement of a second marriage for him. Having then decided to take *sanyas*, he left his home town. His mother and second wife had to face the fury of the orthodox Brahmans of the town who were enraged at Chaitanya's non-conformist bhakti.

There are, in the lives of most male bhaktas, elements of a disavowal of social responsibility to those closely bound to them, elements too of an all pervasive misanthropy and a deep seated misogyny. No less a person than Kabir, strong critic of the caste system and religious hypocrisies, voices this misogyny:

Woman is the refuse of the world,
which sorts out the good and the bad.
Noble men will put her aside,
only the vile will enjoy her.

And again,

Kabir, Maya is a Harlot:
She does not come if you want her
But if you see her falsity and turn away,
She will dog your every step! (Vaudeville, 1974: 298).

The fifteenth century bhakta, Narsinha Mehta, went so far as to declare an inhuman joy at the death of his only son:

Bhalu thayu bhangi janjal, sukh thi bhajshu Shri Gopal.

(It is for the good that these entanglements are broken, we will worship Gopal in peace).

Again, no less a person than Gandhi has lauded Narsinha's stand at the death of his wife and son:

Narsinha Mehta danced and sang with relief—'It is a blessing that the net is cut.' That certainly did not mean that his wife was not dear to him or that her presence did not make him happy. She was of course dear to him. However, when she died he felt there was divine providence in that, even that it was God's kindness (C.W. Vol. L, 'Letter to Narandas Gandhi,' 28-31.7.1932: 313).

There is much sophistry in Gandhi's argument, that Narsinha's wife was 'of course' dear to him, but that he danced and sang with joy when she died. Gandhi actually advocates the emulation of this attitude to fellow supporters (C.W. Vol. L, 'Letter to Rajagopalachari,' 26.7.1932: 292). The seeking of God's kindness here is nothing higher than asking for a disencumbrance from a social and political responsibility to dependants.

Herein lies the main difference between the male bhaktas and Mira. In a closely knit society, ties of responsibility are imposed on men and women alike. But the rejection of this by male bhaktas flows from them being in a position of power over others. This is the power of being providers, the rejection of which role led to the denial of life to those dependant on them.

We do not know at which point in her life Mira accepted Krishna. In the legend, she is supposed to have seen at a very young age, a marriage procession. Mira then turned to her mother and asked her who was going to be her bridegroom. Her mother is then said to have led her to a Krishna *murti*, and to have told her that he was the one. From that time onwards, the impressionable girl child is said to have immersed herself in complete faith in the image of Krishna.

It is instructive that in this story, it is a parental choice which is accepted and taken to heart. I have heard this story repeated again and again by middle class narrators. It is, however, too neat and static a story. It gives no indications as to the circumstances surrounding Mira which made her receptive to the image of Krishna, of the dreams and longings of a young woman seeking fulfillment—of the upheavals these must have aroused within herself and within the ruling Rathod family of Merta. Rao Duda is said to be a Vaishnav, and to have encouraged Mira in her bhakti but no-one could have foreseen the lengths to which Mira was prepared to take her commitment.

Hagiographical writings, and their middle class variants, allow for no slow evolution. They allow for no extended period over which a hazy dream, an ideal held in the imagination can be shaped and strengthened in the face of force and harsh impositions—which dream and ideal would, if it met with a more responsive reality, be honed and acquire a different image.

Whether Mira accepted Krishna from an age of her own conscious knowing, or whether she found the actual experience of marriage to the Rana an unfulfilling one, if not worse, and thus turned more and more to the creation of her own relationship with Krishna, finding courage at the death of the Rana to declare that she would not immolate herself as her mind had never accepted him as a husband, are questions we will never have answers for. It is best to let the historical Mira be. And it is not fit to pry into the intimate life of a woman who has suffered much at the hands of many.

Let us turn to the peoples' Mira. In the peoples' projection of Mira, it is clear that Mira never accepted the Rana as husband. The bhajans often demonstrate a violent conflict between Mira and the Rana, with Mira spurning all the symbols of a marital status and publicly announcing her disaffiliation from this bond. In a very different projection of Mira, she is said to have circled the sacred marriage fire with a Krishna *murti* tied to her *chunri*—and therefore as having performed the marriage rites with Krishna rather than the Rana. The sanctity given through this version to Mira's relationship with Krishna is in fact very much part of the process of ironing out Mira's challenge to the institution of marriage. This is the version Gujarati middle class children grow up with.

Gandhi saw fit to call Mira the 'model wife' who bore with:

> quiet dignity and resignation all the injuries that were done to her to make her bend to her husband's will. (C.W. Vol. XVII, 'Satyagraha', 1920: 152–3).

This is, as we shall see, in complete negation to what the peoples' Mira stood for. The foremost nationalist leader of colonial India, renowned for tapping indigenous idioms, and moving the masses to political action through these, appears peculiarly out of touch with the people's aspirations as voiced through Mira. For Gandhi, Mira was a woman who lived a life of 'absolute love' so that her husband at last became her 'devotee' (C.W. Vol. XIII, 1915–17, 'Letter to Esther Faering,' 11.6.1917: 442). Gandhi also declared that:

> Mira said she paid no heed to what the world said, since she had not left her husband, but only wished to discover the true meaning of devotion to one's husband. (C.W. VOL. XXXII, 1926-7, 'Discourses on the Gita,' 7.4.1926: 144).

Gandhi's words are convoluted, of course, but it is clear that he was extremely anxious to portray Mira as someone who through her stoicism won over her oppressor—rather than as a woman who had left her oppressor to find a more meaningful alternative. There is no evidence that Gandhi's portrayal of Mira has any basis in historical reality (indeed one does not know how he arrived at this particular portrayal), but it was important to him in his attempt to balance finely both revolt and submission in the heady days of the freedom struggle. I will return to this in detail in a later chapter. Here, I am concerned to point out the differential interpretations made of Mira's relationship with her socially ordained husband, the Rana.

Parshuram Chaturvedi, the eminent Hindi literateur and writer on *sant sahitya* has effected his own reconciliation between

Mira's relationship with the Rana, and with Krishna. Chaturvedi states very definitely that Mira's wedding

> took place in V.S. 1573 (AD 1516)... her married life began to pass happily with her husband. But Prince Bhojraj was not to live for many days longer. His death took place sometime during the lifetime of his father (possibly betwen V.S. 1575, AD 1518 and V.S. 1580, AD 1523). In this way, Mira was quickly torn from marital bliss. This unhappy widowhood came at an early age, and because of this came a period of complete transformation for her. But it was as if Mira had come prepared for this from the very beginning. It is said that at her time of wedding, she had brought with her a *murti* of Giridhar Gopal. During Prince Bhojraj's lifetime, she had worshipped this ritually. At the bereavement she felt at her *patidev's* death, she tore aside all her wordly social relations and removing her mind from everything, became even more attached to God. (Chaturvedi, 1983: 20-21, translation mine)

The Rana here becomes Mira's '*patidev*'. Their time together is said to be one of marital bliss. And it is stated, fortuitously for a patriarchal society, that it was only after the death of her husband that Mira immersed herself completely in Krishna.

In Chaturvedi's depiction of Mira, the negation of the Rana as husband which appears clearly in her bhajans is denied. She is said to have been farsighted (sic) enough to have prepared herself for the eventuality of widowhood by bringing a Krishna murti with her—'it was as if Mira had come prepared for this from the very beginning'. Her relationship with Krishna is reduced to a ritualistic, household worship of a *murti* and, like an ideal, upper caste widow for whom there is no other way of life possible, Mira is seen to have embarked upon an intense form of worship at the death of Prince Bhojraj.

In the medieval period, as today, religion pervaded one's whole being. For Mira as for the bhaktas today, Krishna had a tangible presence and reality. This can surprise only those who are so hegemonized by capitalist values that they forget that in a pre-capitalist society, word and idea possessed the same degree of reality as the material world, and the frontier between the concrete and the abstract was not so clearly drawn.[1]

While it is true that the world of the spirit was interiorized so deeply that it held a space of tremendous force, there remained nevertheless a tension when one sought to grasp the inner world and the inner imagination. This was particularly true when the inner relationship was given principal credence over and above the socially structured relationships. One Mira bhajan brings this out with great power and poignance.

(Sung in village Borunda, district Jodhpur, at an informal session within a music workshop. The Langas come from a community of professional musicians, being tied to particular groups for whom they perform. Religious divisions are not important here. Though the Langas are Muslims, they sing bhajans, including Mira bhajans, profusely. Their rendering of Mira bhajans was musically much more sophisticated, but the themes which emerged out of these bhajans were similar to the other Rajasthani Mira bhajans which spoke of Mira's challenge and Mira's dilemma.)

My mother, I wed Giridhar in a dream.
Giridhar coloured me in red,
I wed Giridhar in a dream.

On my feet were anklets, on my body was rubbed *pithi*.
And my hands were all coloured in red.
My mother, I wed Giridhar in a dream.

In the circle of stars were garlands hung up
Within which sat Nandlal.
My mother, I wed Giridhar in a dream.

I wore the beloved's *chunri*, the beloved was present.
I circled the fire four times with him.

Mira, who sang the glory of Giridhar, then said,
This dream is a false chimera.
My mother, I wed Giridhar in a dream.

There is intense longing in this bhajan, within which Mira sees herself in bridal attire, dressed in the *chunri* sent by her beloved, with her hands all red. She sees a marriage taking place between her and Krishna in the heavens, with garlands hung up in the circle of stars. It is a social wedding taking place in the heavens, in which both Mira and Krishna enact and bind their love for each other.

Mira sees herself going round the sacred fire four times with Krishna—but the dream is then shattered and broken by the realization, wrung out of Mira, that it was no more than a chimera.

Herein lies the tragedy to Mira's life—a tragedy which haunted her, but she continued to pursue the dream, for it was so much more meaningful than the relationships society presented her with. For Mira though, the dream became an actuality through the very force of her own commitment, and the deep bond forged by her.

Mira's dream has not gone unrecognized, for it has and continues to strike a chord with all those who recognize the power of this creation amidst a bleak social and emotional domain.

Ranaji came to the forest,
Ranaji came to the market place,
Mirabai, do listen

I am already wedded, they want to marry me off again.
I will not marry another husband.
I will hold an *ektara* in my hand, I will hold a *chautara* in my hand,
I am dyed in the colour of my beloved.

Ranaji came to the garden,
He came to the garden,
Mirabai, do listen.

I am already wedded, they want to marry me off again.
I will not marry another husband.
I will hold an *ektara* in my hand, I will hold a *chautara* in my hand,
I am dyed in the colour of my beloved.

Ranaji came to the riverside,
He came to the riverside,
Mirabai, do listen.

I am already wedded, they want to marry me off again.
I will not marry another husband.
I will hold an *ektara* in my hand, I will hold a *chautara* in my hand,
I am dyed in the colour of my beloved.

Ranaji came to the marriage *pandal*,
He came to the marriage *pandal*,

Mirabai, do listen.
I am already wedded, they want to marry me off again.
I will not marry another husband.
I will hold an *ektara* in my hand, I will hold a *chautara* in my hand,
I am dyed in the colour of my beloved.

This bhajan was not sung within a bhajan gathering, but in the house of Gulabbai Kir. Gulabbai lives in the village of Nagri, district Chittorgadh, where the family own some land by a *talab*. They grow watermelons and cucumber. I had been talking to Gulabbai about the position of women in the family, and I asked her what she thought had been the relationship between the Rana and Mira after the marriage ceremony. She looked disturbed and was silent. I too was searching for words which would make the issue understandable without being gross, when I heard Gulabbai singing softly to herself. She provided the answer in song.

The presence of the Rana within the bhajan is a muted one, where he arrived at different times to convince Mira to accept him. He is in the role of a supplicant in this bhajan. Mira refuses him, avowing that she is already married to Krishna, and will not accept a second husband. She laments the fact that her marriage is not accepted by others who seek to see her socially wedded to the Rana. Although the name of Krishna as Giridhar etc. is not mentioned in this bhajan, it underlies the bhajan.

The main force in the bhajan is provided by the refrain 'I will not marry another husband, I will hold an *ektara* in my hand, I will hold a *chautara* in my hand, I am dyed in the colour of my beloved'. From a time prior to the wedding ceremony with the Rana, right up to the time that social pressures coerce Mira into entering the marriage *pandal*, Mira continues to hold up the *ektara* as a symbol of her commitment to a spiritual relationship and a life based on bhakti. There was no place for the Rana in this life.

For Gulabbai Kir, as for many other bhajniks, both women and men, Mira is a person so integrally committed to the choice of her heart that no social force can make her actually compromise her integrity with the Rana. The quiet strength of the bhajan was enhanced by the fact that it was sung by Gulabbai softly, as if to herself.

Mira's love was not an easy one to live. The bitter hardship involved in living it breaks out particularly intensely in the Mira *bani*, literally Mira's speech. The Mira *bani*—or what has come down to us as the *bani* of Mira—is much less amenable to change and interpolation. Although one does find variations of a particular Mira *bani*, the crucial point is that it is consistently in the voice of Mira. Neither the voice of the bhakta, nor the voice of Mira's antagonist, enters into this articulation.

The Mira *bani* enables us to enter the interiority of Mira's emotions, and thus enables us to understand some of what Mira experienced in her attempt to forge a relationship of her heart.

(Sung by a Kamad, at a Ramdev Pir temple in village Borunda, district Jodhpur.)

Your beak, *papiha*, I will have cut off
And I will have salt rubbed on it.
The loved one is mine, I am the beloved's,
Who are you to call out *piu, piu*?
Papiha, do not speak of love.

Who is this brother who speaks of love?
Who is this brother who speaks of love?
Whoever hears you will twist off your wings.
Papiha, do not speak of love.

Your words are beautiful, *papiha*—oh, if the beloved could be mine!
I would then have your beak cast in gold
And wear you as a crown on my head.
Papiha, do not speak of the beloved.
Do not speak of love.

I will write a letter to my loved one.
Take the letter to him.
Tell the beloved that the one he has wedded is not able to eat.
Papiha, do not speak of the beloved.

Mira *dasi* is Ram's *papiha*.
She calls out *piu, piu* day and night.
Come to me, my beloved,
I can live without you no longer.
Papiha, do not speak of the beloved.
Do not speak of love.

The *papiha* is a popular name for the rain-bird. In Indian lore and legend, it is seen as ceaselessly thirsting for the *Svati* raindrop, as it will drink no other water. It is also a symbol for *viraha*, the anguish of a parted lover (Vaudeville, 1974: 170, footnote 55).

The pied crested cuckoo, as well as the common hawk cuckoo (or brain fever bird) is mostly silent during the winter, but as the hot season advances, it becomes increasingly noisy. It has a loud, monotonous call, which rises in crescendo and ends abruptly. This call is rendered in Hindi as *'piu, piu'* or as *'pee-kahan, pee-kahan'* (where is my beloved) and in Marathi it is said to be *'paos ala!'* (rain's coming!'). The migration of the pied crested cuckoo is controlled by the south-westerly monsoons, and their presence in the locality is heralded by the call of *'piu-piu-pee-pee-piu'* (Ali, 1972: 59, and plates 117 and 118).

The bhajan cited above commences with a Mira crazed at the beloved being called upon repeatedly by the *papiha*. She tells him that unless he stops, she will not only harm him by cutting off his beak, but that she will rub salt on the wound too. The call of the *papiha* is causing her great anguish as it echoes so exactly her own. She beseeches and threatens him at the same time not to bare her longing so plaintively.

There is then an emotional shift. From a tone of authority vis-a-vis the *papiha*, and from a declaration that she has the prerogative in calling on the beloved ('who are you to call out *piu, piu*?')—it becomes a more understanding tone. There is a recognition of a bond between the two of them. This is a recognition that the bird which calls out the same cry of love that she does, will be treated violently by others, just as others have attempted to twist her own being. She fears that anyone hearing him call out his cry will twist his wings.

Mira now says that his words are beautiful, and that as soon as her love is requited, she will ornament his beak in gold. She will then be able to wear the symbol of love on her head.

Mira later solicits the aid of the *papiha* in sending a message to the loved one. But she continues to warn him against making his love public, in case he finds his wings mangled. There is now a pact between Mira and the *papiha*, to assist each other in the same quest, and to aid in each other's survival.

The song culminates in Mira declaring that she herself is the *papiha*, that it is she who calls out '*piu piu*' day and night. What had appeared as a dialogue with a *papiha* singing outside is revealed as a soliloquy with herself. What is actually revealed is her attempt—and inability—to trample on her emotional life in order to conform to that expected of her by society. She attempted to cut off an essential part of herself, to twist herself in order to remain on the ground. Mira's love took its toll on her, but this particular *virahani* demonstrates that Mira rose above her injuries, and continued to be true to her emotional choice of being.

Dula, speak about Ram—speak your heart.
Your longing is intense.
Panchi, speak about Ram,
Speak your heart.
Your longing is intense.

Dula, I will school you and teach you.
And I will remain at your feet.
Dula, speak about Ram.
Speak your heart.
Your longing is intense.

Panchi, I will feed you on a variety of delicacies
And give you *Gangajal* to drink.
Dula, speak about Ram.
Speak your heart.
Your longing is intense.

Listen, *panchi*, your beak is red and your body green.
On your neck is a black band.
Dula, your longing is intense.

Bai Mira sings of Giridhar.
Panchi of the world beyond,
Your longing is intense.

(This bhajan was sung in village Shivrajpur, district Jamnagar, by Ranmalbha Manek at a bhajan gathering held at the house of Hothibha Manek, amidst the community of Waghers.)

The imagery of a bird (*panchi*), is one commonly used for the human spirit, whereby it is deemed that the bird (spirit) is only here transiently in this world, longing to migrate to its real home. Mira is nurturing and giving sustenance to her *panchi*, who lives and speaks of a love beyond, and at whose feet she sits. It is a bird held in captivity, against which it is fretting. What emerges here is her own personal struggle to sustain a relationship frowned upon by her society and impeded by those around her—which is kept enkindled by her own efforts.

Resistance and Personal Liberties

Mira stands up in the bhajans, sharply and unambiguously, for personal liberties. Her resistance to social norms and obligations, and her assertion of liberties based on the dictates of her heart, form a major theme of a large body of bhajans in Rajasthan as well as Saurashtra. In these, Mira spurns the Rana at the very time of the marriage rite, and asserts her own choice of relationship.

(Sung in village Dechra, district Udaipur, by Hakra Nanaji Patel, a young man who owned some land in the village. He sang regularly in a bhajan *mandli*, and also played the *dholak*).

There is dust rising in the distance, Mirabai,
There is dust rising in the distance.
You are bound to the name of Hari.

It is a procession of *jogis*, Mirabai, it is a procession of *jogis*.
There is a lamp lit to Hari in every home.
It is not a procession of *jogis*, Mirabai, it is not a procession of *jogis*
There is a lamp lit to Hari in every home.

Mirabai, it is a marriage party from Chittorgadh arriving,
A marriage party from Chittorgadh arriving.
You are bound to the name of Hari.

Leave aside these tattered rags, Mirabai,
Leave aside these tattered rags.
Drape yourself in the garment sent by the Rana.

Leave aside your *tulsi* garland, Mirabai,
Leave aside your *tulsi* garland.
Tie on the necklace sent by the Rana.

Tie the necklace round your *dasi*, Ranaji,
Tie the necklace round your *dasi*.
This *tulsi* garland is in the name of Hari.
Join your left hand with me, Ranaji,
Join your left hand with me.

My right hand is for Hari.
The Lord of Dwarka has married me, Ranaji,
The Lord of Dwarka has married me.
I have taken to saffron because of him.

I have found a guru in Rohidas,
I have found a guru in Rohidas.
I am bound to the name of Hari.

 A marriage is a socially ritualized and structured affair. It is a highly visible public occasion, whereby social relations between two families are consolidated. It is difficult to imagine a woman—even a woman with the depth of conviction Mira must have held—publicly repudiating a marital tie amidst the weight of social pressure around her on the very day that the wedding party arrives. Yet this is what Mira does in a large body of bhajans. These bhajans mark a stark crystallization of resistance to a marriage with the Rana, and they mark a strong challenge to the symbols and identification of the marriage ceremony.

Amongst the Rajputs of Rajasthan, when the *barat* or wedding party arrives at the bride's place of residence, they bring with them a full bridal wear called the *bari*. This consists of a minimum of four petticoats with gold or silver lace; two red or orange sarees again with gold or silver trimmings; one *dupatta*; one *chunri* trimmed with silver or gold; four blouses with *jari* work on it; one pair of ivory bangles; a pair of footwear; a bottle of perfume; four packets of *kum kum*, henna etc.; four coconuts; some sweet balls; and a *maud*, which is worn by the woman on the head. The bridegroom's party thus brings with it all the necessities needed for the bride to wear on the marriage day, symbolically showing that she now belongs to the family of the bridegroom.

The marriage party, with the bridegroom, is met some distance away from the bride's house by her brother or other male relative. The marriage party is then escorted to the bride's house and welcomed. It is only after the arrival of the bridegroom that the bride has oil rubbed on her body. A bride who has oil rubbed on her body cannot remain unmarried. If, for some reason, the bridegroom fails to turn up and the bride has had oil rubbed on her, then someone else has to be found to marry her. Having had oil rubbed on her body, the bride has a bath, and puts on the attire brought in the *bari*. She is then led to the marriage *pandal*, where the *hath leva*, or joining of hands, takes place. (M.R.M. 1891: 26-31.)

In the bhajan quoted above, the servitude entailed in a marital relationship is brought out sharply. Mira holds in utter contempt the symbols of the social marriage. Give the garment and the necklace to your servant, she says to the Rana!

The bhajan begins with the bhakta singers seeing travellers in the distance. They inform Mira that it is a procession of jogis, come to meet her and perhaps take her away. They are then surprised to find that it is not a procession of jogis, but a marriage party from Chittorgadh. Yet, they hold her fast to her stand, reminding her that she is bound to the name of Hari.

The voice then shifts to one of rebuke for Mira, emanating from someone close to the Rana. Mira, however, answers the Rana direct. She will not wear the garment and ornaments sent by him, she has already chosen tattered rags and the *tulsi* garland, marks of those who have rejected domestic ties.

Her mocking of the wedding ritual, in which she offers him her left hand—one cannot imagine a greater insult in a society which considers the left hand a dirty and inauspicious one—is the ultimate rejection of the Rana as husband.

A different version of this bhajan is as follows:
(Sung in village Ghanti, district Udaipur, by Ruplal Hakraji Patel, a prosperous farmer. There is a *mandli* in the village, which travels widely, outside of Rajasthan too, to take part in the bhajan gatherings. The Patels in village Ghanti are better off than the Anjania Patels in the nearby village of Dechra.)

There is dust rising in the distance, Mirabai,
There is dust rising in the distance.
Hari's tents have been put up by the river.
Worship Hari—cross over to the other side,
Mirabai, worship Hari—cross over to the other side.
You are bound to the name of Hari.

It is not a procession of *jogis*, Mirabai, it is not a procession of *jogis*.
It is the Rano, come from the fortress of Mewar.
Worship Hari—cross over to the other side,
Mirabai, worship Hari—cross over to the other side.
You are bound to the name of Hari.

The Lord of Dwarka has wedded me.
The Lord of Dwarka has wedded me.
My hand was joined with Hari's.

Worship Hari—cross over to the other side,
Mirabai, worship Hari, cross over to the other side.
You are bound to the name of Hari.
The first round of the circle I made through social pressure,
Ranaji, the second round I made in the name of Hari.

Worship Hari—cross over to the other side,
Mirabai, worship Hari, cross over to the other side.
You are bound to the name of Hari.

Watch what you are saying,
Mirabai, watch what you are saying,
Or I'll tear off your outer skin with my nails!

Bhakti is the sharp edge of a sword,
Mirabai, bhakti is the sharp edge of a sword.
Walk the sharp edge in the name of Hari.

Worship Hari—cross over to the other side, Mirabai, worship Hari, cross over to the other side.
You are bound to the name of Hari.

With folded hands, Mirabai spoke:
I have found a guru in Rohidas.
I have found a guru in Rohidas.

The supportive refrain of 'worship Hari, cross over to the other side', provides a constant validation to Mira's stand. In this bhajan, Mira admits that she was forced to go through the marriage rite because of social pressure, but insists that even within this, she gave her hand to Hari. She asserts that it is to the marriage of her heart that she grants legitimacy, not the socially imposed one.

It is very likely that this bhajan has emerged out of the community of leather workers, although it is now sung widely by other peasant communities too. The threat—'I'll tear off your outer skin with my nails!' appears to have emerged out of the labour of those who skin animals. However, the threat put in the mouth of the Rana does not deter Mira. She is held up by the knowledge that her chosen path of bhakti is not for the faint hearted, and the bhajniks continue to uphold her for living out the reality of her faith.

It appears to be an established fact that Mira was married to the Rana at a public ceremony. This no-one disputes. What remains indubitably a social fact though is that the bhajniks have continued to annul this socially imposed marriage, to render it illegitimate, and have continued instead to validate the creation of Mira's own relationship with Krishna.

For Mira, the choice of relationship was not one which allowed her to transcend or escape the everyday, social existence. Her choice brought her into sharp conflict with the people who held power in her life. As we shall see, this included the pressure of her own family, her mother and grandfather. In a society where marriage was an important means of forging political alliances, and was a means of declaring an end to a *vair* and vendetta, Mira stood up against the blind subjection of women to the service of powerful, militaristic patriarchs.

Mira has, indelibly, carved out a path for personal liberties for women. It was not carved out without a struggle, and it was not achieved without facing repression. The bhajans point to an area of personal life harshly governed by those one is closely involved with—one's mother, father, grandfather. On the other hand, the bhajans point to an area of life which leaves one free to conduct one's unfulfilled aspirations. This is the area of the imagination, the world of the mind and spirit, in which the self left empty in actual life can people the inner world with images of one's own making. Herein lies the main challenge of the Mira bhakti, and the main subversion, which has kept alight the tradition of better and more egalitarian social relationships. The powerful spiritual and cultural force of this should not be underestimated.

It is not as if Mira kept her convictions and her love quietly in her heart, accepting unpalatable social relationships in her everyday life while paying homage to the God she held dear. Mira's strength lies in the fact that she made her inner reality the principal one, negating that which was anti-thetical to this. She did not leave her imaginings in the realm of a distinctly separate reality, but penetrated to the very core of this imagining, and lived it out.

In a highly structured, hierarchical, caste-based society, the institution of marriage consolidates and continues caste and community ties. It is not a question of individual choice. Yet, Mira enunciated a choice for herself in precisely this society.

There is a proverb that the Rajput woman 'marries the land not the man' (Enthoven, III, 1922: 289) an instructive proverb when one studies the system of land distribution and the role of inheritance within this. For marriage ties, a Rajput goes outside his *got* to other Rajput *gots*. There are two types of engagements which take place amongst Rajputs. One is called *ekevda* and the other is called *dovda*. *Ekevda* is when one takes a daughter from a particular Rajput family but does not give a daughter in turn. In *dovda*, one gives as well as receives a daughter from the same family. The latter takes place only amongst Rajputs of equal rank as it is deemed by a Rajput that his status will be lowered by giving a daughter to someone who is his social inferior (M.R.M. 1891: 18). This means that by giving a daughter into a particular family, the Rajput is announcing his subservience to that family, and his daughter's with it.

Mira's stand against a relationship (with the Rana) which did not accord with her being, emerged from out of the experience of what the institution of marriage entailed within the society of Rajputs. However, Mira's fierce stand for personal freedoms continues to resonate today amongst other castes too. How has this come about?

It has often been stated that women of the lower castes and working women enjoy more personal liberties than those of the upper castes (Omvedt, 1975: 43–8). On closer examination, though, this statement can be seen to be limited. Although patriarchy assumes a different form amongst the lower castes, labouring women are far from having rights to personal liberties. This explains why the song of Mira is enunciated so strongly amongst the lower castes. For women of all castes and classes, the song of Mira holds within it the hope of desired but unfulfilled aspirations.

Amongst Bhangis, who are considered to be the lowest in social hierarchy, a man who marries a woman of a different caste faces the prospect of being outcasted. A widowed or unmarried woman from the caste of Bhangis is outcasted if she conceives a child by someone of a different caste. She can only escape being outcasted by publicly announcing the name of the father within a caste *panchayat*. If she is not prepared to do this, both she and the child are outcasted. If a married woman from the community of Bhangis decides to go and live with a second fellow Bhangi, she could be ordered by the *panch* to return to her first home. If she is unwilling to do so, she had to pay, at the end of the nineteenth century, the sum of rupees hundred to a hundred and fifty, not an inconsiderable sum (M.R.M. 1891: 583).

Amongst the Meghwals or Bambhis, there are five divisions or sub-castes—the Aadu Bambhi, Maru Bambhi, Jata Bambhi, Baman Bambhi and Charaniya Bambhi. The Maru, Jata, Baman and Charaniya Bambhis marry within their own division, and not outside of this. Once an engagement is decided upon, the uncle of the young man goes to the house of the prospective bride and gives a present of a red cloth, a coconut and *gur*. At the time of the wedding, the bride is dressed in the red *gaghra* and red *odhni* sent for her by the groom. The Garuda, the priest of the Bambhis, joins their hands in *hath leva*, and they then circle the fire four times (M.R.M. 1891: 527–32).

Although the Bambhis, Regars and Chamars share a similar labour and similar skills as we have seen, and although they smoke from the same hookah, marriage relations do not take place between these communities (M.R.M. 1891: 540).

The Jats and the Anjanas, both cultivating groups, have become very closely associated with each other today, but no marriage takes place between the two groups. Amongst the Jats, it is customary to cement a marriage between two families by eating *gur*. Therefore, when a Jat goes to have a meal at a fellow Jat's house, he does not touch *gur* which might be on his plate. If he does, and even if there has been no discussion of a proposed marriage, the person who had given the *gur* can go to the *panch* and demand a daughter from the family of the other man (M.R.M. 1891: 49-50).

In Saurashtra, the Chamars do not marry within their own *got*, but out of it. If a dispute arises between the two families after the engagement, on any personal or social issue, then the engagement is broken off. Neither the prospective bride nor the bridegroom have any say in this. The two families thus sever links (S.P.K. Vol. 1, 1957: 327).

Amongst the Kharvas, if the husband and wife wish to divorce, then both sides have to sign an agreement. If one party is unwilling, no separation is possible (S.P.K. Vol. 2, 1958: 117).

Child marriage is still prevalent amongst the Satvaras. If a child is not engaged by a particular age she/he is looked upon with suspicion by the community, as someone who has got something wrong with her/him. However, the young girl only goes to live at the in-laws after reaching puberty. While engaged, she receives from the man she is to marry, an *odhni* and a plain *gaghro* at every Holi, which she is expected to embroider (S.P.K. Vol. 2, 1958: 281–2).

In the community of the Chunvalia Kolis, the permission of the *panch* has to be sought in order to break an engagement. Even if the two families agree amicably on such a break, the wedding has to take place if the *panch* so sanctions (S.P.K. Vol. 2. 1958: 24).

So amongst each and every community which sings Mira, the power of the internal community in imposing a particular kind of relationship and marital tie is strongly entrenched. Thus, when Mira's choice of relationship with Krishna and the rejection of the Rana are evoked in the bhajans, Mira stands out as a woman who threw aside the particular marriage institution which makes a woman enter into an intimate relationship with a man she does not have an affinity with. While this song of Mira continues to be sung, it continues to point to the domain of a harsh personal repression.

It is significantly this institution of marriage and the symbols embedded within it that the song of Mira pointedly challenges. They are symbols and practices common to all communities—the red *odhni*, the *tika*, bangles, etc.—and they are recognizable and identified as the hall marks of a married woman by all.

The articulation of the Mira bhajans upholds a common experience faced by all women, a common harsh imposition, and a common lack of personal freedom. The community of Mirabai here is the community of all those women who have endured incompatible relationships, all those who have suffered the violence of a forced intimacy, and all those women who have dreamt and continue to dream of relationships in which minds do not remain poles apart and the spirit does not fly out of its house.

In its zeal to form and maintain a marital tie which will guard the existing system of power and community, it is not abstract 'society' that brings the full force of its might on the young woman. Dominant society relies on close members of the family to ensure that the continuity of an ordered society is not shaken. The force of this emotional pressure is not easily repudiated. One can see this clearly in the Mira bhajans.

In Mira's *'Janma Patri'* after Mira has angrily thrown out the maids who had come to dress her in bridal red—she is faced with her mother. Mira's mother holds out her *pallav*, begging that her daughter keep the honour of this:

Bai, rakho palla ri murjad. (Appendix, page 233)

It is a highly emotive scene, the mother asking the daughter to ensure her her personal honour. This is the turning point for Mira. Her anger vanishes—and she agrees to put on the bridal dress.

The holding out of the *pallav* by the mother connotes two things. Firstly, it is a posture in which one begs—a supplication which cannot but be granted by a daughter. Secondly, the holding out of the *pallav* is a gesture that pleads for the continuity of the person's marital status within her family. It is a gesture which asks that her marital status remain inviolate. A refusal would be tantamount to ceding that one does not care what suffering and indignity the supplicant will have to endure. Again this is not a stand that can be taken by a daughter easily.

A daughter's actions reflect always and immediately on the mother who has given birth to her. This is why Mira's mother laments, in a Saurashtrian bhajan, that Mira was ever born to her.

(Sung in village Kesav, Junagadh district, by Bachudas Premdas Dudhrejia, who is a small cultivator. He also performs the worship of Ramdev Pir. The village was a Mer village dominated by a temple to Lirbai Mata.)

Mira's mind was engrossed in Kanudo.
Mira's mind was engrossed in Kanudo.
She was tied to the name of Hari.

From Mewargadh came a marriage procession for Mirabai.
From Mewargadh came a marriage procession for Mirabai.
That Ranoji came to marry Mira.

Mira's mind was engrossed in Kanudo.
Mira's mind was engrossed in Kanudo.
She was tied to the name of Hari.

Let the marriage procession from Mewar arrive, mother,
Let the marriage procession from Mewar arrive.
That Ranoji is like a brother, born of my mother, to me.

Mira, why did you not come out as a stone from my womb?
Mira, why did you not come out as a stone from my womb?
That *dhobido* could then have beaten clothes on it.

Mira, do not utter such words.
Mira, do not utter such words.
Do not blemish the name of our *kul*.

Who is it that has stuffed your ears with ill advice?
Who is it that has stuffed your ears with ill advice?

Rohidas is my guru.
Rohidas is my guru.
Khimdio Kotwal whispered this advice in my ears.
Rohidas is a Chamar by caste.
Rohidas is a Chamar by caste.
He skins hide in service to the bridegroom.

Rohidas' disciple Mirabai replied:
My *sadhuda* will keep me in their *kul*.
My *sadhuda* will keep me in their *kul*.

Mira's mind was engrossed in Kanudo.
Mira's mind was engrossed in Kanudo.
She was tied to the name of Hari

The inter-change in this bhajan, between a deeply unhappy and bitter mother, and her recalcitrant daughter would be familiar to all within a bhajan session. The cry of 'why did you not come out as a stone from my womb' can be heard today in many places, and it is familiar to all living in a tightly-knit society where the family is the bulwark of social and moral norms.

The evocation of Rohidas and Khimdio Kotwal as the instigators of Mira's revolt against the Rana as husband is striking. It does not stand Mira in good stead (within her family) to declare that she has accepted a Chamar as guru. It opens her up to mockery and denigration. It makes her vulnerable to personal vilification. Despite the pressure of close family, though, Mira remains committed to her conviction.

(Sung by Govindram Kapdi, in village Varvada, Jamnagar district. He earns his living by officiating at the worship of Ramdev Pir. The bhajan was sung in the house of a family of Kharvas where there had been a recent death. The bhajan gathering was part of the days of prayer for the deceased relative.)

I am wedded to Shamadiyo,
I am wedded to Vitthalvar.
I will not bind another's *mindhod* round my wrist.

I will not bind it, Rana,
Nor leave aside the one I wear.
I will not bind another's *mindhod* round my wrist.

I have worn my *mindhod*, Rana,
And openly walked in public in it.
I met Dhruv and Prahlad on the way.
I will not bind another's *mindhod* round my wrist.

The Rana ties a *mindhod* round the wrist of a woman he sees is beautiful.
In her heart, there is no feeling for him.
There is no feeling for him in her heart today.
Rana, I will not bind another's *mindhod* round my wrist.

I had known Rana that, that my life partner was...
But fate decreed something else...
Today, fate decreed something else...
I will not bind another's *mindhod* round my wrist.

Beloved, Bai Mira sings the glory of Giridhar.
I have become transformed through loving you.
I will not bind another's *mindhod* round my wrist.

    The setting of this bhajan is the actual day that Mira is to be married to the Rana. It starts by Mira saying that she is already married to Shamadiyo, and that she will not bind herself in marriage to another. The *mindhod* is a bracelet strung with the fruit of the plant *randia dumer torum*, which is tied to the wrist of a woman at the time of marriage. In this bhajan, it symbolizes consistently the commitment (or lack thereof) to a relationship. Mira declares that she cannot break the relationship already formed.

    The song shifts to Mira declaring that she has publicly announced her betrothal to Shamadiyo, that this is well known, and that having established this relationship, she had met two well known bhaktas, Dhruv and Prahlad on the way. She re-asserts that she will not wear another's *mindhod*.

    The bhajan so far has been in the voice of Mira. It has been a voice strong in its pledge, deep in its espousal, at the very time that the relationship that she has formed is to be desecrated. The voice then shifts to that of the bhajnik who is witnessing this desecration—and commenting on it. The witness sees the Rana tying the *mindhod* round a woman of whom he sees only the externality, her outward beauty, but not her inner being. The bhajnik remarks that Mira has no feeling in her heart for the Rana.

    Mira's voice, which continues to assert that she will not wear another's *mindhod*, then becomes a vulnerable voice. It is a voice which continues to assert the truth of her heart, but which has met with a profane reality. Mira's voice breaks. What she had known and recognized remains only half uttered. She had known and accepted... but today fate decreed otherwise...

Her continuing to declare that she would not wear another's *mindhod* is now a matter of her holding on to her own inner truth, retaining her integrity within. The bhajan concludes with the statement that having known her beloved, she has become transformed, and that for her there is no going back on this transformation to being other than what she has become. She reiterates that she cannot accept another's *mindhod*.

This bhajan is sung widely in Saurashtra today. Unlike the Rajasthani bhajans in which the overbearing authority of the Rana, particularly the throne and fortress of Chittorgadh, are sharply challenged, the Saurashtrian bhajans sung by bhajniks who did not, historically, have such a direct relationship with the Rana of Mewar, enter into Mira's inner being. They do this from within their own commitment to her as a bhajnik.

The structure of feeling in the Saurashtra bhajans is much more complex and fraught, more alive to Mira's emotional struggle, than the Rajasthani ones, in which the central force is the challenge to the Rana. The person of Mira emerges in Saurashtra in the full depths of her strivings. I will return to this in greater detail in a later chapter. In the bhajan discussed above though, the Rana is not a threatening, blustering figure, whose authority and power Mira spurns by saying give these clothes to your *dasi*! Rather, the Rana here is an insensitive, blind being who cannot see beyond the physicality of the woman he has come to wed.

The Rana has remained deaf to Mira's public avowal of a relationship with Krishna. He has no understanding of the ideals and longings contained in her heart which his arrival has shattered. He has no knowledge of the world contained within Mira.

One must be wary of interpreting Mira's (and the bhajniks) use of symbols of the marital relationship—the beloved's *mindhod*, the beloved's *odhni*—as a demonstration of the fact that both Mira and the bhajniks consider her relationship with Krishna to be one of that between an actual man and woman who are married. In the realm of spiritual expression, bridal imagery is often utilized to articulate the actual depth of the formation of a commitment—just as the phrase 'wedded to' expresses a strong bond (to a cause, etc.).

It would be facile indeed, to render the relationship between Mira and Krishna as being one in which she saw herself as being within the time-worn and easily identifiable social institution, or to impose on this meanings derived from the social experience of marriage in society. The fact that it is a woman articulating this, that she is utilizing imagery derived from the earthly wedding to encapsulate a commitment she feels deeply, that she seeks to capture this experience within the bounds of a common language, should not make us arrive at an effortless definition of this dream within a neat comprehension of our own well defined boundaries.

Bhakti enabled the bhakta to engage, personally and intimately, into the creation of her own particular relationship with the Absolute. We must grant to Mira her own unique and personal dream and concede her the world that she struggled so hard to create. She too attempted to make the world explicable through the expressions available to her.

I have worn an *odhni*, I have put on a *pachedi*,
I have worn my Giridhar's *odhni*.

Mirabai entered the *mandap*.
The Indestructible sat on the *patlo*.
A vow was pledged between the two.
Rana, I have worn the *odhni* of my Giridhari.

The *chori* is built to the four *yugas*.
Rana, I have circled all four of these and freed myself.

I have worn an *odhni*, put on a *pachedi*,
I have worn my Giridhar's *odhni*.

My heart glows, Rana,
Mirabai's face is radiant.
Mira is in love with the face of Murari.
I have worn my Giridhar's *odhni*.

(Sung by Kanjibhai Punja Salet, who worked as a fisherman, at a bhajan gathering in Subhashnagar, which adjoins the city of Porbander. Others at the gathering were, in the main, Kharvas too.)

The marriage described in the bhajan above is a symbolic marriage through which Mira liberates herself from the burden of existence. Mira, by wedding herself to the Indestructible, survives not only the personal destruction at the hands of the Rana, who tries to poison her, she survives not only the cruelty of an unheeding society—but she survives the ravages of the four *yugas* too. She frees herself from social and historical time. She is able to do this after putting on Giridhar's *odhni*. The bhajniks of Saurashtra have, in their projection of Mira, entered deeply into her world view, from the vantage point of their own bhakti. To conclude, it is important to understand that while Mira posed a very direct challenge to the institute of marriage, she did not then, simply, replace this with a marriage to Krishna. A relationship derived through bhakti must be seen in a more complex way, and within the structure of feeling of bhakti.

On the four corners of this *chundaldi* are four peacocks, Rana of Mewar.
In the middle is a pattern made out of rice grains.
Have this *chundaldi* dyed, Rana,
have this *chundaldi* dyed.

The cotton threads of this *chundaldi* have been spun by my guru.
It was woven in such a way, woven in such a way,
That it took nine months before completion.

Have this *chundaldi* dyed, Rana,
have this *chundaldi* dyed.

The guruji cast an image in the *chundaldi*,
And created a unique design in it.

Have this *chundaldi* dyed, Rana,
have this *chundaldi* dyed.

I put on the *chundaldi* and went in public with it.
I met Dhruv and Prahlad on the way.

Have this *chundaldi* dyed, Rana,
have it dyed.
With the authority of the guru, Mirabai spoke:
Give me abode with the *sants*.

Have this *chundaldi* dyed, Rana,
have it dyed.

(Sung by Vinodbhai Dosa Joshi, at a Ramapir temple in the town of Okha.)

Vinodbhai had, like a lot of other people, left his village to migrate out at the time of drought, in 1986 and 1987. He normally resided with his family in the village of Khatumbha in Okhamandal *taluka*, where they had some land and cattle. However, with the severe shortage of water, resulting from the current drought, he had left with his family and cattle to live in the compound of his sister in the town of Okha. They made ends meet by selling milk to cafes in Okha, as well as delivering milk to individuals in neighbouring Mithapur. Khatumbha was predominantly a town inhabited by Aboti Brahmans. The 1931 Baroda Census states that the other Brahmans do not eat food cooked by the Abotis who are mainly found in Okhamandal *taluka*, and that the Abotis are generally, as a class, poor, who live as confectioners, cultivators, and temple servants (Baroda Census, 1931: 431.)

The imagery of God as weaver, as the creator of the human body (the *chundaldi* is a symbol for the human body) has been so deeply internalized in our culture that it has become part of our common philosophy and language, without us stopping to pay recognition to its origins. The same applies to the imagery of dyeing—'dye my soul in it' and 'I am coloured in the dye of...'—whereby it denotes the immersion of the being in a deep-felt commitment.

Kabir the weaver was the path breaker in the formation of an understanding of the human body being woven with loving care by the Creator, though there may well be other, anonymous bhaktas who contributed too, inspired either by Kabir, or inspired by their own labour, their own act of creativity, to enunciate this imagery.

Mira says that her *chundaldi*, her physical form, was woven with such care by the Creator that it took nine months before completion. On this physical form then, the guru imprinted a unique design, marking her life out as different and memorable from others. She herself became self aware of this and consciously chose the path of bhakti, meeting with fellow travellers, the bhaktas Dhruv and Prahlad on the way.

The refrain of 'have this *chundaldi* dyed, Rana' is a mockery of the phenomenal *chundaldi* with its trite design of peacocks—which is juxtaposed to the creation of Mira's life, with all its depth and pain. The puny power of the Rana who sent Mira a *chundaldi* to wear on her wedding day is pitted against the power of the Weaver who wove Mira's individual being. Mira accepts here the uniqueness of her existence, and shows it to have more depth than the life offered her by the Rana.

What am I to do, Rana,
What am I to do with your rubies and diamonds?
What am I to do with your necklace of gems?

I want to don saffron,
And worship Hari today.
Rana, what am I to do with your rubies and diamonds?

This palace and tall storeys, Rana,
What am I to do with them?
I want to worship Hari in a hut today.
Your rubies and diamonds, Rana, what am I to do with them?

Mirabai sings the glory of Giridhar.
I want to wander wearing the immortal *chudlo* of Ram,
Rana, what am I to do with your rubies and diamonds?

(Sung by Bachudas Premdas Dudhrejia in village Kesav, Junagadh district. On some memorable occasions, one met with individuals who continued to sing Mira throughout the night, each bhajan enhancing the force and power of the other until one was enveloped by the presence of Mira through the singer. By and large, these tended to be older men and women who played on the *ektara*. They held both the authority of experience within a bhajan gathering, and the authority of their commitment. Bachudasbhai was one such person. Vinodbhai Dosa Joshi in Okha, who was in his late twenties, was another such person.)

In the above bhajan, Mira dons saffron and enters, symbolically and irrefutably, into a different sphere of life and being. She throws off the marks of a female servitude and takes to a simpler yet richer mode of life which leaves her free to conduct her own particular search. For the community of Mirabai, a truly integral common life can be evolved only after the emblems of servitude have been discarded, liberating women to create a better self.

An Indestructible Relationship

Mira says:

Why should I wed such a husband who is alive today and dead tomorrow.
I will marry my Giridhar Gopal,
my *chudlo* will become immortal.

This *sakhi* precedes the singing of each Mira bhajan in Saurashtra. It is the indelible hallmark of a Mira bhajan. This *sakhi* articulates the transitory nature of the marital relationship, the fear embodied in the loss of a husband, and makes explicit in a stark way Mira's choice of Krishna as against the Rana. It marks a longing for the breaking of insecurity entailed in the state of widowhood, and holds up a relationship in which the *chudlo*—one of the main symbols of a marital status—will never be broken.

The bhajans are important, crucially, in rejecting the pain and humiliation entailed in being a widow. The *sakhi* quoted above enunciates Mira's experience but it at the same time comments upon each marriage relationship in this society, and comments upon the common condition of large numbers of women whose husbands are dead. It is a common experience and a common condition which is identified and felt by all the bhajniks, as well as those who are encompassed within the fold of the community of Mirabai by the bhajniks' singing.

It is not only women of the upper castes who face a harsh isolation and degradation from the time of the death of their husbands. Though women of the lower castes are not bound by restrictions on what they can eat or not, what colours to wear or not whether and where to go out, and it is commonly cited as a 'freedom' that they are allowed to remarry—there is much degradation involved in this form of remarriage.

Amongst large numbers of cultivating and artisan classes, the remarriage takes place at the dead of night, and it is thought that if anyone sees the face of a widow on her way to the house of her second husband, this person will die within six months (C.o. I. Vol. XXV, Part One, 1901: 214). Within the community of leather workers, the Chamars, the woman is expected to marry the younger brother of the deceased. If she marries someone else, she has to compensate the younger brother of her first husband. The *panch* is then informed, and new bangles are given to the woman by the bridegroom (C.o I. Vol. XXV, Part One, 1901: 214). There is no *homa* or sacred fire, which is reserved solely for the first marriage.

Amongst the leather workers, a bachelor is not allowed to marry a widow. If he wishes to, he must first 'marry' a *shami* plant, (prosopis spicigera) in order to gain the status of a married man (Enthoven, Vol. 1, 1920: 267).

If a woman from the community of Jats is to be remarried, she is dressed in new clothes, with bangles, on the night of Saturday or Sunday, and she is taken to the house of her second husband in the dead of night. This happens if the second husband lives in a different village. If he lives in the same village, then there are two simple practices that they undergo in order to be married. In one, the man brings a load of fodder to the door—the woman takes the load down from his head, and goes inside the house, the man following her. In the second practice, the woman comes to the door with a pot of water—the man takes down the pot, and goes into the house, with the woman following (M.R.M. 1891: 52).

Amongst the Ods, the levirate remarriage to the younger brother-in-law is compulsory. If the woman refuses this, she has to give a dinner to the whole caste (Enthoven, Vol. III, 1922: 147). Amongst Telis, a coconut and a cock are waved in front of the face of the woman before the time of her remarriage, to free her from molestation by her deceased husband's spirit. The second marriage is then performed, whereby the woman wears the new robe and ornaments sent by her intended husband. It is however, another widow who puts a *tika* on her forehead (Enthoven, Vol. III, 1922: 374).

It is a matter of shame that the *natrayat* Rajputs, those who allow widow remarriage, are looked down upon by other Rajputs who consider it a point of honour that a widow be kept under strict restrictions (M.R.M. 1891: 38). There is some humanity displayed in the account as to how the system of widow remarriage originated within the Rajput communities of Rajasthan. The story is that the Chauhan Raja of Jalor, Rao Kanadde, had a daughter who was a child widow. Seeing her friends being married, she expressed a wish to put on red robes too. Her mother was distressed and informed Kanadde and her son Viramde about this. The Rana of Chittor was then invited by Kanadde to marry his daughter.

When the Rana arrived, he was taken inside by Viramde, who said that unless the Rana married his widowed sister, he would kill him then and there, and would also take his own life. The Rana replied that if he were to agree to this, no-one would allow him to return to Chittorgadh—or her. Viramde then suggested that he build a fort in Godvad *pargana* where the Rana could live with his sister. The marriage took place, the Rana staying with her three days—occasionally returning to visit her. After this, all those men who remained unmarried to a mature age, began to marry widows, and were thrown out of caste for this. Slowly, these formed into a separate caste. The Rajputs who married someone from this caste then became part of it too (M.R.M. 1891: 41–3). Even within the *natrayat* Rajputs though, the second marriage takes place at night, with the woman taken secretively to her new home, with no one to see her (M.R.M. 1891: 43).

It is clear that the experience of being a widow is a deeply scarring one, for women of all classes and communities. Thus when the Mira bhajans articulate the pain of this experience, and articulate an opposition to the institution of widowhood, this enters into and validates a negation of the common degradation felt by women.

I have become attached to your face, beloved Mohan,
I have become attached to your face.

The domestic life is a sour and hollow one.
One weds—and then becomes a widow.
Why should I go to his house, beloved Mohan?
I have become attached to your face.

I married my loved one,
and achieved an undestructible relationship.
I annihilated the fear of widowhood.
Beloved Mohan, I have become attached to your face.

Mirabai is blessed.
My one hope rests in you.
Oh, I am fortunate (*badbhagi*), beloved Mohan,
I have become attached to your face.

(This song was sung in virtually every bhajan gathering I attended in Saurashtra, including amongst the women of the *'Gopi Mandli'* in Dwarka, who were from the community of Gugli Brahmans. Women and men sang this bhajan with the same amount of intensity.)

In this bhajan Mira categorically annihilates the experience of widowhood. She obliterates the fear of it, reiterating that her salvation and hope lies in Mohan—that it is the image of his face that allows her to walk unembittered and unfettered in life. The sourness and hollowness of the married life is exposed, and commented upon. This is the most well known and well sung Mira bhajan in Saurashtra—in fact in the whole of Gujarat. The shame of it is that it has been censored by Gandhi and Narayan Khare, the musician who lived at Gandhi's ashram in Ahmedabad (A. Bh. 1922: 168).

In both instances where the still prevalent version has been tampered with, it has been through the deletion of the strong statement made on widowhood—in lines four and eight. I would think that this was done because the Gujarati word for widow is the same as that for a prostitute—*'rand'*—hence the need to delete the phrases from the *'Ashram Bhajnavali'*. Without these particular utterances, though, the bhajan loses its power and indeed its meaning. It is an extremely forceful bhajan when heard in Gujarati *'parni ne randavu pachhu'* and *'randavano bhay bhangiyo re'* are utterances which when heard sung strike at the very core of widowhood.

Gandhi, however, would not have approved of Mira's revolt against widowhood (I will come back to this in a later chapter), and certainly he has not chosen to highlight this aspect of Mira's life in his writings. This act of censorship is much more than a mere deletion of words. It is an expurgation of Mira's challenge to the institutions of marriage and widowhood, both of which make women vulnerable and degraded.

The peoples' Mira continues to stand up in song against an imposed widowhood as well as an imposed marriage. Neither the popularity of Gandhi, nor the widespread influence of the Gadhian ashrams spread throughout Gujarat which continue to propagate the bhajans from the *'Ashram Bhajnavali'*, have succeeded in eroding the particular words and expressions of this bhajan from the peoples' memory. The singing of the unexpurgated bhajan testifies to the force that lies behind the song of Mira—a force which derives from the actuality of women's suffering, from the wish to give expression to a common scar and a common pain.

Chapter Five

Ordeals of Community: The Song Imperilled

There were various elements in Mira's choice of living that made her a figure for opprobrium to the Rajputs, and for which they required her extinction: her public stand in associating with bhajniks of all ranks, her rejection of a life of seclusion, and her public alignment to an emotional life which was antithetical to the decorum demanded of a Rajput princess. When Mira attempted the forging of an alternative community for herself, there were ordeals of survival, to retain life and continue chosen community. Thus, when Mira survived the attempts of the Sisodiya family to destroy her, the community of Mirabai rejoiced and was strengthened. The song of the bhajniks today is essentially a song of this survival, and a song of the continuity of this community.

For an individual woman from a princely family to succeed in breaking out of her social community and forge an alternative one is remarkable enough. What is even more significant is the continuity of the bonds forged to Mira by those who see her as having joined her life to theirs. The history of Mira testifies to her severing bonds with those she was tied to socially—with her family in Merta, and the family of Sisodiyas. She claimed a right to a different association. The rage of the ruling family decreed that a cup of poison be sent to her (a solution often resorted to by princely families when an individual stood in the way of collective honour and advancement). There must have been support for Mira whithin the citadel of Chittor to ensure that the cup which reached her did not contain poison. The bhajans say that Mira drank of this cup, knowing that it contained poison and knowing that her destruction was desired. In the peoples' rendering of Mira, there is no distinction made between the Rana who sent Mira an *odhni*—and the Rana who sent Mira a cup of poison. They are one and the same person.

Attempts were made on Mira's life not because of her devotion to Giridhar, but because embedded in Mira's complete commitment to this worship was her public affiliation to an alternative form of being, and an alternative association. The concept of honour, of *izzat*, so essential to the maintenance of Rajput power, was dealt a body blow by Mira's actions.

In a pre-capitalist society, one's social community was ordained by birth, making dissent to this community and survival outside of it extremely difficult. Romila Thapar has pointed out that the key to the functioning of rights and obligations, and therefore the key to everyday survival in Indian society lay in belonging to a particular group. It was this group which sought and claimed rights—rights as a caste, rights as a family, rights as a guild. A member of a particular caste could then claim the rights to economic and social maintenance from his or her group, *provided* that she/he observed the rules of this group (Thapar, 1984: 35–6). Once a person broke and thereby threatened the cohesion of this group, she/he was isolated and vulnerable. If this particular dissident attempted to carve out a different way of being, the group would draw in together against him/her and condone a harsh reprisal.

Examples of social communities holding together against a violent punishment of someone from within their midst abound. In the early twentieth century, the British found it almost impossible to gain convictions in Kheda district against those suspected of murder, because the Patidars shielded each other (M.S.A., R.D. 1904, Vol. 27, *Assistant Collector's Report*, 1902-1903: 244). Chakrabarti, the Collector of Kheda stated in his first report that the key to understanding the complexities of society in that region was that murders were usually carried out as a form of village justice, and it was therefore deemed an offence to assist the authorities in bringing the offenders to justice (M.S.A., R.D. 1911, Vol. 10, *Collector's Report*, 1909-1910: 39). Such 'justice' was often highly brutal, involving the use of men from the lower castes to perform the destruction of someone within the dominant caste (M.S.A., R.D. 1914, Compilation 511, Part III, Collector's Report, 1912-1913: 40). In the village of Ashamli in the district of Kheda, the head of a Patel was publicly chopped off by a fellow Patel. In Moholel similarly, the body of a murdered man was dragged in public (M.S.A., R.D., 1912, Compilation 511, Part II, *Collector's Report*, 1911-1912: 41–2).

The crucial point to note in the above examples is the public demonstration of punishment, with the body left lying in an open place—a reminder to all those present not to digress in a similar way. This reinforced norms, values and existing power structures in society.

An individual need not, necessarily, have flouted a community norm to be thus extinguished. Amongst the Jadeja Rajputs of Saurashtra, the birth of a girl child is unwelcome. In the nineteenth century, the Jadejas systematically eliminated girl children, and this was condoned and accepted by the whole community. The occurrence of such a murder within a family drew no surprise or inquiry. If a person asked the outcome of a pregnancy, the answer 'nothing' said all (Walker et al, 1856: 330).

Other women within the Sisodiya fold who have not, unlike Mira, posed a challenge to Rajput values or the rule of the Ranas, have still been obliterated. The murder that took place in the nineteenth century of Krishna Kunwari, the Sisodiya princess, has been described by Tod with his customary pernicious hypocrisy and the false beating of breast. The circumstances surrounding the murder of Krishna Kunwari are as follows:

It was a time of internecine warfare in Rajputana, Sindhia's troops having overrun large areas. A contingent from Jaipur camped near Udaipur with a troop of about three thousand men, awaiting acknowledgement of the proposal of Krishna Kunwari's hand. Raja Man of Marwar also advanced a claim to the hand of

Krishna Kunwari, saying that the princess had been promised to his predecessor, which meant to the occupant of the throne, and not the individual occupant of it. Sindhia aided the demands of Raja Man and sent a corps of eight thousand men into the valley. The Jaipur forces were crushed by the Marwar force, but neither side was prepared to give up its claim to Krishna Kunwari, considering this to be a loss of face.

A 'solution' was then thought of—to dispose of Krishna Kunwari, in order to let all the contenders retreat with their miserable honour intact. Tod comments on this grandiosely—and viciously:

When Iphigenia was led to the sacrificial altar, the salvation of her country yielded a noble consolation. (Tod, 1971: 539.)

The brutal, senseless murder of the 'virgin' princess is portrayed in a portentously noble tone by Tod.

Krishna Kunwari's brother was then sent to stab her. He displayed an un-Rajput emotion by being unable to perform the deed when he was actually face to face with his sister. Krishna Kunwari was, subsequently, poisoned. According to Tod, her dying words to her mother who was half crazed with grief were:

Why afflict yourself, my mother, at this shortening of the sorrows of life? I fear not to die! Am I not your daughter? Why should I fear death? We are marked out for sacrifice from our birth; we scarcely enter the world but to be sent out again; let me thank my father that I have lived so long! (Tod, 1971: 540.)

The bitter irony contained in Krishna Kunwari's words make it very clear that Rajput women were well aware that their lives were in the hands of their fathers, brothers and husbands.

When the gift of life is itself at the mercy of predatory patriarchs, the onus is on the woman of courage and integrity to seek an alternative life. Mira did so, seeking a life of emotional fulfilment which was marked by a long drawn out struggle to retain life and community.

The formation of the community of Mirabai however, was beset with repression. The song of Mira was imperilled, yet it has remained continuous in its force. Nevertheless, this song has remained confined to the sphere of bhakti and it has not spilled out to engage in an active combat with the hierarchies embedded in society. For this though, we have to look to more sustained political organizations. The importance of the people's Mira lies in her crystallization of ideals upheld by the mass of bhajniks, and it lies in her giving form to a different structure of relationships and values.

In the past, dissident religious movments have often ended up by becoming a sub-caste or separate caste, the Lingayats and Bishnois but being two examples of this process. This did not, however, happen with the Mira phenomenon. The force of Mira has not been directed by a small elite who head a *sampraday*, living off the fruits of the initial impetus and bending this to commercial gain. The song of Mira exists outside of formal *sampradays* and it has been kept alive within the condition of the degradation of the vast majority of people. It remains enfolded within the lives of the people—and it is also a leap into a future which has not yet come.

Chapter Six

Privation in Community

The creation of an alternative community is not one that can be evolved without a political and emotional battle. Even for a person who assumes *bhekh*, who dons saffron, picks up an *ektara*, leaves her social domain and moves into another, to live within that alternative community and sustain it without reference to the past is not possible. The past, at the same time as it is rejected, continues to burden the present. The conception of the future remains dim. The much struggled for present, when it arrives, holds hardships, and holds dreams which continue to elude one.

Mira broke with her *kul*. She broke with the ruling family of Merta and Mewar. She left the fortress of Chittor, swearing never to set foot in the land of the Rana. She did not tarry in Merta either, riven as it was with conflict with the house of Jodhpur.

She embarked on a life of an itinerant bhakta, a wandering singer. Thus, she reached Dwarka. The bhajniks in Saurashtra show a strong empathy with the predicament of Mira the exile. They enter the emotions of Mira the woman in a deep way, paying heed to her disjunctured ideals and vulnerabilities, so that Mira emerges not just as a rebel of strength, but as a person who having fought a battle against entrenched powers, began the life of an itinerant singer, and was scarred by her experiences. Mira's historical mooring in Saurashtra is as a person who had sundered herself from the community which had oppressed, as well as given birth to her. There is a compassion expressed for her in the bhajans sung in Saurasthra, a sympathy for her situation in exile—and there is an anguish voiced by her at the life of penury she is leading.

Hermann Goetz, in his reconstruction of the life of Mira, states that Mira arrived in Dwarka circa AD 1537 at a time when the Ranchhodji temple there was in ruins, and deserted, after having been sacked by Mahmud Shah I, the Sultan who became known, popularly, as Mahmud *Begadha* after his conquest of the two forts in Pavagadh and Junagadh. Goetz attributes to Mira the ambition of setting herself up as the *'Gosaiyni'* of the temple at Dwarka, by preaching her own interpretation of the Krishna bhakti (Goetz, 1966: 29). Goetz portrays Mira to be a powerful, single-minded person, who might have

if she had not been a woman... become the founder of a sect of her own. (Goetz, 1966: 30.)

The grandiose ambitions that Goetz attributes to Mira, including that of being the architect of Akbar's plan to bridge the gulf between Hindus and Muslims, and

organizing an empire in which people were expected to find peace and justice (Goetz, 1966: 38)

are lofty indeed, and must be left in that realm. For our purpose, we must, in time, descend to the common recognizable experience of alms-seekers and beggars to make sense of the peoples' Mira as she emerges in Saurashtra.

That Mira should have chosen to go to Dwarka is not surprising. It was a popular place of pilgrimage—Madhavacharya, Nanak, Kabir, Chaitanya, Jnanesvar, had all visited Dwarka in their lifetime (Thakar, in D.S., n.p.d: 67). Mira had already visited Vrandavan and come in conflict with the Gaudiya Vaishnavs there. The Vallabh *sampraday* she had rejected. Whether the Shardapith at Dwarka set up by the Shankracharya in the eighth century A.D. welcomed Mira or not is not known.

It is unlikely that Mira would have remained permanently established at Dwarka. If she had, she would have had to enter into alliances with the orthodox religious leaders as well as the political rulers of the time, and we would have been left with some documentary evidence of this. Saurashtra has a strong network of pilgrimage places, especially around the Girnar, and it is much more likely that Mira frequented these, given her particular propensity to sing and compose.

Dwarka was ruled at this time by the Waghers (Maniks) who were an important sea power. Sultan Mahmud is said to have sacked Dwarka because he heard complaints that pilgrims, who were on their way to Mecca, were captured and harassed by the Wagher pirates. Dwarka however was placed on the vital sea trade route with the Middle East, and having captured Junagadh, it was obvious that the Sultan would turn his attention to the control of the area of Dwarka. Dwarka was thus taken (Chaube, 1975: 66). The Waghers quickly regained it though, (K.G. 1884: 592) and even in the early nineteenth century, British officers reported that the Waghers lived mainly by plunder, retiring in the monsoons to their villages to cultivate *bajri* and *juvar*, millet and a kind of corn (MacMurdo, 1809-1810: 12).

James MacMurdo remarked that the peninsular coast of Dwarka abounded in creeks and inlets, where the pirates sought refuge. He went on to say that the pirates were encouraged in their trade by their faith in the God of Dwarka. The priests and attendants of the Dwarka temple instigated piracy, whereby they granted the protection of Ranchhodji to the pirates while they were out at sea, gaining in return a certain share of all plundered property. Many pirate vessels were fitted out in the name of Ranchhodji, which in reality belonged to the temple *ashrams* which received all the plunder that was brought ashore (Mac-Murdo, 1809-1810: 12–9).

As can be seen, the temple authorities worked hand in glove with the Waghers in their piracy. Mira might well have found refuge in the Wagher state for reasons which are not as lofty as those conjectured by Goetz. Dwarka attracted a rich and numerous population, which also included the trading and moneylending community of Luhanas, offering them a safe asylum from foreign danger. The Waghers continued to revolt against the imposition of British rule right into the 1860's, when their support for the revolt of 1857 was crushed (K.G. 1884: 165).

The Nath influence had been strong in Saurashtra from the eighth century onwards, one of its main bases being at Gorakhmadhi (Gaudani, 1973: 530). A number of verses attributed to Mira contain Nath symbolisms, not surprising in an age when there was conflict between the wandering, non-householder *jogis*, and the settled population. However, it was not only an age of conflict between the Naths and the medieval bhaktas, but conversely, an age of borrowing too. Kabir's verses are replete with Nathpanthi allusions, and there is a community of weavers in Uttar Pradesh who are called Jugis, who, earlier, had been Nathpanthis (Dwivedi, 1985: 22).

The fifteenth and sixteenth centuries saw a struggle between the bhaktas and the Tantric based sects for influence over the people. Tukaram declared that the mother of the *shaktas* was a sow, an ass (Deleury, 1960: 119). Jnandev's disciple, Nivritinath was a disciple of a Nath yogi at Trimbak (Deleury, 1960: 9). Sixteenth century Bengal was rife with *shakta* rites. One day, the chief of the *shaktas*, who was a Brahman, smeared wine and meat on the door of Chaitanya's neighbour, Srivasa, when he heard *kirtan* coming from within (Dimock, 1966: 113).

Not only was there hostility between the bhaktas and the *shaktas* as well as the Nathpanthis, but the Sufi literati was hostile to the 'yogis' too (Maxwell Eaton, 1978: 153). While the Nathpanthis were Shaivites of a Tantric tradition, and ascetics, eschewing the company of women, the *shaktas* were in the main house-holders, who took part in ritual sexual activity.

The main *shakta* tradition in Saurashtra is called the *mahapanth*. This *mahapanth* has given a far ranging number of revered *lok sants*, and it has also provided strong female figures, who, although they have been harnessed to a process which allows their male partners to gain salvation, nevertheless emerge as socially courageous beings in themselves. Here, one can cite the examples of Toral, Lirbai, Amarbai, etc. (Rajyaguru, 1986: 556).

Outside of the ritual sexual activities, the women of the *mahapanth* appear to have made remarkably independent decisions.

The influence of the *mahapanth* on the cultural life of Saurashtra has been immense—primarily on the tradition of bhajan singing and even more on the tradition of providing sustenance to pilgrims and wayfarers on their journey. One of the hallmarks of the Nath tradition is the provision of food and shelter for travellers of all castes and creeds (Briggs, 1973: 45). The *lok sants* of Saurashtra, influenced by the Nath tradition, provided the first attempts at social and welfare provision and thus became embedded in the lives of the people.

Sant Devidas was a Rabari who set up an *ashram* at Parab Vavdi, after rescuing an old woman who suffered from leprosy from being drowned in the sea by her son. Devidas' reputation attracted others suffering from leprosy to the place. Devidas ministered to them with care, and provided for them by travelling around various villages seeking alms. Amarbai, a young Ahir woman was on her way to her marital home after the day of her wedding. Getting out of the bullock cart to rest for a while, she heard a cry of someone in pain and on investigation she saw Devidas looking after a group of lepers. The young woman decided then and there to remain at Parab Vavdi and do the same. She was steadfast in this resolve, Devidas then enduring a murderous beating by the Ahir community for inciting Amarbai to be unfaithful to her marriage vows.

In time Parab Vavdi ceased to be a place catering for the needs of those who suffered from leprosy but continued to act as a *sadavrat*, as a place at which all travellers could obtain food and shelter. Other *lok sants* set up *sadavrats* too, providing food for the hungry and needy in times of famine, and providing for pilgrim and travellers at all times. And thus it is within this tradition—not in its formal association or institutional base—but in the strong feelings of sympathy for the wayfarer, of provision of nurturance to the impecunious wayfarer, that the figure of Mira begins to take shape in Saurashtra.

We are not fortunate, Rana, we are not fortunate,
With my being scarred, Rana, I am most wretched.
We are not fortunate, Rana, we are not fortunate,
With my being scarred, Rana, I am most wretched.

We came into this world, and were caught up in a whirlwind.
We are birds that seek to fly to the other shore.
With my being scarred, Rana, I am most wretched.

In shallow waters, we are unable to survive.
We are fishes of the deep waters.
With my being scarred, Rana, I am most wretched.

By becoming a *jogin*, I lost a life.
By becoming a *jogin*, I lost a life.
With a *jholi* in my hand,
I wander house to house, begging.

We are not fortunate, Rana, we are not fortunate,
With my being scarred, Rana, I am most wretched.

My love was bound to someone not of this land.
I washed my eyes with tears,
I washed my eyes with tears.
With my being scarred, Rana, I am most wretched.

Mirabai sings the glory of Giridhar.
We attained happiness through worshipping you,
With my being scarred, Rana, I am most wretched.

(Sung by Vinodbhai Dosa Joshi and by a person who came from the community of Kharvas who was referred to as Kanjibhai Khataravada, in the town of Okha. Most bhajans in Saurashtra are sung solo, but here, the supportive refrain provided by Kanjibhai added weight to the pathos of the bhajan.)

Mira by now has left Chittor. The imposed ties no longer fetter her. She has made her choice of donning saffron, and she is with the community of mendicants who do not impede her inner search. And yet, what it is to be a *jogin*! There is no reason for anyone to idealize the lives of these seekers after love. It will not do to exalt this path. By becoming a *jogin* Mira has 'lost a life', she is cut off from the everyday world of social relations, and the everyday security of a house-holder. All those belonging to the company of mendicants are caught up in a dilemma whereby they cannot accept the constraints of a rigid and emotionally superficial society, whereby they are unable to survive in shallow waters—and yet the choice they have made imposes its own hardship on them. A flight of birds wanting to cross over to the other shore, they are trapped in a present in which they attempt to be true to their commitments.

Mira's being is scarred by a thousand injuries—the trials at Chittor, the mockery of dominant society as she wanders an indigent, and the destitution involved in being part of a community of mendicants. Mira has bound herself to a love in which there is no going back, to a person she is not able to see as he is not of this land. Although she states that happiness is to be attained through worshipping him, walking through life carrying her scars, she is unable to say that she is fortunate. She is wretched. The people's Mira is neither one of ambition to be a propertied Vaishnav and a *sampradayic* leader nor is she a transcendental mystic. She chooses the path of emotional and political integrity and pays the price exacted. She lives a life of material and social hardship and recognizes that no true alternative can be evolved without going through these hardships, the necessary outcome of tearing asunder social and economic privileges.

The alternative community that emerges in Saurasthtra is that of the community of mendicants, who share a common penury with the common beggars and itinerant singers. There is a commonality in the condition of mendicants who have left family and community, and those house-holder bhajan singers who come from the lower castes and who have kept alive the tradition of singing bhajans within particular social contexts. These lower class bhajan singers who earn their livelihood from this live in a position of dependancy on the communities who act as their patrons, just as alms-seekers are dependant upon individuals and families who give some sustenance in the form of food or money.

In the experience of the bhajniks of Saurashtra, Mira the *jogin* is not a grand pure soul who does *tapas* in the mountains. Their Mira, the bhajan creator and singer, forms part of a condition of lower class bhajan singers. It is a Mira who has broken with the life of pretty versification at the court—and who has taken to the road, travelling, singing and sustaining herself on the depth of her emotions.

In Saurashtra, there is an itinerant group known as 'Nath *bavas*' who travel around playing on a string instrument called the *ravan-hatho*. These Nath *bavas* who earn a living by singing bhajans on the *ravan-hatho* were originally celibate Naths who gradually formed into a house-holder caste. Travelling as families, they make their base on the outskirts of a particular village, and then go out to surrounding villages from there, singing and seeking victuals. The Nath *bavas* sing in the main of Bharathari, Gopichand, Jesal-Toral and Mira. They are also renowned for removing the effect of snake poison through *mantras* (S.P.K., 1958: 398-507).

The Nath *bavas* occupy a peculiar position in the caste hierarchy in Saurashtra as they were not considered untouchable but deemed socially just as inferior. They consider themselves to be slightly above the dalits as well as Dhobis and Mochis (S.P.K., 1958, 412). The gazetteer of Kathiawar classifies the 'Jogis' as

> wandering religious beggars, who also earn their living by selling *baval* toothbrushes, brooms, salt and *indhonis*... They also cast out evil spirits and catch snakes. (K.G., 1884: 159.)

In the experience of the people of Saurashtra, the Naths form a body of people who are associated with mendicancy.

The Turis of Saurashtra are another group of itinerant singers. They perform the Ramlila, and enact stories of Harishchandra, Narisinha Mehta, etc. too. The Turis as a group are specifically tied to the dalits, for whom they put on performances, as well as sing bhajans. At the end of the monsoon season, the Turis travel in troupes to various villages where they are invited by the dalits (from the weaving communities) to stay in their *vas*. They perform at night, where others from the village apart from dalits come to participate. At the end of the performance, those attending give to the Turis according to their means (S.P.K., 1958: 448–50).

The Dhed *bavas* were originally celibates from amongst the weaving community. Those who became house-holders formed into a caste group and lived amongst the weavers. They do not don saffron, nor do they have the external trappings of a *bava*. When they go seeking alms, they are given a pinch of flour. Otherwise they do agricultural labour (S.P.K., 1958: 461–2).

All of the above groups are alms-seekers who are sustained in the main by the lower-caste communities to whom they are integrally tied. Dominant society, even as it enjoys the musical skills of various singing groups, does not accord much dignity to them. The hereditary singing communities have invariably been ostracized and spurned socially, much as their musical skills have been harnessed at weddings, etc. There has been and continues to be stigma attached to the profession of singing, whereby whole communities of hereditary singers are assigned a low status in the caste hierarchy.

The hereditary singing communities are in a position of dependance on their *jajman*. Not having access to the right of cultivation in land, they were tied in dependancy to the 'giver' communities, similar to the communities who provided 'service'. In Rajasthan, a Dholi (who plays at weddings) will ask from every caste—but no Bhangi or Dhobi will give of his service to a Dholi. The Dholis make *dhols* too, and are everywhere branded as liars and cheats (M.R.M., 1891: 367–8).

The community of Dhadhis are similar to the Dholis. Unlike the Dholis, though, they do not ask from the Rajputs, but are tied to the Jats, Raikas, Bishnois and Sunars. They play primarily the *sarangi* and *rabab* (M.R.M., 1891: 369–70). Like other hereditary singing communities, they too are socially degraded and humiliated, and are not allowed to cross the threshold of a caste home.

Groups of itinerant singers and itinerant mendicants are not 'beggars', yet they rely on the giving of money and grain in order to survive. Though the giving of charity is seen to be an entrenched principle of Indian society, it makes the receiver no less the degraded one. Mendicant singers are looked upon as not much different from the ordinary beggars who go from house to house seeking victuals.

Often individual alms-seekers are tied to particular families, who set aside a certain sum each week to give away. In turn, the alms-seekers invoke a blessing on the house of the giver, especially on the children—or, appositely, curses if they have been badly received. There are also those amongst the poor who turn to begging as a last resort, and a temporary one, when they are unable to meet the expense of a funeral or a daughter's wedding (Campbell Oman, 1972: 234–8). The pilgrim places of Saurashtra bring into the province large groups of alms-seekers on their way to Dwarka, Girnar, Shatrunjaya, etc. (K.G., 1884: 154).

Thus, when Mira sings of wandering from house to house to seek alms, *'mangi bhikhia'*, this feeds into a variety of notions concerning the position of alms-seekers, itinerant singers, and paupers.

Burn, *hansla*, burn.
The body's *dalal*, *hansla*, keep on burning.

Recognizing you, *hansla*, I freed you,
Feed on pearls, *hansla*, feed on pearls.
The body's *dalal*, *hansla*, keep on burning.

For nine months, *hansla*, for nine months,
You were enfolded in the womb.
Look after the needs of your mother and father, *hansla*.
The body's *dalal*, *hansla*, keep on burning.

Through effort and through extortion,
You have accumulated a lot of wealth.
Make sure you give out charity with your right hand, *hansla*.
The body's *dalal*, *hansla*, keep on burning.

Mira sings the glory of Girdhar.
Bai Mira sings the glory of Giridhar.
Keep on drinking the *ras* from the bhajans of Ram, *hansla*.
The body's *dalal*, *hansla*, keep on burning.

(Sung by Vinodbhai Dosa Joshi, in the town of Okha, at the Ramapir temple which had recently been constructed by the community of Kharvas.)

There are two layers of thought and emotion which are simultaneously being enunciated in the above bhajan. One is of a suffering Mira, who daily faces the fire of privation, and whose spirit is kept alight by the life she has chosen. The symbolism of the *hans*, the swan, feeding on pearls alone and rejecting the chaff, is a common one for the soul—whereby the spirit, through which the body perceives the finest issues, sieves the essential from the inessential. Mira, wandering as a mendicant, is experiencing a harsh privation in her alternative community, whereby she has attained freedom from social bondage to the Sisodiya family, yet she recognizes that she has to walk through fire to continue on her chosen path. And here, another message interlaces with Mira's own experience.

The songs of alms-seekers contain one common theme—that of being excluded from the realm of ordinary social relations, from a life based around hearth and home and of being an outsider to the fortunes of a house-holder yet dependant on the body of house-holders.[1] The wandering alms-seeker, through giving expression to her condition, simultaneously negates the condition of the house-holder and at the same time teaches him the value of that particular life, as compared to that of a mendicant. Thus, the injunction to look after the mother and father, to give charity out of ill gotten gains, draws a polarity between a difficult but spiritually satisfying existence—and the world of a corrupt prosperity which bolsters up the world of stable, domestic relations. It is important to understand that those who have placed Mira within the condition and emotions of alms-seekers, with all the depth of deprivation that this entails, are not themselves mendicants, or alms-seekers, or ordinary beggars. Those who have understood Mira's situation to have been similar to these groups (as articulated in the bhajans) are the ordinary peasant and artisan bhajniks of Saurashtra, who have entered into the being of Mira the mendicant singer, and expressed her experiences within that condition.

Rana, I have no-one to accompany me on the journey of my life.[2]
All these ties are dust.
They are poison.
Rana, I have no-one to accompany me on the journey of my life.

Mira, leave aside these saffron robes.
Adorn yourself, in rubies.

I will not lay aside these saffron robes,
I will not adorn myself in rubies.
Rana, all these ties are dust.

Mira, leave the company of *sadhus*.
Come and live as princes do.

The company of *sadhus* suits me, Rana,
I will not live as princes do.
Rana, all these ties are dust.
They are poison.
Rana, I have no-one to accompany me on the journey of my life.

Mira wore anklets round her feet.
She picked up an *ektara*.
Rana, I have no-one to accompany me on the journey of my life.

(Sung by Pacchabha Manek in the village of Shivrajpur, district Jamnagar. The whole village was inhabited by the community of Waghers, except for the few families of Ahirs who had come from more drought-stricken villages further inland, and rented in some land from the Waghers on which they kept their cattle.)

Mira is here refusing to live as princes do, not at a time when the demands of the princely family are oppressing her, but at a time when she has left this realm, when she is living out a choice of a relationship with Giridhar, and where she is driven to continuing the life she has chosen almost despite herself. There is a hint here in the bhajan of a will stronger than her own which is driving her forward. No-one could have barred her from her chosen path—but there is no-one to lighten the burden of this either. The Mira in Saurashtra is learning that a life of rejection entails not just privation, but an acute loneliness too.

Awaken, Jadvpati Rai.
For a moment, inside my veil, I will smile,
and take the name of Hari.

I have given of my mind and body.
I want to reach the door of the beloved.
Giridhar, I have left the *marjad* of the *kul* for you.

I left my mother and father.
I brought grief to the children.
I have come to seek shelter with you, my Shyam, I have come to your door.

You are the highest.
Take compassion upon me.
Awaken, Jadavpati Rai, for a moment, inside my veil, I will smile,
and take the name of Hari.

(Sung by Vidhabha Manek in the village of Vasai, district Jamnagar. He was the younger son of a cultivator and worked on the family land.)

I have only heard men sing this bhajan, not women. It is a deeply moving experience, to hear an individual man, and those supporting him, being able to enter so profoundly into the emotions of a woman, singing her experiences in the first person. All the Saurashtra bhajans are sung solo, the instrumentalists lending sustenance and lift, the *ektara* being handed from one singer to the other, usually after the singing of two bhajans, without any break to mark the end of one bhajan and the beginning of another. The bhajans detailed in the chapter 'A Dream Validated', which describe Mira's anguish when faced with the Rana in the *chori*, and which show Mira facing a bitter mother were all sung by individual men too. And yet these bhajans are not an 'individual' expression, in the full modernist sense of the term. For this, one has to hear the renderings of radio artistes and the individual outpourings of middle class women as described in Part Four of this work.

The solo voice within the gathering of bhajniks in Saurashtra gives full expression to the personal being and the personal suffering of Mira. The Mira here is a fully complex and a fully angular being, without the edges smoothed over.

In the above bhajan Mira sings solely to Giridhar, looking forward to a moment of pleasure when she will be able to see him, when she will smile inside her veil and take the name of Hari. She has given herself fully to her own inner search, away from the power of the Rana, but discovers that this involves pain and grief too. It is not just the pain of material deprivation, but of finding that the instances of seeing her Beloved on her veil are momentary.

It is not that Mira is not part of a collective articulation in Saurashtra. She is. But within this collective articulation and projection is a person expressed in the fullest depth of her being. The solo voice nurtured within the collective gathering of bhajniks, expresses this perfectly. The content has found the form. And the form the content.

The special nature of the artist's work is his use of a learned skill in a particular kind of transmission of experience. His command of this skill is his art (we remember that the traditional meaning of 'art' was, precisely, 'skill'). But the purpose of the skill is similar to the purpose of all general human skills of communication: the transmission of valued experience. Thus the artist's impulse, like every human impulse to communicate, is the felt importance of his experience; but the artist's activity is the actual work of transmission. There can be no separation, in this view, between 'content' and 'form', because finding the form is literally finding the content—this is what is meant by the activity we have called 'describing'. It is, in the first instance, to every man, a matter of urgent personal importance to 'describe' his experience, because this is literally a remaking of himself, a creative change in his personal organization, to include and control the experience. (Williams, 1961: 42.)

Raymond Williams is here describing the process of individual artistic creation. I have been concerned with describing in this part of the work the process of an encapsulation of Mira whereby large numbers of people have taken to Mira out of their own experiences, and have embodied through her a powerfully collective vision.

The bhajniks in Saurashtra have transmitted the valued experience of a woman who has stood up for personal liberties, and the valued experience of itinerant singers, giving us some of the finest renderings of Mira. They have projected all of themselves, collectively and individually, into the task of describing the emotions of a woman who left her kin and tore off her privileges to seek out her own truth.

The bhajniks of Saurasthra and Rajasthan have given of their impulses and energies to remake Mira, and through this have remade themselves—they have remade the world giving to it their stamp, and their hope for a better form of relationships. They have encapsulated a vision of Mira through whom they project their own history, as well as showing the centrality of Mira in cementing alternative bonds. There is a collective, political, and deeply personal bonding here.

It is necessary to undertake the fight for a recognition of a morality which has emerged out of the history and experiences of those oppressed and humiliated. It is not only necessary to grant recognition to the peoples' morality, but it is essential to attempt to retain it too, for to deny this strong current is to collude with the process of expropriation undertaken by those upholding an official morality.

The Mira who exists in hegemonic society, who forms the subject of Part Three of this work, has been built upon the destruction, as yet only a partial one, of a peoples' culture which has arisen out of the deep rooted strengths of peasant and artisan communities.

I leave the peoples' Mira here: leave her in the visions and voices of those whose minds have not yet been plundered by an expanding commercial media, whose traditional creativity has not yet been usurped, and whose hearts have not been ravished by a rapacious film industry.

PART THREE

Chapter Seven

Incorporation

Mira, who had challenged the whole basis upon which the Rajput polity was based, and who had refused to subordinate herself to the patriarchal system of domination, began to be incorporated, slowly and tangentially, within the official history of Chittor in the nineteenth century. However, this incorporation remains incomplete to this day, as incorporation always does which has not undergone a transformation. Mira remains as a wound within the social fabric of Rajput society, the touching of which elicits a sharp response.

It is instructive that it was a colonial agent who laid the basis for the myth that one of the temples within the fortress of Chittor was erected under the patronage of Mira, and hence that she was supported in her choice of Krishna bhakti by the Rana that she was married to, Rana Kumbha. Colonel James Tod, the Political Agent of Mewar between 1818-1822, wrote his influential '*Annals and Antiquities of Rajasthan*', which were published in three volumes between 1829 and 1832. In these, Tod describes Mira as being the wife of Rana Kumbha, from whom she may have

imbibed her poetic piety

and

whose excess of devotion [to Krishna]... gave rise to many tales of scandal.

Tod's depiction of Mira as

> the most celebrated princess of her time for beauty and romantic piety... [whose] history is a romance (Tod, 1971: 337–8.)

places her firmly in the romantic tradition and creates a particularly idealized nineteenth century view of Mira. Much more than this though, Tod, in his writings on Mira, separates out the realm of the spiritual from the profane, driving a wedge between the two and enabling them to occupy different spaces as well as co-exist at the same time. It is a highly bourgeois rendering of an expression that arose within a radically different ethos. For all Tod's championing of the cause of the Rajput princes of Rajputana, (Tod, 1971; 'Dedication' vii) though, he has been unable to perceive that Mira's bhakti posed a strong challenge to the patriarchal rule of the Rajputs which he (Tod) strongly endorsed—and he has thus been unable to perceive that Mira could not have given rise to 'many tales of scandal' (Tod, 1971: 338) without suffering the repercussion of this.

Tod's description of one of the temples at Chittorgadh as being built by Mira paved the way for the official recognition of this as being the 'Mirabai temple', placing Mira centrally within the history of Sisodiya rule in Chittor. Tod describes two temples built to Krishna in Chittor

> one being erected by Rana Kumbha, the other by his celebrated wife, the chief poetess of that age, Mira Bai, to the god of her idolatry, Shamnath. (Tod, 1971: 1818.)

This is the first reference we have to a temple officially patronized by Mira in Chittorgadh, and therefore officially sanctioned by the Sisodiya rulers. By 1905, though, the *'Progress Report of the Archaeological Survey of Western India'* (for the year ending, 30.6.1905: 59), was referring to

> what is called Mirabai's temple

indicating that this temple was generally referred to as Mirabai's temple by this time. The same report, however, went on to say that this temple appeared to have been erected by the Guhila prince, Kumbhakarana,

and probably had no connection with Mirabai, daughter-in-law of Rana Sanga. (30.6.1905: 59)

Confusion reigned, as there were two temples within this particular complex, the larger of which was revealed by investigation to be an Adivaraha one, which had images consecrated within it, and a smaller, unconsecrated temple to the side of this which continued to be referred to as 'Mirabai's temple'.

In 1955, this smaller, unconsecrated temple was publicly declared open as the Mira *mandir*, and a card-board cut-out figure of Mira in worship to Krishna was installed within it. Let us see how this took place.

Interest began to be shown in the archaeological remains of Chittor in the nineteenth century. It was not, however, till the early twentieth century that attempts at conservation began. Significantly, the emphasis was at first on renovating the Tower of Fame (built by Rana Kumbha after the defeat of Mahmud Khilji) the 'Udaipur Darbar' bearing the costs of repair and reconstruction of this 'triumphal pillar' (*Annual Report of the Director General of Archaeology*, for the year 1903-1904, 1905: 4). The Udaipur princes, though, bore no responsibility for the renovation of the Mira *mandir*, and made no attempt to consecrate this temple as befitted its rising status.

Shree Radha Krishnaji, a ninety-two year old priest of the Nimbark *sampraday*, gave a clear picture of the process whereby the Mira *mandir* officially came into being (discussion with Shree Radha Krishnaji at the Radha-Krishna temple, Bauji-ka-kund, Udaipur, 17.2.1987). Lalsinha Shaktawat, an Arya Samaji barrister who later became a staunch Vaishnav, was in Shree Radha Krishnaji's company constantly. It was Lalsinha who through his political influence, and emotional affinity to Mira, made the Mira *mandir* what it is today.

Lalsinha Shaktawat was a Settlement Officer for the State of Mewar, and was later called to Ajmer. He reports that having visited Chittorgarh as a Settlement Officer in 1933, he was eager to pay his obeisance at the Mira temple, and he received a severe shock when he saw that this was

neglected and void. (Shaktawat, 1982: i)

He decided then and there that a Mira *murti* should be installed within it.

However, Shree Radha Krishnaji described how the temple was in a ruinous state even when he visited it with Lalsinha Shaktawat. How did they come to the conclusion that this was indeed the Mira *mandir*?

Lalsinha had read a lot of histories, and he had at first thought that the Kumbhashyama *mandir* [the larger temple within this complex in Chittorgadh] was the one Mira had worshipped in. However, seeing that this was an Adivaraha temple, he estimated that the one to the left of this must have been the one where Mira sang bhajans, immersing herself in Krishna bhakti. Everyone I met asked me—Are you certain that this is Mira's *mandir*? And I would answer in the affirmative.

Radha Krishna paused, wiped his eyes, and continued:

But just as there is fear in the mind of a thief, so there was fear in mine. How *could* I be certain? It was then that I decided to do *tapascharya*.

I fasted within the precincts of the temple at Chittorgadh. I stayed awake all night, singing bhajans. I remember that it was the night of *sharad purnima*. I was half asleep and half awake, when I saw a figure approaching me. She was dressed in white, and had long, unbraided hair. I knew it was Mira. She carried an *ektara* in her hand. She came to me, told me to still the doubts in my head, and said this was indeed her *mandir*. After saying this, she vanished. From that time onwards, I had no further doubts.

It is not difficult to see how an evidently sincere person such as Shree Radha Krishnaji, beset by the trauma of a reality he had created, could have had the vision he did. This particular vision was enclosed within the boundaries of a depiction of Mira which is peculiarly modern—a Mira who is dressed neither in tattered rags nor in saffron, but in the white of a high-caste widow, with her hair left romantically unbraided.

Lalsinha Shaktawat had been a member of the Rajasthan Legislative Assembly from 1952-1962, representing Chittorgadh between 1957-1962. He thus had the power to bring pressure to expedite certain kinds of work to the temple at Chittorgadh. Lalsinha ensured that the Archaeological Survey Department at Chittorgadh renovated the Mira *mandir*. Seeing the completion of these works, the question that arose next was—how should this temple be consecrated?

Lalsinha Shaktawat and Radha Krishnaji both believed that a small Krishna *murti* which was in the possession of the Sisodiya family in the palace at Udaipur was the actual *murti* that Mira had worshipped within her lifetime. They felt that it rightfully belonged to the Mira *mandir* in Chittorgadh and asked that it be installed there. From the palace at Udaipur, Bhopalsingh initially agreed to the transfer of this *murti* to Chittorgadh, but later dragged his heels. A struggle ensued between the palace and Lalsinha on this issue. All this time, the inner sanctum of the 'Mira *mandir*' remained empty, and Lalsinha thought this very amiss. A compromise was reached, whereby Bhopalsingh had a court painter paint a card-board cut-out of Mira and of the Krishna *murti* housed within the palace. These were installed within the inner sanctum of the Mira *mandir* by Lalsinha Shaktawat in May 1955. A painted sign was then installed outside the temple proclaiming it to be the 'Mirabai *mandir*'.

The whole saga is a shoddy one, showing the lack of respect to the memory of Mira by the Sisodiya family, and showing too their lack of imagination in being unable to assimilate her within their midst. The Sisodiyas, though, have never been renowned for achieving hegemony through sophistication and finesse.

Today, the tourists who flock to Chittorgadh to view the remnants of Sisodiya rule, are greeted by a signboard which designates a small temple as being the one where Mira spent her time in worship. Directly facing the Mira *mandir* is a raised platform with the footprints of a person carved on them. These are said to be the footprints of Rohidas, the Chamar bhakta who became Mira's guru. A concession has been made to popular opinion on this issue.

Today too, the printed maps of Chittorgadh have the pictures of two figures to bind the contours of this region—Rana Pratap and Bai Mira. Both Rana Pratap and Bai Mira have become symbols pliably bent to political exhortations which attempt to engender regional solidarities, within the rhetoric of abstract principles. Political meetings held in Chittorgadh invariably begin by acknowledging that this was a land which gave birth to 'shakti and bhakti'. Mira's name is invoked by power-mongers who seek to gain legitimacy through an appropriation of the past.

So has Bai Mira been laid to rest within dominant society in Rajasthan, her name and message harnessed to suit ruling blandishments?

Chothuji Nat comes from a family of travelling puppeteers. His father had died when he himself was a child, and Chothuji had thus travelled with his uncle to earn his keep. Chothuji said that whenever the two of them entered a new village, his uncle used to strike up a Mira bhajan to attract people round about to the puppet show. The Mira bhajan invariably brought people crowding around. When Chothuji began travelling on his own with his wife and children, he retained his uncle's practice of striking up a Mira bhajan before the beginning of a performance.

In 1972, Chothuji was travelling in the region of Chittorgadh, and he entered a *Sisodiyon ka kheda*, a cluster of hamlets belonging to some Sisodiya families. As was his custom, he struck up a Mira bhajan. The inhabitants of the hamlets crowded round him, shouting at him to stop, and jostling. Chothuji was dazed and confused, unable to understand what had stirred up such anger. An old man then approached him, and explained that as this was a village of Sisodiyas, he should not sing Mira bhajans there.

'You are a poor man, come here to earn something to feed yourself with. Go away from here quickly. You have made a mistake in singing a Mira bhajan in a village of Sisodiyas. Make sure that you do not sing a Mira bhajan where there are Sisodiyas. People here still think that Mira brought shame on their name'. All this time, the shouts of those enraged at my singing a Mira bhajan continued. They were saying that by singing Mira, I had insulted and humiliated them. No, they were not *rajvi* Sisodiyas, they were poor Rajputs who laboured on their fields (they keep their women under strict *purdah*, though.) In that region, there were about ten or fifteen villages of Sisodiyas. I made sure that I did not sing of Mira in those villages. I could not afford to, could I? [Discussion with Chothuji Nat, at the Tilonia Social Work and Research Centre, 21.4.1987.]

Chothuji's experience is not untypical. Travelling in the region of Chittorgadh on field-work in February 1986, I stopped at *Dagla ka kheda*, a small village. I asked a group of Bhatti Rajput women whether they would consider naming one of their daughters Mira. This inquiry brought a hostile response which bordered on the abusive. A negative could not have been uttered with greater force. The blow that Mira struck against governing rules of Rajput society is raw and bleeding to this day, and it has remained unhealed.

Even in the land of *sanyasinis*, a woman who chooses a relationship with God in opposition to the socially designated patriarchal ones, who asserts her convictions, and who actively seeks association of the spirit, is looked at askance. In commom usage, the term *'bhaktani'* or *'bhaktin'* (a female bhakta) is a derogatory one, levelled by those who wish to put a woman down because they see her as having loose sexual morals. Professor Bhayani remembers a widow in his home village of Mahuva in Bhavnagar district, who was referred to as a *bhaktani*. She was from the Bania community, and associated with ascetics and those who gave religious discourses. She was also a woman who took her own decisions and was non-conformist.

If a woman associates with *sadhu-sants* then she is looked upon in a particular way. Yes, she was called a *bhaktani*. A *bhaktani* does not mean a prostitute exactly, but a woman who is loose, free. [Discussion with Professor Harivallabh Bhayani, Ahmedabad, 29.7.1987.]

Professor G.D. Sharma remembers that in his home village of Dhanagaji in Mewat, northern Rajasthan a young woman who struck up friendships of her own will, or a young woman who did not listen to the wishes of the elders in the family, would be taunted with, 'So, you have become a Mira?' Similar taunts would be levelled if a young woman sang aloud (singing itself connoting a freedom of spirit) or if she kept her hair unbraided. (Discussion with Professor G.D. Sharma, Baroda University, 23.6.1988.)

It was in Nagri, Chittorgadh district, that I heard a Brahman priest tell others in my presence that Mira was a *bhaktin*, on a par with dancing girls and singing women. In a society which aims to rein in womens' imaginings, womens' faith and womens' deepest giving to the satisfaction of male desire, a *bhaktin* is a prostitute. In Bengal, the women singers who sang *Dhap*, a new development of the Vaishnav *kirtan*, such as Bami Kirtani, were regarded as whores (Chakravarti, 1985: 466).

There is a caste of women in Rajasthan who earn their living through singing and dancing, and who give of their bodies too. This is the caste of Bhagtan. Their daughters, nieces, etc. are taken on by the practitioners and initiated into the skills of the trade. Sons marry within the community of Bhagtan (M.R.M. 1891: 379–80).

It is clear that in dominant society which has not yet accepted Mira as a saintly, mystical figure, the life and actions of Mira feed into notions of woman as the satisfier of male desire.

Purushottam Palwal, the main librarian at Gulabbag, Udaipur, when hearing of my search in the libraries said:

You will find no trace of Mira in the written records here, for how can a person rejected by the rulers have her history preserved? You do not know the strength of feeling here against Mira. And it is not only in the silencing of her name and history. I remember less than twenty five years ago, and it is so even today, the word Mira was a term of abuse directed at a woman who did not act according to custom. (Discussion with Purushottam Palwal, Udaipur, 4.2.1987.)

I met D.S. in the town of Chittor. His name had been given to me by a voluntary organization, as being someone who could introduce me to the complexities of Rajput society. He did.

What is so great about Mira that you want to write about her? Why are you travelling around in the way that you are doing to find out about her? What will you achieve by it?

Mira did not just worship Krishna in the temple. She had reached the streets (*vo sadak par jha pahunchi tthi.*) When other Ranis did bhakti, they did so within the palace, with other women. Not amidst men outside. Mira did not keep to the decorum of a Rajput princess. Therefore, whoever sent her the poison was not at fault. He did the right thing. Even today, if my wife did something to overturn the prestige (*pratishttha*) of my family...

Mrs. S. gave a start and looked down. The conversation had taken a very different turn and I was concerned about Mrs. S.'s self-pride. She was a dignified woman who spoke quietly but firmly. She looked at me and said:

The decorum of a bhakta is very different from the decorum of a house-holder. For a bhakta, the decorum of a house-holder means nothing. But if you ask a house-holder about Mira—the answer will be that she was insane (Chittor, 4.6.1987).

Chapter Eight

A Nation Cleaved: The Song Betrayed

The song of Mira had lain latent within the lives of various subordinated groups in society—leather-workers, women, itinerant singers, etc. Acting as a force which provided strength and solace, which bound people together in a community of shared suffering, and which articulated a vision of better relationships, the song of Mira remained (and continues to remain) as a powerful hope seeking realization. These deeply-held visions and aspirations could have been actualized in the process of transformation of society during the struggle for national liberation. Instead, the song was betrayed.

In the twentieth century, during the creation of an independent nation state in India, attempts were made to give the message and significance of Mira a new direction. The manner in which Gandhi in particular took up this task forms the subject of this chapter.

It is difficult to know where Gandhi gained his knowledge of Mira from, and to gauge the extent to which he consciously moulded her figure to suit his political philosophy and how much of this was evolved through a process of cogitation upon the Mira bhajans available to him. It is clear though, that the figure of Mira was close to Gandhi from as far back as his days in South Africa. One of Mira's bhajans, *'mere to Giridhar Gopal dusro na koi'*,

(Giridhar Gopal is mine, I have no other), was very popular in Gandhi's Phoenix ashram in South Africa. Prabhudas Gandhi, who lived at the Phoenix ashram and who noted down Gandhi's discourses on the bhajans sung there, states that this was one of the most important bhajans which enabled Gandhi to gain strength in the evolution of his fight against tyranny (Prabhudas Gandhi, 1978: 99). Prabhudas Gandhi's interpretation is that Gandhi learnt to face social and political obstacles from this bhajan of Mira, and that he also learnt to transform the draught of poison into ambrosia from this particular bhajan (Prabhudas Gandhi, 1978: 100). It is not unlikely that Gandhi read this into the bhajan and it is also likely that he saw in Mira's rejection of her wealthy apparel and attire a stirring precedent for his own vow of poverty which he took in 1905. Mira would have appealed to Gandhi on a number of counts—her fearless strength against oppressive authority, her determination to pursue the truth of her heart despite hardship and repression, and her taking to a life of simplicity, all of which were in clear resonance with his own self.

However, Gandhi had scant knowledge of the basic history of Mira. As late as 1926 Gandhi admitted to hearing just the

day before yesterday

that Mira had met Jiva Gosain in Vrandavan where she chided him for refusing to see her, as she was a woman. Mira's response to Jiva Gosain, in which she said the only male in the universe was Krishna, all others being *gopis*, was very attractive to Gandhi, late as he came to it (C.W., Vol. XXXII, 1926-1927: 486, 'Talks to Ashram Women'.)

Mira, however, as interpreted by Gandhi, became a crucial lynchpin for him upon which turned his commitment and faith throughout the twists and turns of the momentous anti-colonial struggle. That this involved moulding and remoulding Mira into a cast completely at odds with the peoples' Mira, is a comment both on Gandhi's removal from the aspirations of the community of Mirabai, as well as his removal of her from the context within which she had been nurtured. I will go through Gandhi's upholding of Mira within particular junctures of the anti-colonial struggle, and in relation to particular ideas and values as propounded by him.

Gandhi had begun to practice the politics of *satyagraha* in South Africa in the first decade of the twentieth century. Later, in India, where he was to develop this political philosophy more cogently, he invoked the name of Mira again and again in his speeches and writings. In order to show that *satyagraha* was an age-old weapon in the fight against tyranny, Gandhi invoked a number of historical precedents

> Just as light and darkness are opposed to each other, just as cold and heat can never exist together, so also justice and injustice are incompatible... Prahlad non-co-operated with his wicked father, Mirabai with her husband and Narsinha Mehta with fellow members of his community. Today, we revere all three...
>
> Co-operation and non-co-operation have been accepted policies in use since times immemorial—co-operation, always with the just and non-co-operation with the wicked. It cannot be invalidated by any number of manifestos. (C.W., Vol. XVIII, 1920: 125–7, 'What the Scriptures Say' in '*Navajivan*', 8.8.1920.)

This statement stressed the moral rightness of the practice of *satyagraha* within the Indian polity. In 1917, Gandhi had written in a letter

> You may not know that the Gujarati word for passive resistance is truth-force. I have variously defined it as truth-force, love-force, or soul-force. But truly there is nothing in words. What one has to do is live a life of love in the midst of the hate we see everywhere. And we cannot do it without unconquerable faith in its efficacy. A great queen named Mirabai lived 200 or 300 years ago. She forsook her husband and everything and lived a life of absolute love. Her husband at last became her devotee. We often sing in the Ashram some fine hymns composed by her. (C.W., Vol. XIII, 1915-1917: 442, 'Letter to Esther Faering', 11.6.1917.)

Mira has here become a 'great queen' who lived at a somewhat indeterminate time, though elsewhere Gandhi referred to Rana Kumbha as being the husband of Mira (C.W., Vol. XXI, 1921: 519, 'Master Key' in '*Navajivan*,' 4.12.1921).

The English phrase 'passive resistance' does not suggest the power I wish to write about; 'satyagraha' is the right word. *Satyagraha* is soul-force, as opposed to armed strength. Since it is essentially an ethical weapon, only men inclined to the ethical way of life can use it wisely. Prahlad, Mirabai and others were *satyagrahis*. (C.W., Vol. XXXIII, 1915-1917: 517, 'Letter to Shankerlal on "*Ideas about Satyagraha*"', 2.9.1917.)

Gandhi, in his firm intent to forge an 'ethical weapon' as against 'armed strength' with which to fight the colonial power, did all that he could to mould the precedents he held up as beings who suffered stoically and who won over the enemy through 'love'. In his eagerness to enjoin Mira into an evolution of a pure, ethical practice, Gandhi wiped out both the tensions and strengths which existed in the life of Mira, eradicated the deep subversion inherent in her message, and made her into a very different being.

In a letter to Raojibhai Patel on 25.7.1918, Gandhi wrote:

Against Manibhai, you are only offering *satyagraha*, and *satyagraha* can never be wrong. It is not ill-will against Manibhai, but your love for him which keeps you away. Mirabai forsook her husband out of her love, and so, in his love, did Lord Buddha leave his devoted wife and his parents. (C.W., Vol. XXIV, 1917-1918: 506.)

It is a tortuous argument, in which it is difficult to escape the conclusion that Gandhi was convinced that Mira 'loved' her husband. He is unable to see that Mira held a radically different love which entailed the complete rejection of the Rana.

Mira said she paid no heed to what the world said, since she had not left her husband, but only wished to discover the true meaning of devotion to one's husband... (C.W., Vol. XXXII, 1926-1927: 144, '*Discourses on the Gita,*' 7.4.1926.)

There is a chasm here between Gandhi upholding Mira as a fighter and a *satyagrahi* and in depicting her as a woman who went to seek 'devotion to one's husband'. Gandhi is attempting to walk a tight rope here, in firstly ensuring that the challenge of Mira remains within the bounds of an unarmed struggle, and secondly in keeping safe the institution of patriarchy which was to be the bulwark of Gandhi's future society.

Non-co-operation without love is satanic: non-co-operation with love is godly.... It was certainly not hatred which impelled Mira to non-co-operate with Kumbha Rana. She lovingly submitted to the punishment which the Rana inflicted on her. Our non-co-operation also springs from love. (C.W., Vol. XXI, 1921: 519, 'Master-key,' in *Navajivan*', 4.12.1921.)

Gandhi is at odds here with the community of Mirabai, which had sought to negate through Mira imposed marital relationships, and which posed a challenge both to the institution of marriage and of widowhood. Gandhi's Mira, who sought 'devotion to one's husband' and who 'lovingly submitted to the punishment which the Rana inflicted on her' is far removed from the Mira who, through bitter struggle, established a life independent of the Sisodiya princely family, and who led a life of hardship which was nevertheless a transformative one. This Mira, instead of breaking the boundaries of established hegemonic relationships, in effect props up these relationships by refusing to over-turn them.

In Gandhi's view, Mira left the Rana not in order to seek a different love, and a different life, but in order to guide the Rana along the correct path. A Mira who curses the throne of Chittorgadh, who states that the Rana is like a bitter *kair* fruit, who uncompromisingly rejects any kind of relationship with the Rana is unknown to Gandhi.

In relation to jail treatment, Gandhi said:

Mahadev Desai carries with him a heart of love which has place in it for his torturer and carries too a stock of spiritual anaesthetics in the shape of sacred bhajans which he will sing to ward off all feeling of pain. I do believe it as literally true that Mirabai never felt the pains inflicted upon her at the instance of her husband. Her love of God and conscious repetition of that precious name kept her cheerful forever. (C.W., Vol. XXI, 1921-1922: 128, 'Jail Treatment' in *Young India*', 5.1.1922.)

A transformative self-expression is hereby reduced by Gandhi into a purely self-conscious repetition, as an instrumental means of warding off all thought and pain. Bhakti, which had broken the bounds of conventional self-expression, which delighted in its own expression, in communal singing and dancing, is reined in an iron grip to serve an individuated self-control.

Gandhi re-iterated again and again that *satyagraha* was

an extension of the rule of domestic life to the political. (C.W., Vol. XVII, 1920: 153.)

The kind of society envisaged by Gandhi was a village-based, community-oriented patriarchy, within which the 'rule of domestic life' could follow. Gandhi's vision of a future society as a self-sufficient village-based patriarchy is open to the same criticism as Lenin made of Leo Tolstoy

Tolstoy's ideas are a mirror of the weakness, the shortcomings of our peasant revolt, a reflection of the flabbiness of the patriarchal countryside and of the hidebound cowardice of the 'enterprising muzhik'. (Lenin, 1978: 15.)

Lenin's evaluation of Tolstoy as someone who on the one hand had

merciless criticism of capitalist exploitation, exposure of government outrages, the farcical courts and the state administration, and unmasking of the profound contradictions between the growth of wealth and achievements of civilization and the growth of poverty, degradation and misery among the working masses.

And who on the other hand preached submission,

'resist not evil' with violence, (Lenin, 1978: 13)

applies forcefully to Gandhi too.

Gandhi consistently sought to inculcate a moral being which would suffer tyranny cheerfully, a moral being which would not consume itself in hatred of the oppressor, and which would in fact serve as the instrument for the moral transformation of the oppressor. His depiction of Mira as someone who won over the Rana to her side through 'love' so that the Rana at last became her 'devotee' (C.W., Vol. XII, 1915-1917: 442) flouts the message of the peoples' Mira, but is essential to him in propagating the 'truth' of his philosophy whereby

there is no human being in the world who is beyond all hope of change. Love is a kind of force of attraction... that is why Mirabai sings about the bond of love. (C.W., Vol. XXXII, 1926-1927: 187, *'Discourses on the "Gita"'*, 5.5.1926.)

Mira's challenge to the princes, her sharp rejection of patriarchal political authority was deeply threatening to Gandhism, as it sought to negate existing unequal relations not through entering into a process of negotiation and change with them, but through repudiating these and embarking upon a radical restructuring of relationships. Mira's challenge and her subversion of the social order were contained by Gandhi, and her life and message were given a different twist by him.

The peoples' Mira did not express a 'love' for the Rana. The peoples' Mira profoundly challenged the imposed marital relationship, and showed a transformative fearlessness in rejecting patriarchal prescriptions. This message of the peoples' Mira could have been invoked to generate the deepest stirrings of society in the course of the freedom movement, when the nature of a future society was an appropriate matter for debate. However, this aspect of Mira, which was of the utmost importance in placing value on the grave need to attain personal liberties, as against rigid community demands, was wiped out by Gandhi, and a message which could have been vital and powerful in changing fundamental social relations was distorted and made to serve patriarchal illusions of harmony within the domestic and political realm.

The song of Mira, which echoed the choice of heart over and above the claims of family, legislators and jurors alike, remained unheeded. This unheeding was a blow struck against the deepest aspirations of all those men and women seeking release from damagingly imposed marital relationships, and it lay at the very core of the betrayal of the people. The institutions and practices that mould our most intimate being are always the most difficult to dislodge, and hence are the ones which need the most attention.

An attack on this iniquitous system of marriage could have dealt a body blow to values of subservience to those who wield power in the domestic realm, it could have challenged the very basis of patriarchal authority, and it could have undermined misguided notions of suffering in the pious hope that it would transform the other. Most importantly, it would have brought into question the first and most vital rung of legitimation of the caste system, and it would have freed the hearts and minds of all those people whose spirits are confined and imprisoned.

Gandhi upheld the existing institution of marriage as one through which individuals could face control

I submit that marriage is a force that protects religion. If the fence were to be destroyed religion would go to pieces. The foundation of religion is restraint and marriage is nothing but restraint. (C.W., Vol. XXX, 1926: 364, 'Abolish Marriage!' in *Young India*, 3.6.1926.)

Gandhi attempted to put up fences which would be deeply interiorized in the innermost recesses of one's existence. This concept of marriage does not protect an abstract 'religion', but a very particular one based on *varnashramdharma*, on the four-fold hierarchy of the caste system, and the 'restraint' that is advocated on its behalf is one that ensures that this *varnashramdharma* is not challenged. It also limits the capacity of a human being to give of herself, or himself fully. Gandhi was utterly consistent in paving the path to the kind of society he had envisaged in his strivings, for his authoritarian moral being could brook no liberationary thrust.

Gandhi evoked the person of Mira in his attempt to involve women within the nationalist movement:

In Hinduism devotion of wife to her husband and her complete merger in him is the highest aim, never mind whether the husband is a fiend or an embodiment of love. If this be the correct conduct for a wife, may she in the teeth of opposition by her husband undertake national service?... I think there is a way out. Mirabai has shown the way. The wife has a perfect right to take her own course and meekly brave the consequences when she knows herself to be in the right and when her resistance is for a nobler purpose. (C.W., Vol. XXXI, 1926: 511–2, 'Tough Questions', in *Young India*, 3.6.1926.)

While the argument above is ostensibly for the right of a married woman to her own political life and decision, it in fact negates this. It is a tightly controlled right, only legitimate when it is for a 'nobler purpose', the judge of which will be the patriarchal moralist himself.

In his own relationship with his wife Kasturba, Gandhi subjected her to a coercive tyranny. Kasturba was told that she should either observe the rules of the Ashram and accept the entry of untouchables into it, or she should leave the Ashram.

But the argument that a woman in following in her husband's footsteps incurs no sin appealed to her and she quietened down. I do not hold that a wife is bound to follow her husband in what she considers sinful. But I welcomed my wife's attitude in the present case, because I looked upon the removal of untouchability as a meritorious thing... I had therefore no hesitation in accepting my wife's renunciation of untouchability not as an independent person but only as a faithful wife. (C.W., Vol. L, 1932: 222, *'History of Satyagraha Ashram,'* June-August, 1932.)

Herein lies the root of reaction—the belief that a dominant and benevolent despot can impose moral choices on someone who is subordinated to him. This conception was so deeply rooted in Gandhi that he was not even aware of the moral and political issues involved here.

Let us now turn to the other major challenge to the established social order that is posed by the community of Mirabai: the challenge to the institution of widowhood. The bhajans sung about Mira express a deeply felt anguish at the life of widowhood. This expression of course takes place in the context of bhakti, but it would be a grave mistake to see this as confined to the sphere of religion, bearing no relation to actual daily existence. It is precisely because daily existence is structured in a particular way that an expression is articulated to overcome this. Mira, having refused to recognize a social relationship with the Rana, takes this further at his death, and refuses to conform to the socially defined rules of widowhood. In Gandhi's rendering of Mira (as in Tod), Mira is the wife of Rana

Kumbha, and nowhere is the popularly accepted rejection of the Rana mentioned by Gandhi anywhere. Rather, for him, Mira remains a figure who reconciled the Rana to a love for Krishna.

Yet Gandhi's Mira lends herself well to his notions of widowhood. Gandhi named his English follower, Madeleine Slade, Mirabai. It was at Gandhi's behest that Madeleine Slade undertook to have her head shaven—this being both the mark of an ascetic and a widow. And it was for his English disciple that Gandhi undertook to translate the bhajans sung at the Ashram. In one of the greatest travesties, Gandhi expunged the refutation of widowhood in one of the most widely sung of Mira bhajans.

D.B. Kalelkar shared a prison cell with Gandhi in Yeravda in 1930. During this time, Gandhi translated one verse each evening from the 'Ashram Bhajnavali'. Kalelkar shows how Gandhi did not hesitate to take liberties in his interpretation of bhajans and prayers (Prasad, 1965: 211–12). It appears that the particular Mira bhajan which has been drastically purified was sung by Gandhi and Kalelkar in Yeravda Central Prison often on an evening and early mornings (Prabhudas Gandhi, 1978: 218). It is worth noting the major differences in content of the popularly sung Mira bhajan, and Gandhi's translation of the one sung in the Ashram.

I have become attached to your face, beloved Mohan,
I have become attached to your face.

The domestic life is a sour and hollow one.
One weds—and then becomes a widow.
Why should I go to his house, beloved Mohan?
I have become attached to your face.

I married my loved one,
and achieved an undestructible relationship.
I annihilated the fear of widowhood.
Beloved Mohan, I have become attached to your face.

Mirabai is blessed.
My one hope rests in you.
Oh, I am fortunate, beloved Mohan.
I have become attached to your face.

As discussed on pages 199 and 200 of this work, this particular bhajan is still extant, and widely sung, despite the attempt to tamper with it and popularize a different version of it. The English translation of the altered version as it appears in the *'Ashram Bhajnavali'* is as follows

O dear Lord, I love Thy face; as soon as I saw Thy face, the world became useless to me and my mind became detached from it. The happiness that the world gives is like a mirage, one should move about deeming it of no account. Mirabai says: Blessed Lord, my only hope is in Thee and I consider myself fortunate (in that I have seen Thee face to face). (C.W., Vol. XXXXIV, 1930: 449–50, *'Ashram Bhajnavali'*, 11.11.1930.)

In the bhajan as printed in the 'Ashram Bhajnavali' (above), both couplets relating to the condition of widowhood (*randavu*) are expurgated. Instead, a flaccid phrase as to how the happiness of a house-holder is like a mirage is inserted.

In Gujarat, even amongst the middle classes, the original version of this powerful bhajan is still widespread, its vitality lying in the utterance of a condition of degradation, which is not masked by polite words. Not only is this degradation sharply voiced—it is sharply refuted too. The community of Mirabai has continued to uphold this refutation, inspite of the attempts of those with a variant morality to tame this.

We have seen how Gandhi was unable to accept the rejection of marriage to the Rana by Mira—equally, he could not have accepted her rejection of the very institution of widowhood. Gandhi again attempted to imposed a moral veneer to a condition of degradation

I read a profound meaning in widowhood; equally, I also see how it can be turned to good account... To the widows, therefore, I would say—'Look upon your widowhood as sacred and live a life worthy of it'. (C.W., Vol. XVI, 1919-1920: 233–4.)

Mira of course did not 'read a profound meaning in widowhood'—she rejected the status of widowhood as being a humiliating one, refuting it completely and irrevocably, positing in its stead a relationship of her heart. If this message of Mira was to be taken further, if it was to be realized in everyday social relations, then instead of putting widows on a pedestal as pure beings, they would be supported in a clear choice to establish their own self-chosen association. This, however, was antithetical to Gandhi's philosophy.

If a fifty year old widower may remarry with impunity, it should be open to a widow of that age to do likewise. That in my opinion both will be sinning by remarriage is quite another matter. I should anyday subscribe to a reform in the Hindu law making sinful the remarriage of a widow or widower who voluntarily married after maturity. (C.W., Vol. XXXI, 1926: 493, 'A Catechism' in *Young India*', 14.10.1926.)

The Mira bhajans have emphasized the governing of personal relationships by the choice of an active and liberated will—not by the harsh moralisms of those who decide after a

profounder consideration about *dharma*. (C.W., Vol. XXX, 1926: 36, 'Widow Re-marraige' in *Navajivan*', 21.2.1926.)

The peoples' morality as it emerges through the Mira bhajans, is profoundly opposed to the dominant *dharma*. However Gandhi reneged on the community of Mirabai, abrogated on the opportunity to take the message of this community forward in realizing itself, and attempted to consolidate a dominant *dharma* within the process of establishing an independent bourgeois rule.

Mira's breaking of caste had resonated with the bhajniks from peasant and artisan communities alike. Gandhi persistently alludes to Narsinha's transgression of caste, but he does not seem to be aware that Mira is deemed to have done so too. Within his own particular context, Gandhi's commitment to the removal of untouchability cannot be doubted. He had the integrity to make this one of the most central issues while many in the Congress would have been comfortable with limiting themselves to political, not social objectives. Gandhi nevertheless stopped short at attacking the roots of the system of untouchability. Rather, he wanted to remove the concept of pollution and stigma attached to particular tasks.

Gandhi's Ashram contained even a tannery. However, he reiterated his basic support for *varnashramdharma*. The spectre that haunted upper-caste Hindu society was that of inter-caste marriages. While Gandhi came down in favour of remarriage of child widows, (and not those widows whose marriage had been consummated), he stated categorically that this should not take place across caste lines (C.W., Vol. XXX, 1926: 110, 'Letter to Kasturchand Marfatia, 12.3.1926).

The spirit of the Mira bhajans is a profound right to personal association, in many and varied ways—with God, with those society stigmatizes as 'polluted', with ragged wayfarers and poor bhajan singers, with those on the fringes of society—governed by the right to enter into these associations unchained by the fetters of a dominant social system. To understand the spirit of the Mira bhajans and to take this understanding into the entrails of society would require a closer listening to the voices of the bhajniks, and would make for a deeper transformation of social relationships as we know them today.

There are visionary moments in Gandhi when he does precisely this, when he looks to the bhaktas not as figures to be plucked and moulded according to his religiosity, but when he sees them concretely within their own specific context of lived community, and performed labour. He extends this to creating and evolving a society where this labour would receive valued recognition:

The university which I visualize will consist of masons, carpenters and weavers who will be truly intellectual social workers—they will not only be masons, carpenters, and weavers having a knowledge of their trades sufficient merely for them to earn their livelihood. From this university I look forward to seeing a Kabir rise from the weavers, a Bhoja Bhagat from the cobblers, an Akha from the goldsmiths, and a Guru Govind from the farmers. I regard *all* these four as having received intellectual education. (C.W., Vol. XXXVI, 1928: 422, 'Questions on Education' in '*Navajivan*' 17.6.1928.)

Homage is here paid to the bhaktas as being organic intellectuals, who spoke out of and to the conditions of the people, who struggled and visualized a different form of knowledge, a different way of being and who were, in a rigid feudal society, pathbreakers for individual conscience and liberty. However, on essential issues of restructuring the social order, Kabir and Nanak, like Mira, are betrayed.

The Khilafat movement gained in strength in India between 1919-1920. The major demands of the movement was that the Caliphate in Turkey should be preserved. We are not concerned here with the complex interplay of contradictory forces that lay behind the Khilafat movement, which in fact was opposed to the aspirations of Turkish nationalism, as well as the stirrings of Arab nationalism. For Gandhi, it was a means of drawing in the mass of the Muslims into the anti-colonial struggle in India, and within the support that he gave to the cause of Khilafat, he drew a sharp line between the two religious communities, Hindus and Muslims.

I know that the Khilafat agitation is not a political weapon. It is the duty of all Muslims to defend the Khilafat... Of course, fighting for the Khilafat will increase the power of Islam. It is no crime to rejoice at this. The Muslims cannot but be glad, and, if we wish that people of other faiths should be happy at the awakening of a new spirit in Hinduism and its regeneration, we Hindus should also be glad at the regeneration of Islam.

I hope that nobody will bring up here the history of the attempts made by Guru Nanak and Kabir to unite Hindus and Muslims; for the effort today is not for uniting the religions, but for uniting hearts, despite the differences in religion... The attempt today is for the cultivation of tolerance. Its aim is to see that the orthodox Hindu remains what he is and yet respects an orthodox Muslim and sincerely wishes him prosperity. This attempt is altogether new but it springs from an ideal which is at the very root of Hinduism.

Let us assume that the Muslims will betray us even after this effort... The law does not bind the party that breaks it, but love may bind even the person so breaking it.

'Hari has bound me to him by a slender cord,
As He pulls me so do I turn.
My heart by love's dagger has been pierced.'

Thus sang Mira and proved by her actions that it was so. The same slender cord will suffice to bind the Muslims and to save the cow. (C.W.,

Vol. XIX, 1920-1: 305–7, 'Why I have been working for Khilafat So Seriously' in *'Navajivan'* 30.1.1921.)

Tragically, the forces of orthodox Hinduism and of orthodox Islam were encouraged, in a flawed bid to 'unit[e] hearts, despite the differences in religion'. The looser, popular, anti-hierarchical strands that continued to exist on the ground were discouraged. Mira's message—or a particular variant of Mira's message—was tied to the cause of cow protection. And Kabir and Nanak were to be forgotten.

While the entrenchment of consolidated religious identities has wrenched the polity of the sub-continent, it is significant that ratified religious orthodoxies have not managed to smother the very real shared beliefs and faith of people from both religious communities. Hindus continue to worship Pirs, and Sufi *qawwals* continue to sing in praise of Mira.

Gandhi continued to preach of love and non-violence. He saw the programme of spinning of *khadi* as not only an economic necessity, but also as symbolizing and inculcating values of *satyagraha*. Gandhi invoked Mira again and again in his exhortations to take up spinning. I have shown in an earlier chapter Mira's specific alignment to the weaving communities. It is unclear whether Gandhi was aware of the affiliation of the weaving groups to Mira, although this appears unlikely, as he did not seem to be cognisant of the very powerful base that Mira held within the untouchable groups. It seems more likely that Gandhi mulled over the lines of particular Mira bhajans over and over again, as he demanded that his followers do too. In this way, Gandhi came up with his own unique interpretation of Mira

'God holds me with a slender thread and I turn in whichever direction He pulls me.' Mira knew this thread because she was filled with love. If she had not been a skilled spinner, how could she have given the beautiful simile of a thread to the bond of love uniting her with Lord Krishna: (C.W., Vol. XXIV, 1924: 167, 'There is no Enthusiasm' in *'Navajivan'* 1.6.1924.)

Mira thus becomes one of the foremost *khadi* bhaktas, who, 'filled with love' overcame all obstacles.

In a different speech, Gandhi said

Whether Swaraj is attainable through your spinning or not, if you have a fellow feeling for the beggar, I shall require you to spin out of sympathy for him. You should identify yourself with the beggar and develop a bond of sympathy for him. Mira has chanted,

'God has bound me with a string of yarn,
I am a puppet in his hands,
I have been stabbed with the dagger of love.'

If you have such love for millions of your brothers and sisters, you should all tie yourselves up with a string of yarn. I know only this economics and nothing else. (C.W., Vol. XXV, 1924-5: 61, speech at Excelsior Theatre, Bombay, 31.8.1924.)

There is a serious point to what often reads as garbled interpretations by Gandhi. This point is that Gandhi attempted to instil a highly abstracted love of humanity, of all classes, and of all affiliations, through his preachings and practices. There is a sharp disjuncture between this love, and one which in the course of evolution, led to an affinity between Mira and those who valued her. The latter arose through a process of shared struggle and suffering—not through an imposed high philosophy.

In Gandhi's writings, Mira remains the foremost *satyagrahi* and the foremost non-co-operator. However, in the political conjunctures when Gandhi upheld Mira most strongly, she emerges in actual political circumstances not as a powerful figure leading liberationary struggles—but as a symbol marking the stark defeat of the mass movements in this period. I have shown in this chapter how the social and deeply imaginative message of Mira was neutered by Gandhi. In the political realm too, Gandhi's Mira marked a betrayal of the people.

On the sixth of April, 1919, Gandhi called for a day of national strike against the Rowlatt Act, which attempted to make wartime restrictions on civil rights permanent. The response to this call was widespread, resulting in a popular and violent groundswell against British rule. In the cities and towns of Punjab and Gujarat, in Delhi and Bombay, there were large-scale agitations.

In Ahmedabad, fifty-one government offices were burnt down by rioters who were, in the main, textile workers. In Amritsar, there were massive demonstrations which united Hindus and Muslims alike. When a peaceful demonstration was fired upon in Amritsar on the tenth of April, crowds attacked banks, the railway station and the town hall. Martial law was imposed in Amritsar on eleventh April, and on the thirteenth April, an unarmed group of villagers who had come to the town to celebrate a fair, and who were unaware of the martial law, were fired upon, leading to a brutal massacre of civilians (Sarkar, 1984: 187–95). News of this massacre led to further expressions of mass resistance.

Gandhi was shaken by the wide-spread violence, described the whole strategy as a 'Himalayan blunder', and called off the *satyagraha*. The biggest mass upsurge since 1857 had ground to a halt. In his contribution to the *Congress Report on the Punjab Disorders*, Gandhi wrote a statement on *satyagraha* in which he said

When Daniel disregarded the law of the Medes and Persians which offended his conscience, and meekly suffered the punishment for his disobedience, he offered *satyagraha* in its purest form... Prahlad disregarded the orders of his father because he considered them to be repugnant to his conscience. He uncomplainingly and cheerfully bore the tortures to which he was subjected at the instance of his father. Mirabai is said to have offended her husband by following her own conscience, was content to live in separation from him and bore with quiet dignity and resignation all the injuries that are said to have been done to her in order to bend her to her husband's will. Both Prahlad and Mirabai practiced *satyagraha*. It must be remembered that neither Daniel nor Socrates, neither Prahlad nor Mirabai had any ill will towards their persecutors. Daniel and Socrates are regarded as having been model citizens of the states to which they belonged, Prahlad a model son and Mirabai a model wife. (C.W., Vol. XVII, 1920: 152–3, '*Satyagraha*' in the '*Congress Report in the Punjab Disorders*'.)

The emphasis here is on a cheerful forebearance of 'tortures'. It is a grotesque admonition to the masses to resign themselves to injuries. In a context where the colonial authorities had deliberately utilized a policy of repression, whereby in the Punjab alone more than one thousand two hundred had died, and three thousand six hundred had been wounded (Sarkar, 1984: 192), it appears as a deliberate buckling under to British rule, for fear of what the alternative could entail. The bitter hardship of war exactions, and low wages, which had provided the spark for the rioting in Punjab, and which were later compounded by the knowledge of the brutality of the colonial army, were to be quietly borne, and the persecutors were not to be hated. An attempt was made to turn aside the legitimate anger of the people by giving them the figures of Prahlad and Mirabai, one a 'model son' and the other a 'model wife'. A patriarchal philosophy which had arisen out of an evaluation of relationships in the domestic sphere was carried through to its logical conclusion in the political domain.

Gandhi, while purporting to hold up historical precedents who stood up against tyranny, in fact put brakes on the growing protest against harsh exploitation. After the Chauri Chaura incident, where twenty-two policeman had been killed by a crowd enraged at them having fired into a peaceful picket, Gandhi quoted a Mira bhajan

In 1919, Ahmedabad and Viramgam, Amritsar and Kasur showed my error and *satyagraha* was suspended. Last November, I witnessed in Bombay man's barbarism and again suspended mass civil disobedience. Even then I did not learn the lesson completely. Now it is Chauri Chaura which has punished me.

'If the King gets angry, the city will shelter me; if God is displeased, where shall I turn?' I do not know if Mira actually composed any song with this line, but she certainly lived her life in that spirit. We may bear the world's reproaches, but we should not be guilty in the eyes of God. We should heed His warning. (C.W., Vol. XXII, 1921-2: 424, 'Divine Warning' in *'Navajivan'* 19.2.1922.)

In the above bhajan, Mira is in fact flouting the authority of the Rana, in which she says that he can keep his kingdom, that she is removing herself from his power—Gandhi, though, utilized the bhajan to curb the passions of those enraged at the arbitrariness of an unjust rule.

The process of subversion of the Mira message was completed when Gandhi turned to her and to other bhaktas to distance himself from the horrors of the partition. The bloodshed which accompanied the period preceding partition, the stabbings in Calcutta, Bombay, Ahmedabad, made Gandhi announce in a prayer meeting in New Delhi, that the Mira bhajan that they had just listened to during the prayers, taught them that God was the only one who could rid them of their woes and heal them of their pain. (C.W., Vol. LXXXV, 1948: 382, 'Speech at Prayer Meeting', New Delhi, 26.9.1946, appeared in *The Hindustan Times* 27.9.1946.)

Given that Gandhi had lost faith in the power of mass movements to bring about change, given that he saw it as a shortcoming in himself when he realized that the practice of *satyagraha* was unworkable—Gandhi took recourse to the Absolute to seek solace.

The potential to change fundamental social relations pertaining to the innermost lives of the people, which would have taken into account their imaginings and their aspirations, the power to take the Mira message into the forming of actual social relationships was lost, and Mira was turned into something which was not of the peoples' making. The community of Mirabai, though, continued to be tied to her, finding no other deeper expression for their visions.

Chapter Nine

Amplification

The cultural upsurge that accompanied the nationalist movement mobilized the endeavours of intellectuals, singers, film-makers and other artists, all of whom were intent on building up a cultural and social climate more in keeping with the needs of an emergent society. Within this, while attempts were made to overthrow the values contained in the old order, nevertheless these artists failed to break away sufficiently from the continuing contradictory forces of feudal reaction and bourgeois interests. The process of establishing a thorough capitalist society in India, which had been begun by the British, and which was continued by the new rulers, utilized the most divisive elements of religion, caste, community, and male domination, giving these forces a new form and harnessing them to the benefits of the powerful. The incorporation and appropriation of Mira firstly by artists who were closely aligned to the nationalist upsurge, and later by the commercial media, gave Mira a new social base and a new social turn. This marked a wider rift with the people's Mira, even as it created a widening differentiation amongst the bhajniks.

Amongst those who did so much to provide a powerful cultural voice to nationalist aspirations, Vishnu Digambar Paluskar stands out as adding a zest and vitality to the anti-colonial movement with his patriotic songs. He defied the ban on the singing of *'Vande Matram'* at the Kokanada Conference, and he popularized too Gandhi's much-loved bhajan, *'Raghupati Raghav Raja Ram'*. V.D. Paluskar brought Mira into the tradition of classical singing and it was his pupil Omkarnath Thakur who sang in the classical style *'pag ghunghru bandh Mira nachi re'*, a much renowned and powerful rendering. In 1958, when Vinoba Bhave, leader of the Sarvodaya movement, visited the Mira temple in Chittor, Omkarnath Thakur's singing of this particular Mira bhajan was extremely important in consolidating the occasion (Shaktawat, 1982: iii).

V.D. Paluskar visited the Sabarmati Ashram in 1926, and at Gandhi's request, Paluskar's pupil, Narayan Khare came to live at the Ashram, and became an important initiator at the morning and evening prayer sessions there. Khare sang the Mira bhajans, as others, on a *tanpura* (Prabhudas Gandhi, 1978: 22–3). Gandhi wished to encourage the growth of classical music in Gujarat, which did not compare well with other states such as Maharashtra, but he wanted music to inculcate certain values through its expression. 'Shri Khare is fully conducive to improvement in moral standards and is steeped in the spirit of prayer', he approved. (C.W., Vol. XXXVII, 1928: 317–8, 'Music in Gujarat' in *'Navajivan'* 30.9.1928). The role of music in contributing to a disciplined morality continued to be stressed by Gandhi.

Gradually in the North, bhajans which had earlier been sung in the regional dialects and within a gathering of devotees, began to be set to Hindustani classical *ragas* and began to be sung at music conferences, at music concerts and at private gatherings. This removed the bhajans from the sphere of a community religious experience and expression, and placed them in the realm of sophisticated aesthetics, which in both content and form was at once removed from the domain within which these bhajans had originated. A bhajan rendered in a classical *raga*, sung solo, does not contain within it the force of a common historical experience jointly articulated, and in the classical style, the recurring musical lines are used much more to demonstrate the musical virtuosity of the singer.

The setting of regional bhajans also meant a standardization of these bhajans, which borrowed from regional dialects but translated these into a language accessible particularly to those in urban areas who patronized classical singing.

There emerged a hierarchy of professional bhajan singers too, with the classical singers catering to the tastes of the upper middle and the middle class, while singers such as Lata Mangeshkar, Hari Om Sharnam, Anup Jalota and others, with their phenomenal popularity as bhajan singers, were tied to the voracious need of the lower middle classes for more and more renderings of sentimentalized bhajans. A number of these latter singers have been prominent in the assertion of the lower middle classes to defend (as they see it) their position against those from the lower castes and against Muslims (Mukta, 1989: 2472).

In 1947, Mira bhajans were appropriated in a yet new context. M.S. Subbulakshmi (a powerful exponent of the songs of Subramanya Bharati, 1882-1921, who had written a number of Swadeshi songs) pioneered the breakthrough of Mira bhajans into the world of films. Subbulakshmi acted the lead role in the film *'Meera'*, and sang the bhajans in it. The film first appeared in Tamil, but the Hindi version which appeared in 1947 was immensely popular in the North. Sarojini Naidu praised the film lavishly, and it catapulted Subbulakshmi into prominence.

The strength of the *'Meera'* film was undoubtedly Subbulakshmi's voice. This outlasted the film, with the songs being available on a gramophone record, as well as on a prerecorded cassette. The emotions expressed in Subbulakshmi's voice are intense, yet restrained and controlled. They are very much in the context of a person of dignity who voices a mature love. Even when singing *'taat, maat, bandhu, bhraat, apna na koi'* (HMV India, HTC 03B 1615, *'Mere to Giridhar'*) she offers a controlled rendering. The song *'Hari Awan ki Awaz'* (HMV India, HTC 03B 1615), with its high point of *'dharti rup nava nav dhariya'* betokens the culmination of the love of a woman who has gone through the fire of pain and emerged stronger. The film, which appeared in black and white, continues to evoke the gentler and more controlled days of Indian cinema.

It is instructive, though, that in this film on Mira, was shown as living in comfort and ease in Chittor, sharing an enjoyment of music with her husband, the prince. He is then shown as having been misled and inflamed by advisors who were unhappy with Mira's actions, particularly in accepting a gift from the Mughal Emperor Akbar, then in conflict with the Rajput rulers of Chittor. The prince is also seen as repenting of his actions, much in keeping with Gandhi's version of the Mira story. The film made no attempt to grapple with Mira's throwing aside of the marital relationship, her refusal to accept a socially prescribed widowhood, and her transgression of caste and class allegiance. All in all, it was a staid film, brought to life by the songs, which did not pose challenging ideas—but which did not degrade the person of Mira either, in terms of a voyeuristic portrayal. This was to come later.

The most significant early film in the South was *'Bala Yogini'* (1936), made by K. Subramanyan, in which Subbulakshmi played a leading role. The film attacked the caste system, exposed the hypocritical Brahmans, and showed the plight of a Brahman widow who took shelter with her daughter in the house of a lower caste servant. In the 1930's and 1940's, films had not yet succumbed to the crippling pressures of the financiers, and many socially aware films were made. *'Devdas'* and *'Duniya na mane'* (1937) were indictments of arranged marriages, and *'Badi Didi'* (1939) exposed the plight of widows. But, as in *'Achut Kanya'* (1936), a film about a dalit woman in love with a Brahman youth, a tragic and pessimistic ending was projected—in this case the death of the dalit woman crushed under an oncoming train.

Directors of films were sensitive to dominant prejudices, and even when they attempted to highlight social griefs and personal suffering, they treaded warily. Where they did take up social injustice, the themes recurrent were untouchability, arranged marriages (including child marriages) and widowhood, themes which had been central to the Mira bhajans.

The films *'Eknath'* (1939) and *'Bhakta Chetha'* (1940) created a furore. The former dealt with the Maharashtrian bhakta who served the food intended as an offering to God, to hungry untouchables. The latter showed the offerings made by Chetha, a cobbler, actually being accepted by God (Baskaran, 1981: 111, 123–4).

The 1979 production of the film 'Meera', directed by Gulzar, and starring Hema Malini in it, was thus in a long line of films which centred around the lives of bhaktas. Hema Malini is a well known dancer too, and in this film she depicted a Mira who half-fainted at the time of the marriage ceremony, who was engrossed in composing verses in the palace of Chittor, and who, having left Chittor, sang and danced on her own on the sands of Rajasthan. In the denouement, Mira is charged with having discourse with the enemy of the Rajputs, the Badshah Akbar. Mira refutes these charges, putting loyalty to Krishna above the claims of the state—and making her way to the nearby Krishna temple, vanishes within it. What is instructive is that in conversation with middle-class, middle-aged women living in small towns such as Jodhpur, when talking about the subject of work, they began to refer immediately to this film, which has been shown on Doordarshan more than once. While women bhajniks spontaneously burst into a Mira bhajan when informed of my work—those who did not participate in this form of worship used the Gulzar film as a point of reference.

Till the growth and expansion of the mass media, Mira had remained enfolded within the community of bhajniks, and had been remembered and re-evoked through time by the bhajans sung in her name. It was a medium whereby the figure of Mira was preserved and passed on by the bhajniks, who kept her deep in their heart, gaining sustenance through the message of her bhajans which spoke to their lives. These bhajans had emphasized and continue to emphasize not appearance, but inner worth, not external form, but spiritual depth, not an objectified comeliness—but a life of struggle unadorned, irradiated by its intensity of seeking, and brilliant in its self-illumination. With the growth of a commercial art, though, with the sale of records with illustrated jacket-covers, the sale of calendars, Diwali cards etc., the inner being of Mira was thrown away, and her image was translated into an ever-changing and gross physicality. Within thirty years of this development, as the profiteers grew rich on the exploitation of the sale of womens' bodies, as society became deadened to the effects of this and as warped eyes which remained unfulfilled sought further revelations, so the depictions of Mira became more and more base.

A nineteenth century painting of Mira shows her seated opposite a Krishna *murti*, with a *tanpura* in her hand (see photograph I). It is an alert, wide-eyed Mira, gazing steadily at the world in front of her, her attire enhancing the choices she has made in her life, and accentuating the solidity of her character. While obviously in opulent surroundings, the person of Mira has force and vigour here, compared to the soft domesticity as in Rawal's Mira (see photograph IX).

Ravishankar Rawal and Kanu Desai were both artists, who were creative at the time that Gandhi was active in the anti-colonial movement. While both purported to paint, to inculcate Gandhian values, both set a precedent for a highly refracted and contradictory image of Mira.

Gandhi's views on art too were very specific. '[He] is the greatest artist who leads the best life. For what is life without the background and setting of a worthy life? An art is to be valued only when it ennobles life' (C.W., Vol. XXIII, 1922-4: 193–4, 'Interview to Dilip Kumar Roy' in *'Bombay Chronicle'* 2.2.1924). Similarly, Ravishankar Rawal wrote in an article entitled 'Art in the Time of Gandhi', that art should satisfy the soul (Rawal, 1947: 161). Rawal argued that Gandhi's teachings had made it clear that art which created dissatisfaction, or which led to a lack of contentment was destructive. Hence Rawal's work lacks tension. His Mira (IX) was adopted by the Gujarat government after Independence as its calendar photo, and it depicts Mira as a chaste middle class figure immersed in *murti-puja*, who hovers ambiguously between the figure of a pious house-wife and a widow.

Kanu Desai was another painter, educated at the Gujarat Vidyapith, who won a lot of praise from many countries for his paintings of Gandhi, whom he had observed at close quarters (Rawal, 1947: 164–5). Kanu Desai painted a set of portraits of Mira entitled, 'Mirabai: Ten pictures from the Life of India's

Greatest Poetess of the Past' (Desai, 1943). Both Rawal's and Desai's portrayal of Mira consolidated her embourgeoisement in the visual arts.

The first painting by Kanu Desai is entitled 'Dedication' and shows the face of a woman with half-closed eyes, holding a lamp on a lotus-leaf, the flame curling round her face. The second, 'Ranee Mira' depicts a plump, soft-faced figure standing looking out of the windows of a palatial room, with a hand on her cheek and a slight smile on her face, a full moon outside. 'Devotion' shows the back of a white-clothed figure bending down to do an *aarti*. 'The Poison Cup' shows two women, both dressed in white, one with a cup of poison to her lips, the other bending towards her, both looking intent. A flower pot stands on the table.

Mira 'In Quest' shows a figure standing by the sea-shore, gazing across the sea, the Dwarka temple in the background. The figure is of a mature woman dressed in white, her hair streaming out behind her, at once romantic and seductive, the white lending this an aura of self-conscious purity. (see photograph X) 'Mira dancing' and 'Mira in ecstasy' (photographs XI and XII) pandered to middle class male voyeurism and debased the figure of Mira, turning her into a sexually charged figure, at once flamboyant and supplicating. The social base of this art form became more and more entrenched within the logic of profit-making, and the morality of a two-faced bourgeoisie.

These artists, whose middle class background and commitment refracted their vision, sought to modify and change the popular culture and its values. They worked from the outside, practicing a didactic and prescriptive art. They were removed from the deepest aspirations of the people. Gandhian ideology did induce some of them to look at rural life with some respect, instead of the previous contempt (Rawal, 1947: 163), but even so it was a refined and highly idealized depiction. In paintings in Gujarat, this developed into a portrayal of rural life as rustic simplicity (as in Rawal's *'Krishikanya'*,). This and similar pictures were to decorate the living rooms of the well-to-do. Rural life was shown to be soft and idyllic, in which toil and hard labour were transmitted into a joyous activity, breathing a clean and unexploitative air. Such paintings pandered to the nostalgia of the middle class urban dwellers of Gujarat.

Highly conflicting and contradictory images of Mira and of women bhaktas in general continued to abound. This was not surprising, given that the prevalent notion of women who had left home to embark on a spiritual path was that they were 'loose'. Yet the opposite and equally chastening notion of the purity of women who had foregone all physical desire was introduced and propagated by visual artists and verbal moralists alike. Both of these conflicting images existed side by side (see photographs XIII and XIV), leaving it to the eye of the beholder to come to terms with the tensions and opposing pulls of social values, whereby 'modernity' was much sought after, while a particular kind of 'traditionality' was eulogized and harked back to.

Visually, the image of Mira garbed in white (both in paintings and in plaster of Paris models—see XV) has led to a creation of a climate whereby Mira is seen as a pure widow, a white saree being indelibly the badge of widowhood for upper caste widows. The other pictorial depiction of Mira though, as in a 1990 calendar, places her in a hazy area between what a princess-courtesan, a bedecked heroine of the film screen looks like.

No attempt was made to replace the dominant religion by a humanistic and secular morality, creative artists harnessing religiosity to profit-making. Film makers who made films on the lives of bhaktas, and other moral figures, such as '*Raja Harishchandra*' ended up glorifying miracles and godly tricks. Novelists and writers like Jhaverchand Meghani utilized the language of the subordinated in rural areas, yet propagated a feudal culture with his stories of the *baharvatiyas* of Saurashtra, and his stories of the *lok sants* of Saurasthra, which again emphasized miracle-mongering. There was a warping of the potential in both the crucial sphere of culture which dictates one's deepest strivings, as in the political sphere.

The incursion of the commercial media into the heart of society has made for a differentiation amongst the bhajniks. Sale of pre-recorded cassettes became widespread in the 1970's. This began to change the content and the form of bhajan singing, so that it is not unusual now to hear in the Jagdish temple at Udaipur, the Charbhuja temple in Merta, and amongst lower middle-class housewives in Dwarka, people singing the bhajans of Hari Om Sharnam and Anup Jalota, with similar inflexions, and dramatic pauses. Bhajans sung by these two singers are widely available on cassettes, on gramophone records, and much more recently, on ubiquitous video recordings. The taking on of these readily available song expressions has displaced even the creativity of middle-class housewives who used to compose their own words and music and share these with other women in afternoon bhajan sessions. The emphasis is very much now on listening to recorded music and bhajans—and viewing them on the video and on films, with the filmi bhajans gaining ascendancy. These have begun to displace the earlier expressions of community and self.

The community of Mirabai has not put up a fight against the encroachment of this insipid and predatory deformation in any direct way. The older bhajniks amongst the peasant and artisan communities continue to offer resistance by holding on to what they have always sung, by continuing to play the *ektara* rather than the harmonium, by turning their backs on this instrusion. These bhajniks, and they are not always only the elderly, continue to provide voice to the community, and to articulate a common history.

The kind of person who has taken to this mass-produced culture and to the individuation of Mira with greater ease, is a different kind of person. He is typically in his twenties, with aspirations of upward mobility, residing in a small town who does not have pride in self and community, and who is without the strength that emerges out of the struggles and lives of his people. Some of these singers have become absorbed in the local 'All India Radio' network, they are referred to as being 'radio artists' and they sing for an audience which is not closely-knit within a collective and emotionally-charged atmosphere of a bhajan gathering, but for a distant audience which is acclimatized to a light entertainment as they listen to the radio while going about their routine.

This has led to changes amongst the community of bhajniks, and to divisions amongst them. The singing of bhajans, and a sharing of a joint experience, which had been valued for itself (and which continues to be so valued amongst certain sections of bhajniks) whereby a person achieved recognition for the intensity with which he played the *manjiras*, or for his repertoire of *'jooni vani'* (older sayings which bore witness to a particular condition) has now begun to be overlaid by the status and fame attached to those who sing for the radio, or those who go abroad to give concerts.

A Brahman school teacher noticed that one of her pupils had a facility for singing. The teacher encouraged her young dalit pupil to sing on the radio, which she did. She has become quite a celebrity in the dalit qurters in Porbander, and at the bhajan session that I attended (which had three radio artists there) these bhajan singers were showered with coins and notes, which is unheard of and considered unseemly in an ordinary bhajan gathering. This cuts away at the group roots of a gathering, and elevates a particular person above the rest, attaching a monetary value to the voice and the bhajan.

The community of Mirabai has been cut into. It has not responded to this at a concrete, political level, but at the level of the spirit, for those who are tied to Mira in close bonds and who are bound to each other by a faith in a different social order continue to uphold and validate a liberationary Mira. This retreat into itself when faced with an onslaught is the shortcoming not of these bhajniks, but of political movements which have failed to link up with deeply held values of alternative relationships. But the community of Mirabai continues to sing of its visions and imaginings, in the face of grave pressure of an acquisitive society.

Chapter Ten

The Rainbird Thirsts

Amongst middle-class women in Rajasthan and Saurasthra, Mira and Krishna bhakti are a potent force marking an alienation within the marital relationship as well as marking a quest to seek individual satisfaction in an imagined relationship. An active creation of a relationship in the mind through bhakti (and bhakti is, essentially about the forming of relationships), negates unfulfilling relationships around one and acts as a bulwark against a harsh emotional privation. The seeking of love through bhakti by women of the lower middle and the middle class shows in its articulation both the strength of bhakti to resist the daily aridity arising out of a patriarchal oppression, as well as the limits to such resistance. This form of bhakti is an individuated expression, a socially isolating one, which is sharpened and accentuated by a commercial media whose main thrust has been to prey on the very real yearnings for meaningful human associations, and warp these into virulently slick formulae, posing these as the universal ones. The fragmenting of the community world of bhakti, the appropriation of bhakti in film songs which tap the bhajan form but distort this at the same time, changes the structure of feeling and the kind of relationships that are sought, so that the notion of God as the Beloved is overlain and a bhakti which laments a separation from God becomes associated, on the big screen, with a pining after an uncaring lover. This process has sharpened the individuation of the Mira bhakti—an individuated and alienated form of bhakti which at the same time broadcasts the personal to the ears of millions.[1]

Manglaben Mulji Padh is an elderly widow in her seventies. She lives in Dwarka, in a tiny, one-roomed place, half of which is partitioned off to house a Krishna shrine. Her husband died over thirty years ago, but in the last twenty years of his life, he had been seriously ill. She had sewn clothes to make ends meet.

I have never asked anyone for anything.

Now people in the *mohalla* come to do *darshan* at the Krishna shrine in her house, and they leave behind some food-stuffs for the meals which she prepares for Krishna. Manglaben has children, but she does not see much of them.

I gave birth to them, but that is all. Now they have all gone their own way. I have only one *dhani*,

pointing to the Krishna shrine,

my sole trust is in him. I talk to him, and address him as *tu*. Who else can I claim as my own and say *tu* to? I tell him everything. He relates only through love (*te prem no sago chhe*.)

When Manglaben goes to the town market place, women who meet her ask

What are you buying for Lala (*bal* Krishna)?

because they know that she does not have anyone else to shop for, or cook for. Looking after Lala's needs enables her to look after herself. She eats what she places before him, drinks the same, and goes to sleep after putting him to bed. If she did not have this to bind her to day-to-day living, she would not be able to get up to face the next day.

Ranjanabehn Deval lives with her younger son and daughter-in-law in Udaipur, in a run-down *haveli*. She was alone the morning that I visited her, and got up from reading the Valmiki *'Ramayan'* to greet me.

Although we were not educated, my sister and I taught ourselves to read. Now I spend most of my time in reading the *'Ramayan'* and in doing *puja*.

On the subject of relationships, Ranjanabehn said

I had a *mausi*. She gave me a lot of love, as did my grandmother.

She began to cry.

My *mausi* was blind from birth. She used to compose bhajans, but she never claimed these as her own. She would say, 'There are innumerable bhaktas. They have all created them.' I used to like singing bhajans too, but after my marriage, I had to leave aside bhakti. My husband, the family, all made demands on me. Now, though, I have a lot of time to do *puja*. When I sit down to do so, I think, how shall I convey my feelings? Then I start singing a bhajan. I do this when I am on my own. No, no, I never sing in a group. You know, God will do anything for his bhakta. All he asks is that you remember him, that you love him. I think the lines of a bhajan to sing, I write these down, and then I sing them to him. Try this yourself. While singing a bhajan, think that he is near you, and you will see him. He is not so heartless that he will not give you *darshan*.

Her voice breaks.

Mira loved Krishna. Bhakti lies in loving. You know, there is no meaning in the life of a house-holder. But there is meaning (*saar*) in bhakti.

My *mausi* was married at the age of fifteen. Who would marry her, blind as she was? He was an older man, who had a wife and children (you know that in our community, they often have more than one wife). After the marriage ceremony, when her husband came to her, my *mausi* said, 'I will leave my body if you come near me.' He left her alone from then on, and though she lived in the same house as him, she had her own room, and she used to stay up till the early hours of the morning, singing bhajans.

Unequal, patriarchal relationships can brutalize through their everyday working. Rejection of these intimate relationships, with husband, with children ('I gave birth to them but that is all'), the turning towards bhakti to furnish sustenance to a self starved of active caring relationships shows a profound turning away from personal bonds which are not mutually nurturing. The forging of love through bhakti, the seeking of love through bhakti, and, significantly, the ceding that this relationship lies outside the realm of unequal giving ('all he asks is that you remember him') is a testimony to the grave need to evolve relationships which are not based on an inegalitarian property system which penetrates right into the depths of an emotional giving, in a society where women have their beings drained in constantly looking after the needs of others.

Bhakti provides here the strength to resist dehumanized relationships. It can resist by refusing to consummate the relationship (as did the blind *mausi*), or, more commonly, it resists by keeping a part of one's mind separate and apart, holding on to the self-forged relationship with god to displace the other unsatisfactory one. This relationship with god takes on an actual reality and benumbs the pain of the other. It is a self-created reality which is profoundly and intimately personal even as it is socially circumscribed, enabling the self to regenerate its capacity to face, endure, and at times overcome the harshness of an unloved existence.

What this form of bhakti does not do, though, is combine with others similarly unloved to evolve a collectivity within which to resist the basis of these shackles. This form of bhakti is a double-edged weapon. While it keeps alive the torch of the imagination, sustaining and rekindling the hopes for a betterment in social relations by its rejection of the present ones, positing in its stead a relationship based on a self-directed love, there is tremendous pessimism in this kind of bhakti in that it sees no possibility of any change in altering relations between men and women in the present. The lack of trust, the lack of faith in being able to change the existing relations around one is announced constantly by

He [God] is the only true relation that I have (*aij sacho sago chhe.*)

And also

There is none else in this world who can be yours (*duniya ma biju koi sagu nathi thatu.*)

Bhakti provides the rationale for the acceptance of unequal relations and posits an alternative which is pure and unsullied precisely because it lies in the imagination and is not involved in the grime of everyday life. An uncontaminated relationship which remains in the mind, outside the realm of power and emotional strife, while it does not challenge patriarchal relations actively, bolsters the oppressed and helps her to continue surviving within the existant relationship. There is power in the subordinated self to create her own imaginings and seek fulfillment in order to overcome an empty emotional existence.

Bhavanibai, (photo VI) an elderly Brahman widow, while leading a bhajan gathering at the temple in Merta, pointed to the *murti* of Krishna and said,

He is my *dhani* (husband).

The acceptance of Krishna as *dhani* by widows is condoned by relatives and the family around, who see the formation of this relationship as a safe expression for emotions and longings which might otherwise break through the boundary of chastity. Widows who spend a large part of the day in bhakti are reminded when they attempt to intervene in earthly family affairs that they would be better occupied worshipping God. It is a reminder that they do not have the right to participate in the struggles over matters of this world, but that they must withdraw from life and prepare for their end.

The articulation of a personal relationship with Krishna is a bond which is forged by the woman bhajnik. When it is forged within a context in which there is a withdrawal from life itself, this relationship bolsters widowhood, and negates all social relationships. The alienation of widows implodes—rather than explodes. While this reverberates internally, socially it offers despair and resignation.

Bhavanibai sang a Mira bhajan which throws some light on her own marital relationship:

Ranaji, when did you ever know what was in my mind?
In my mind, in the *sadha's* mind,
In my mind, in the *bhakta's* mind.

Mira's father arranged her marriage. Before this was formalized, Mira had refused it.

Ranaji, when did you ever know what was in my mind?
In my mind, in the *sadha's* mind,
In my mind, in the *bhakta's* mind.
Ranaji, when did you ever know what was in my mind?

Mira's father made her sit in the *chanvri*.
My bangles, the *ghunghat*, I discarded them all.
Ranaji, when did you ever know what was in my mind?
In my mind, the *sadha's* mind,
In my mind, the bhakta's mind.
Ranaji, when did you ever know what was in my mind?

Mira's father sent her to her marital home.
My beloved's face remained in front of me.
Ranaji, when did you ever know what was in my mind?
Bai Mira sings of Giridhar.
Without Hari bhajan, my heart thirsts.
Ranaji, when did you ever know what was in my mind?

The shift in the bhajan, from singing of Mira in the third person, to the first person identifies the singer with Mira and her experience. The main thrust of this bhajan, when sung by Bhavanibai amidst a group of women bhajniks, shows the inability of a father or husband to enter into the sensibility and sensitivity of a woman. A bhajan sung in Udaipur, by a married woman born into a Rathor family, is a lament that loving parents could marry off a daughter to someone like the Rana.

Come, Mohan, Mira Mertni calls you.
Mira Mertni, the Rathori calls you.

My mother and father lavished affection on me.
They lavished affection on me, Rama, they lavished affection on me.
God knows why Dudaji married me off.

Come Mohan, Mira Mertni calls you.
Mira Mertni, the Rathori calls you.

Your love, Rana, is not acceptable to me.
It is not acceptable to me, it is not acceptable to me.

Come, Mohan, Mira Mertni calls you.
Mira Mertni, the Rathori cals you.

Hari's *viyogan, jogan,* has become a *divani.*
I do not know you, Rana, my love is an old one.
Mira Mertni, the Rathori calls you.

The above bhajan was sung by Himatkumari Chundawat, accompanied by Jashodra, who came from the community of Damamis, and played the *dhol*. Jashodra was paid to come once a week to the house of Himatkumari, in order to sing bhajans. Those Rajput women that I spoke to, when they did not demonstrate an overt hostility to the very name of Mira, said that they had heard Mira bhajans sung by the women servants in their house-holds. These were, of course, a specific class of women, some of whom received a servant as part of their dowry. It was these women servants who had taken the name of Mira into the *havelis* of the Rajput nobility.

Mrs Ladha is a lecturer in a college in Chittor, who teaches Hindi literature. Married to a doctor, she was initially involved in the Lions' Club, and in voluntary work, but she felt that this did not give her a stature for herself. It was not until she started teaching that she found this. She had no children, and said that she felt very close to her students. She taught the works of Kabir, Surdas, Mira and others to her class. Did she know anyone around her who loved Krishna as Mira had done? She answered, after a pause

Even if a woman did love in this way, do you think she would publicize this to others? What happened to Mira when she made her love public? All she got was abuse. What is one to learn from this? Any other woman would keep this inside herself.

A relationship like this, kept secretively inside oneself, threatens nobody. It is only when women begin to assert the relationship of their imagination over and above the unwanted ones facing them, and rejecting the latter, as did Mira, it is only in the refutation of the imposed relationship in favour of living out the self-created ones, that immediate patriarchal relations are challenged, for society finds it difficult to accomodate this challenge within its existing structures. A married woman, or a widow, who enters into a relationship with God through bhakti, while remaining within the socially ordained relationship, carves out an area of life which sustains her, but which is assimilated into the workings of domestic relations, albeit with tension.

There is a sphere in which there is a direct transference of exploitative and humiliating norms of subservience of the wife/lover to the man, to the field of bhakti. This is reflected in the kind of Mira bhajans sung.

Mohan, do come, Giridhar do come,
Mira is waiting alone in Madhav's *mandir*.

If you so bid, beloved, I will become *kajal*.
I will become *kajal*, beloved, and remain in your eyes.

Mohan, do come, Giridhar do come,
Mira is waiting alone in Madhav's *mandir*.

If you so bid, beloved, I will become a necklace.
I will become a necklace, beloved, and remain on your heart.

Mohan do come, Giridhar do come,
Mira is waiting alone in Madhav's *mandir*.

If you so bid, beloved, I will become a *bansuri*,
I will become a *bansuri*, beloved, and remain on your lips.

Mohan do come, Giridhar do come,
Mira is waiting alone in Madhav's *mandir*.

If you so bid, beloved, I will become an anklet,
I will become an anklet, beloved, and remain on your feet...

(Sung by Sivri Kalal, within the Kalal colony, Jodhpur).

I was told that one could add as many of one's choice ornaments as one liked to the words of this bhajan. It is significant that all the images of the woman cast her in an ornamental role. It is a servile surrender—'if you so bid'—and it is a stark adoption of the role of becoming an objectified ornament in order to enhance the beauty of Giridhar.

The Kalal community, within whom I heard this bhajan sung, is not a prosperous community, being traditionally a liquor-brewing one, and socially looked down upon. The majority of women in the Kalal colony rolled *beedis* in their own homes, the men working as vegetable vendors or were in casual employment. Widow remarriage has been a practice amongst Kalals, but this is now frowned upon in certain house-holds as they rise in material conditions.

Lachhamibai Kalal is in her fifties. She narrated the story of Kankubehn, a child widow in the Kalal colony. Kankubehn had been married into a family which was held in regard by the Kalal community. She did not remarry as the in-laws thought that remarriage would not accord with their status. Now she spends a lot of time in *puja*. Lachhamibai was admonished by the other Kalal women for providing this information. She should have said, they insisted, that it was Kankubehn who refused to remarry as she was immersed in bhakti. Lachhamibai nodded her head at this, but continued with her argument. Kankubehn's father-in-law was looked up to by everyone, she said. He owned a shop. That is the reason Kankubehn did not remarry.

The Kalal women met in the house of a particular person with their tobacco and leaves, and often sang bhajans together as they rolled the *beedis*. Sivri Kalal who had sung the Mira song which made her into ornaments for Krishna (above) said

Mira lived on her own. She did not need anyone else. As one does everything to please one's husband, so Mira did everything to please God.

The Mira bhakti, which had blazed up against submission to patriarchal norms, which had burnt on through years of struggle against this, is, in this interpretation, extinguished and made to legitimize patriarchal norms.

Amidst these Kalal bhajniks, and amidst some of the housewives gathered together in the Merta temple, the most powerful of the Mira bhajans sung in Rajasthan, 'Mira leave aside the company of the *sadha*, your Merto is humiliated, Mewar is humiliated,' (*Mira sadha ro sang chhode re, chhodo re, laaje tharo Merto, Mewar laaje ho,*) has been enfeebled. The main strength of the bhajan has been weakened by changes in the words of the bhajan

The anklets they jingle, they jingle.
In the temple is Mira dancing. (*Ghunghru chham chhamachham baje re, baje re,*
nij mandir re mai Mira ubhi nache re).

The constant repetition of the refrain, 'the anklets they jingle, they jingle', changes the whole quality of the original bhajan, giving this a feminized, seductive quality. It is telling though, that the original bhajan retains its hold. On each occasion that I heard the feminized version sung, at times the main singer, at times one of the other women in the group would lapse into the original refrain, would attempt to pull herself out of this, or change in the middle of the line, or alternatively, the other women would raise their voices to drown out this 'mistake'. This slipping back to the original happened on every occasion that I heard this version of the bhajan.

Housewives often meet together of a morning or afternoon, in the midst of their domestic chores, to sing bhajans. This is a city and town phenomenon, not one of villages. The bitterly drab lives of lower middle class housewives, whose living revolves round the kitchen is brought home by the painfully limited visions encapsulated in the bhajans that they sing.

I see Mohan in the *mooli*, Kanha in the *karela*,
I see Damodar in the *dudhi*.

The naming of Krishna in various ways, the alliteration of his names with the names of vegetables, actually seeing him in these vegetables, is pitiful. This bhajan was sung in the town of Dwarka, by a group of women who come from the communtiy of Gugli Brahmans, which makes a living from the pilgrims who come to Dwarka, feeding them, keeping their records, etc. The women had formed themselves into a 'Gopi *mandli*', and in fact sang more songs in Gopi *bhav* than they did Mira. When they did sing Mira, it was to the tune of a film song.

The structure of feeling of highly sentimentalized filmi relationships has penetrated the world of bhakti. It has created a drastic change in the very nature of the evolution of bhajans—and in their singing. It is not now unusual to hear bhajans sung to a filmi tune, so that one will hear *'Krishnaki divani ban kar Mira ne ghar chhod diya, ek Rathor ki beti ne Giridhar se nata jod diya...'* which is an imitation of a film song *'Chandiki diwar na todi, pyar bhara dil tod diya...'*. This song describes the story of a rich girl who was unable to break away from her wealthy life-style, and spurned the love of a poor boy. Anyone in Indian society who hears the 'Mira' song which is based on this film song, will immediately recognize the original that it is derived from, and though the words are changed, the structure of feeling is circumscribed by the film song, and this becomes the standard against which other emotions flowing out of the song are set.

Cheap booklets are sold at pavement stalls, within temple precincts, at places of pilgrimage, in old parts of cities such as Ahmedabad, Baroda, etc. These have not become standard fare at bhajan sessions, but it bodes ill for the survival of a genuine peoples' culture. These booklets have a written collection of bhajans, either made up by a particular individual (such as the son of a *sevak* in the temple at Merta), or they are a collection of bhajans heard around particular towns. The problem of the musical transmission of bhajans has been neatly solved. At the beginning of the song appears simply the first line of a film song, which sets the tune and pace of the bhajan that follows. This provides the basis to which the bhajan should be sung to.

Thus, one can have the first line of a popular tune such as *'dil ke arman aansuon mein beh gaye'* which is then followed by a long bhajan which begins, *'Mira Krishnaki divani ho gai, Krishna Krishna ratte kho gai'* (Kathavyas, n.p.d.: 25). Whatever the merits or otherwise of these film songs, the bhajans set to them are often banal. They cannot but be otherwise when they arise within a process of an imitative creativity. These 'Mira' songs lack depth, and the fraught tightness which gives tension and strength to the other Mira bhajans. The bhajans which arose out of a common expression and a common aspiration, the bhajans of the struggle to evolve a different kind of relationship, are not in evidence in this form of singing.

The co-existence of filmi songs with bhajans, and the blurring of lines between them means that there is no clear demarcation between bhakti and commercialized entertainment. In fact, bhajans (on cassettes) blare out in the same manner as other songs of entertainment: casually, intermittently, endlessly—outside a *paan* shop, in tea places and even within temple precincts. Being able to broadcast songs in and around one's precincts, and to provide free entertainment is to be able to satisfy one's customers. There are temples now which broadcast music to the surroundings of an evening after *aarti*. In the town of Jamnagar, I heard loud bhajans (from various films) being broadcast over a stereo tape-recorder from within a Jain temple. At Kabirvad, which is a small island off Bharuch, after *aarti* the curtains were drawn over Kabirsaheb, and an assortment of Hindi film songs were blasted from within the new temple complex right across the island.

The acceptance and introduction of this form of music within temples is extremely significant because it makes very clear the conflation of the world of bhakti with the world of commercialized relationships. There is no space for the seeking of relationships based on like spirits. The accent is on an alienating gratification, and on pulp pleasure.

The bhajans sung by lower middle and middle class housewives in Rajasthan and Gujarat today are greatly influenced by, not to say bound, by the tunes and sentiments of Hindi film songs, which attempt, through the power of broadcasting, to make a particular norm of the man-woman relationship universal. The bhajans sung by this section of housewives mark a disaffection with the marital relationship, and mark their need to live within relationships which are much more of their making, and of their own imagining. As far as the reality of their daily lives is concerned though, they inhabit a murky world of a sphere where human labour is vivified and reproduced, without there being any respect or value attached to this perpetual, grinding work. It is an area of life which they inhabit without any satisfaction.

For the women who inhabit these conditions, the prospect of liberation is bleak. A yearning after an imagined love within the walled existence of domesticity furthers disenchantment and discontent—it does not fulfill. It can enlarge these walls slightly—it does not break them. Seeking comfort in a relationship which is permanent by nature of its very immutability provides strength in a harsh and emotionally lonely existence—but it transforms neither the self nor the Immutable. Bhakti provides sustenance to the soul to rise above drudgery. Holding the image of the Beloved close to one can stop the wells of the heart from drying up. But the rainbird continues to thirst.

Epilogue

Earthly Life and its Completion

Mira spent her lifetime struggling against the authority of the Sisodiyas, and she searched for love and liberties throughout her travail. Not only did she survive outside the domain of Rajput power, but she gained in power and influence over a large mass of people for having flouted Rajput authority. The Rana cast a long shadow over the life of Mira—and ultimately blighted the completion of her earthly life. Just as Mira was discovering that a life lived amongst pilgrims and wayfarers was a bitterly hard one but that this was, nevertheless, nearer to her quest, the Rana threatened her hard-gained freedoms. It was the Rana who was responsible for the death of Mira, the person who had strived constantly to carve out a life separate and apart from dominant might.

But how did Mira end her non-conformist existence? Hagiography does not shed adequate light on the question. The oral tradition does not provide an answer either. It is significant that while the bhajans ring out the survival of Mira in the face of the Rana's attempts to kill her, there is not a single bhajan which mentions the ultimate destruction of the person of Mira. The bhajniks keep alive the *life* that was Mira's, not her death.

Again, how did Mira die? If one leaves aside for the moment the transcendental end attributed to Mira—that she merged herself in the Krishna *murti* in the temple at Dwarka—then one is left with two stark alternatives. Self-destruction, or destruction at the hands of the Rana. An exploration of the death of the earthly life of Mira makes us confront the question of violence done to a seditious life: the violence of a ruling power whose vendetta stretched a long way. In what way does bhakti provide a counter to hatred and *vair*?

Mira had left the fortress of Chittorgadh, having survived various attempts on her life. She had spent some time in Braj, and had then reached Dwarka. In the meantime, Chittor was sacked and taken by Akbar in 1567. Udai Singh set up a new capital at Udaipur (Tod, 1971: 378–84). It might have appeared judicious to the Sisodiya ruler to try and appropriate the moral authority of Mira during this period of political crisis. Equally, it might have appeared best to eliminate a person who continued to exist as a canker to Sisodiya power.

Be that as it may, the story has it that Udai Singh sent two Brahmans as emissaries to Dwarka, stipulating that they bring Mira back. The two emissaries reached Dwarka and put the Rana's case to Mira. They appear to have exerted maximum pressure on Mira to return to Mewar, refusing to eat or drink when Mira did not concede to their initial appeal. Mira then sought refuge in the sanctum sanctorum of the temple. The Brahmans waited for her to re-emerge. She did not. When they went inside to ascertain what had happened to her, they are said to have seen Mira's outer garment wrapped around the Krishna *murti*—and there was no other sign of Mira. The two emissaries are said to have returned to Udaipur, proclaiming that Mira was merged into the Krishna *murti*, that she had become one with him, and that she had attained her ultimate salvation.

It seems unlikely that this particular legend could have been started by the Rana's men, given their close links to the Sisodiyas, for whom the hallowing of Mira's name was not tolerable. Certainly the Sisodiyas never utilized Mira's miraculous end to bolster their own power. They did not even in the end claim that she was one of them. As we have seen, the superficial incorporation of Mira by the Rajput establishment was not begun till the nineteenth century, and even that remained disjunctured. The Sisodiyas did not reap the reward of a miraculous death attributed to Mira. They continued to disown her. In a manner true to a feudal principality, they continued to retain a silence about a person who had left their system of values behind. The official history of the Mewar rulers, 'Vir Vinod', (Shyamaldas, 1986: 1-2), makes no attribution of sainthood to Mira.

History obscures for us the truth of what happened within the temple at Dwarka. The only fact that emerges clearly is that Mira did not wish to return to the land she reviled. Did Mira perhaps take her own life rather than return to a life she had abjured? Was Mira eliminated by the Rana's men? Or did she slip away from the temple at Dwarka, away from the powers who had come to know where she was—and live anonymously in the South as Hermann Goetz avers (Goetz, 1966: 33-40)?

Rational explanations are useful in that they demolish demagoguery. They do not, however, aid us in entering the turbulence of emotions which precedes a sudden death, nor do they enable us to understand the nature of power at particular junctures. The subjectivity of death is not pan-human either, acquiring, in a class society, varying political meanings. Let us take each of the possible ends to Mira's life.

The story of Mira's mergence into the Krishna *murti* is one that marks the ultimate negation of worldly relations. It is also an annihilation of self. It is in fact a negation of the very basis of bhakti. Bhakti demands a social relationship. This requires that the two within the relationship remain separate beings in order to experience the presence of the other. Bhakti does not require that the bhakta blots herself out in the other. The bhakta strives to sing of the glories in order to demonstrate and act out a love for god in association with other bhaktas. The bhakta seeks opportunities to demonstrate a love through bhakti. A flight from this—to a mergence with the Ultimate—is a flight away from acting out this relationship.

It is significant that the bhajans do not attribute to Mira a glorious, sudden death. For the bhajniks, glory belongs to Mira for living out a relationship with Krishna in the teeth of opposition—forging, within this process, other bonds in society too. It is not in fact the bhajniks described in Part II of this work who place such fervent faith in Mira's mergence into the Krishna *murti*. Those who do this come from a different strata of society. They are those privileged for whom securing a life after death is instrumentally important—rather than a securing of a better form of relationships here. Unlike the bhajniks who have given us the powerful figure of the peoples' Mira, they accord much more importance to the manner of Mira's death than to the strivings in Mira's life. To them Mira is a saint shorn of her subversiveness. She is a smooth, smiling face moulded out of plaster of Paris, who graces their living-rooms and radiates purity in their lives.

Today, the bhajniks who come in groups from Mewar and Marwar to Dwarka, enter the town with '*Mirabai ki jai ho*'. They call out for the victory of Mira. These pilgrims associate Dwarka with Mira, not with the seat of rule for Krishna the King. These bhajniks have not forgotten the antithesis of Mira to Rajput rule. They particularly venerate the place which offered sanctuary, for a time, to Mira. The townspeople recognize the specific affinity of these humbler pilgrims from Rajasthan to Mira. The *pandas* earn their livelihood from this association.

Mira's power lies in flouting the values embodied in Sisodiya rule—and in showing an affiliation which refuted relations based on inegalitarian power. For these bhajniks, Mira's life and the struggle that this embodied is more important than the manner of her death. They continue to affirm the bonds forged by her in her life through the bhajans that they sing. The power of the Mira bhakti has not been tested because it has not openly confronted political authority. But this bhakti has provided an enduring strength to those subordinated to resist a dehumanized existence. It has also given a vision of social relationships which are more optimistic because they are not based on degradation. The Mira bhakti has engendered solidarity between the oppressed, and it has kept alive a vital tradition which affirms active relationships and which disowns humiliating ones. This affirmation continues to be vivified through the singing of the Mira bhajans and these attest to the very real need to achieve transformative relationships.

Did Mira actively take her own life perhaps rather than return under pressure to Udaipur? However fashionable this theory may be in certain modernist circles[1], to pose this question is in itself bitter. One takes one's life only when there is no hope around or within one. Mira had fought back tenaciously against the despotism of Sisodiya power. She had forged an alternative community for herself, showing a clear light forward to all those brave enough to follow their innermost convictions, and drawing to herself a large number of people who saw in her a part of themselves, and who sought in this a betterment of their conditions. To conceive of Mira giving all this up is to concede defeat, a defeat for the liberties that she had striven to chart. It conjures up a picture of a Mira in despair and in a void. A Mira without community. A Mira without fellowship.

No bhajnik worthy of the name would grant the possibility of Mira taking her own life. The suicide theory derives from a mentality which is not in accord with the resilience and vigour of the Mira challenge, but from a mentality supercilious in its sophistication, which does not hesitate to brand Mira both a suicidal and a schizophrenic[2] person. This portrayal strikes at the very core of the peoples' Mira. It is a desecration of the person of Mira, and of the faith that arises out of the Mira bhakti. Not only is the power of Mira negated through this—what is extinguished and made impotent is the very survival of a non-conformist life which engenders and sustains its own fellowship.

If Mira had ended her life so desolately, it would lay a mark, a stain on all our lives today. It would be a negation of hope for the creation of liberties, and for the formation of an alternative community. It would be a victory for those whose power is bloated through the crushing of an oppositional life, showing the futility of challenge and a victory for the Sisodiya rulers who battled down the strengths created by Mira in association with fellow bhajniks. It would be a stamping down on a woman of courage who had attempted to follow the dictates of her heart, and sought to realize them. This additional scar would lend a greater pain to all the scars caused by the innumerable suicides of women unable to face the bitter violence of a daily privation. It is a historical burden that all of us carry, bearing responsibility for lives unable to continue because society does not pay heed to their needs and wants. The self-destruction of Mira would be a bleak message for those struggling to evolve better social relationships, dealing a blow to the common owning of that precious historical legacy.

Was Mira killed by the Rana's men who finally wrought vengeance? It is not as fantastical a suggestion as it may appear. The Rajput code of vendetta operates across time and geographical boundaries. Despite an ideology that abjures the use of weapons in cowardly acts of violence against those unarmed, the Rajput chronicles are replete with acts of just such cowardice and treachery against the defenceless (Tod, 1971: 858,539). Tales of cynically planned slaughter abound too (M.G., 1908: 132). Mira refused to return to Udaipur. It is a point of integrity and pride with her, as well as some apprehension perhaps. She refuses to be incorporated in a life within the palace. What does murder mean to Mira? It means death at the hands of a power she had so fiercely rejected and stood up against. It means the ultimate victory of *vair* against a person who had held on to its opposite.

The murder of Mira would show the inability of bhakti to overcome and transform deeply-embedded values of vengeance. The bhajniks though, have a complete faith in the power of Mira to survive against the Rana's vindictiveness. For them, the question of the possibility of Mira being murdered does not arise. To pose this question is to remove Mira from the sphere of regenerative values, and it is to bring Mira into the arena of power politics which the bhajniks eschew. Within this domain of the Mira bhakti, political authority is nullified by a higher morality and spirituality. The peoples' morality has tremendous strengths to envisage and claim a more equal order, to forge a conscious community welded to better social relationships. But when directly threatened, it often retreats into itself, being equipped solely and remarkably with the weapon of a hardy trust in self and God.

Do we want our historical figures to die before their time so that their integrity is saved from decay by a glorious end (Warner, 1983: 27)? Is it necessary that our symbols of liberty become martyrs? I have had to struggle long with this question, and at last I leave Mira alive amidst the bhajniks, unviolated by self or the enemy, travelling, singing, in a community drawn from those on the fringes of society. It is a resilient community, which has provided shelter and refuge to all those rejected by dominant society.

There is evidence of an underground passage from within the temple of Dwarka to the outside.[3] It would not have been difficult for Mira to slip away when faced with the Rana's emissaries, and later join up with groups of itinerant singers. So Mira travels on, with her *ektara* in her hand, embracing her liberties and inspiring others. Her songs continue to reach those scarred and humiliated and who grasp from these songs a message of emancipation.

Appendix

Mira's 'Janma Patri': An Epic Poem on the 'Birth and Life of Mira'

It was the ninth month of the Rani's pregnancy. A girl child was then born of her, under the most auspicious stars. Preparatory celebrations began, to greet the birth of this child.

The aunt visited the astrologer in order to know the future of the girl child born in the house of Dudo Mertiyo. He foretold a bright future for her. The aunt then visited the carpenter, and asked for a beautiful cradle, made out of sandalwood. In return, she promised a gift of a saree for his wife, and a colourful turban for himself.

Having grown a little older, Mira went to the outskirts of Duda's palace, and asked Rivdas to bless her. At first, he refused, answering that she was the daughter of a prestigious family, and that Dudo Mertiyo would be wrathful if he found out. Rivdas asks Mira to keep her distance from his hands.

At last, though, he consented to accept Mira as his disciple. He showed her around the quarters of the Jatiya Chamars, and told her that he earned his living through dyeing the skin of animals.

One day, while Mira was playing with her friends, she constructed a temple for Hari—while others built toy mansions.

The groom rode on his horse, and was asked to give dues to the cow-herd, the water-carriers, the carpenter who had put up the wedding pavilion, and the priest who officiated at the wedding ceremony.

Some maids were sent to Mira, and they asked her to discard her saffron clothing and don bridal attire. At this, Mira became filled with rage. She hit the maids violently, who went out crying and shrieking. Mira called upon Giridhar to deliver her.

The mother then came in and beseeched Mira to keep the *marjad* of her mother's *pallav*. Otherwise, she said, she would have to bear the wrath of Dudo Mertiyo. She ended by appealing to the fact that she had given birth to Mira—and again begged her to put on the bridal attire, and agree to the marriage.

Mira and the Rana arrived in Chittor and were greeted by his sixteen Ranis. That night, the Rana knocked on each of the sixteen Rani's door, but none would answer. Each was afraid that Mira would bewitch her with her magical powers. When the Rana arrived at Mira's door, he found her in worship.

The Rana asked Mira who it was that she was worshipping. She replied that her guru was a Jatiya Chamar—and that she was worshipping Krishna.

The Rana asked Mira to leave his palace immediately, accusing her of polluting it. Mira asked him not to make her leave the palace. She said that she would build a small hut at the side, and spend her time in spinning and weaving *dhotis* for him. She called upon Giridhar for assistance.

Mira then broke the ivory *chudlo*, threw away the clothes given by the Rana, and wiped away her *tika*.

Rivdas in his dream saw all his disciples deeply asleep—except for Mira, who was alone in a forest. He went in search of her. Each step measured a hundred *kos*. He reached Mira just as the sun rose in the sky.

Rivdas lamented the fact that she was in this unhappy position due to his influence—but Mira was lost in contemplation of Hari.

Footnotes

ACKNOWLEDGEMENTS
1. A bhajan which brings this out very clearly is Narsinha Mehta's
   sukh dukh man ma ne aaniye
   ghat sathe re ghadiyaa
   taadiya te koyina nav tade.
   It continues to be a referent point in the family history, demonstrating the times of earlier want—now past—linking up the family experiences with the experiences of those from a more ancient (and royal) genealogy who represent iconic figures of those who have undergone a harsh privation.

1: INTRODUCTION
1. The first written reference to Mira appears in Nabhadas' *'Bhaktamal'* (composed circa AD 1600) which was followed by Priyadas' commentary in AD 1712. The late nineteenth and early twentieth centuries saw an increasing interest in the history of the bhaktas, with many litterateurs utilizing the Mira verses to compile a biography of Mira. G. Tripathi's *'The Classical Poets of Gujarat and their Influence on Society and Morals'* (1892), was followed by, amongst others, K. M. Jhaveri's *'Milestones in Gujarati Literature'* (1914), and the

1935 publication of *'Gujarat and its Literature'* by K.M. Munshi. P. Chaturvedi's treatment of the figure of Mira remains influential (*'Mirabai ki padavali'*), as does P. Shabnam's *'Mira, ek adhyayan'* (1951). H. Goetz's *'Mira Bai: Her Life and Times'* (1966) is an important imaginative construction of Mira's position within a volatile political climate, and John Stratton Hawley provides a sympathetic study of Mira in Hawley and Juergensmeyer *'Songs of the Saints of India'* (1988). There exists besides many articles in journals, and many small pamphlets and chapbooks provide reworkings of the life of Mira as well as note some of the more popular bhajans.

2. Many writers did not feel compelled to limit themselves to drawing up a picture of Mira through the extrapolation of 'evidence' from the published Mira verses, but embellished many stories around Mira's childhood, her growing up years etc. Swami Anand Swarup's *'Mira Sudha Sindhu'* (1958) thus has a long account of Mira's mother being concerned about her indifference to beautiful clothes and ornaments even on her birthday, and who thereby started to think of arranging a marriage for her (Swarup, 1958: 21). Kaka Kalelkar, who was closely associated with Gandhi from 1916 onwards called Mira 'Hindustan's most important martyr' (Kalelkar, 1974: 30). The nationalists' concern with the power of the Mira rebellion is in strong contrast to the accounts of those like Swarup who were anxious to point to Mira's philosophical and spiritual prowess. The foregrounding of Mira's experiences as an outstanding example of women's creativity is present in M. Kishwar and R. Vanita *'Poison to Nectar: The Life and Work of Mirabai'* (Jan-June 1989).

3. Colonel James Tod's *'Annals and Antiquities of Rajasthan'* conceptualized Kumbha as Mira's temporal lord (Tod, 1971: 337–8). Most writers accepted the Sisodiya chronicler's version of Mira being married to Bhojraj, which appeared in the nineteenth century compilation of *'Vir Vinod'*. See for ex-

ample K. Shekhavat *'Mirabai ka jivanvrat evam kavya'* (1974: footnote one, 58) and N. Bhagat *'Mira'* (1982: 4).
4. E.P. Thompson has a critique of Keith Thomas' *'Religion and the Decline of Magic'* (Weidenfeld and Nicolson, 1971), in which he takes objection to Thomas' depiction of popular magic as being a collection of miscellaneous recipes, which is not informed by a comprehensive world-view. Thompson argues too that the presupposition of a unilinear, progressive 'decline' of popular beliefs may be unhelpful (Thompson, 1972: 51–4).
5. The phrase 'vale of tears' is borrowed from Karl Marx's *'Introduction to the Contribution to the Critique of Hegel's Philosophy of Right'* (Marx and Engels, 1975: 39).

2: OPPOSING LOYALTIES: MIRA'S BHAKTI AND RAJPUT DHARMA
1. Nainsi was born in AD 1611 and was an administrator and military commander for the state of Jodhpur. He was dismissed from office, together with his brother in 1667, and both men committed suicide in 1671. Nainsi's historical writings are meticulous.
2. For the previous discussion on *samm dharma*, I have drawn heavily on the excellent analysis by Ziegler, (1973).

3: A COMMUNITY FORGED: THE BIRTH OF A SONG
1. Discussion with Bhattnagarji, Chittor, 16.2.1986.
2. Goetz thus contends that Mira 'belongs to the greatest figures of mankind. And I, personally, know only one other similar person, Jesus, the Christ, shrouded in the presence of his Divine Father, as she in that of her Divine Husband, pure, loving and misunderstood and misinterpreted like her' (Goetz, 1966: 42).

4: A DREAM VALIDATED
1. A.J. Gurevich has an insightful discussion on the notion of time in medieval culture (Gurevich, 1985, 26-38 and 94-151). The notion that linear time is only one of the possible forms

of social time is an important one in rejecting the dominance of linear model time.

6: *PRIVATION IN COMMUNITY*

1. The relationship between alms-seekers and givers is described in wonderful detail in the novel *'The Beggars' Strike'* (Sow Fall, 1986). The death of old Gorgui Diop during a police raid in which the authorities had attempted to 'clean' up a post-independent city in W. Africa had shaken all the beggars in the city—who decided to go on strike. Nguirane, a blind man who played the guitar on street corners crystallized the argument for striking:

> It's not because of our rags, nor our physical disabilities, nor for the pleasure of performing a disinterested good deed that people deign to throw us the money we get as donations. First of all they have whispered their dearest and most secret desires to the alms they tender: 'I make you this offering so that God may grant me long life, prosperity and happiness...' 'This donation is so that the Creator may remove all the difficulties I might encounter on my path...' 'In exchange for this contribution may the Master of heaven and earth help me climb to the top of the ladder, make me the Head of my Department...' 'Thanks to this offering, may the Almighty drive away all my cares as well as those of my family, protect me from Satan, from man-eating sorcerers and all the spells that might be cast upon me...' That's what they say when they drop a coin or a little gift in the palm of your out-stretched hand. And when they are kind enough to invite you to share their steaming, odorous calabashes of millet porridge and curdled milk, do you imagine it's because they thought you might be hungry? No, my friends, that's the least of their worries! Our hunger doesn't worry them. They need to give in order to survive, and if we didn't exist, who would they give to? How could they ensure their own peace of mind? They don't give for our sake; they give for their own sake!

They need us so that they can live in peace! (Sow Fall, 1986: 36–8.)

The unholy nature of giving alms is brought out sharply in the words of old Nguirane.

2. The phrase here is *'karma no sangadhi'*, which connotes a companion who supports one's deeds, choices, actions. I have translated it, broadly, as 'life'.

10: *THE RAINBIRD THIRSTS*
1. Richard Hoggart has provided details of the appropriation of working class cultural forms in England in *'The Uses of Literacy'* (Hoggart, 1962, see especially chapter seven, 'Invitations to a Candy-Floss World: The Newer Mass Art', pages 206–46).

EPILOGUE: EARTHLY LIFE AND ITS COMPLETION
1. I first heard this theory propounded by a lecturer in Hindi Literature in Udaipur.
2. The example of Mira is often cited to describe the symptoms of 'schizophrenia' by college lecturers teaching psychology.
3. Discussion with Pushkerbhai Gaukani, editor of *'Dwarka Sarvasangraha'*, (n.p.d.), January 1988.

Krishna by Other Names

Bal-Krishna
Giridhar
Giridhari
Hari
Jadavpati Rai
Kanudo
Lala
Madhav
Mohan
Murari
Nandlal
Raghunath
Ranchhod
Shamadiyo
Shyam
Vithalvar

Glossary

Aarti	Worship entailing the circling of an image with a lighted wick
Abhang	Marathi religious verse
Amiri	wealth, as also spiritual wealth
Amrit	ambrosia
Ashram	refuge, a place where those tied to a particular set of beliefs live together
Badbhagi	fortunate
Baharvatiya	outlaw, in Saurashtra a member of a warring patriarchy who went into exile in rebellion against a local ruler
Bajot	stool upon which the bride and groom sit during the wedding ceremony
Bal-Krishna	child Krishna
Bambh	carrying the stigma of forced labour (a stick etc.)
Bandh	stopping of work in protest
Bani	authoritative speech
Bansuri	flute
Bapota	ancestral land to which a particular community held a strong right
Bari	clothes etc. presented to the bride by the groom

Barat	marriage party
Bat	narrative
Batai	division of crop for tax purposes
Bava	ascetic
Baval	stick from baval tree, used for cleaning teeth
Beedi	tobacco wrapped in a conical-shaped leaf
Begar	forced, unpaid labour, imposed by those in power
Bhai-bandh/ bhaiyad	Rajput brotherhood
Bhai-bandh chakar	a subservient member of a brotherhood
Bhai-bant	system of land division where male members of a clan had right of control over territory which they had either conquered, or acquired from the head of the brotherhood
Bhaktani/ bhaktin	female bhakta, but commonly a term of abuse—loose woman, prostitute
Bharud	Marathi verse which is acted out, depicting the persona of the subject of the song
Bhekh/ bhes	to donn saffron, renounce worldly relations
Bhog	share of crop taken by ruler
Bhomiya	person holding ancestral land which could not be resumed by the state
Chakar	servant, denoting the relationship between a ruler and those who performed military or administrative duties
Chanvri/ chori	pavilion where wedding ceremony held
Chautara	four-stringed instrument used to accompany bhajans
Chunri/ chunddi/ chundaldi	outer garment worn by the woman. If she wears one sent by a particular man this signifies her betrothal to him. It is also a symbol for the human body—the weaving, dyeing of the human form and spirit.
Chote	small

Chowkidar	watchman
Chudlo	woman's bracelet—signifies marital status. At death of husband, the *chudlo* is, symbolically, broken.
Dalal	intermediary
Darshan	visitation by god, sighting of god
Desh	country
Dhani	lord, master, husband
Dharma	religious duty, officially sanctioned code of morality
Dharna	exertion of moral force by staging a sit-down protest
Dasi	woman servant, woman subordinated to an overlord
Dhediya-panth	derogatory term for the sect which has a lot of untouchable (Dhed) followers
Dhobido	washer man
Dhol	large, double-headed drum, played with hands
Dholak	small, double-headed drum, played with hands
Dhoti	male garment, long strip of cloth wrapped around the legs
Divani	a woman crazed with love
Doha	couplet, a verse form utilized by many bhaktas
Dovda	system of marriage whereby one takes as well as gives a daughter to a particular family
Dudhi	white gourd (vegetable)
Dula	bird
Dupatta	scarf
Ekevda	system of marriage whereby one takes a daughter from a particular family without giving one in return
Ektara	one-stringed instrument, used as an accompaniment to bhajans
Fakiri	mendicancy
Fauj	army
Garibdi	a poor woman
Garibi	poverty

Gaghra	long petticoat
Gaun-Bambhi	someone assigned to carry out forced labour in the village, for example act as watchman
Gangajal	water from the river Ganges, which is invested with sanctity
Garusa	honorific (in Rajasthani), for guru
Ghunghat	veil
Gimvara	peasant
Gopis	women from the cow-herd community in the Braj area (Uttar Pradesh) who were devotees of Krishna
Gosain/ goswami	preceptor, guru, head of a particular sect
Got/gotra	sub-division defining exogamy
Grahasta	house holder
Gur	molasses
Hakim	governor in charge of administration
Hans/ hansla	swan: symbolizes the purity of the human spirit
Hath leva	joining of hands in Hindu wedding ceremony
Hasil	land tax
Haveli	mansion. The places of worship of the Vallabh sect are called havelis, being opulent mansions
Indhonis	worn on the head by women who carry a load on the head, to act as a break against the weight
Izzat	patriarchal honour
Jagir	land held in return for service to a king (Rajasthan)
Jagirdar	those who held land in return for service to the king (Rajasthan). Under the Mughals, those who were assigned the right to tax-collection of an area for a limited period
Jajman	patron of a village servant, or Brahman
Jari	gold thread
Jati	an endogamous group
Jholi	border of garment held out in mendicancy
Jogin	female ascetic
Jogi	ascetic
Johar	collective death undertaken by women of a royal

	family when faced with an on-coming, victorious army of another ruler
Johar-jund	place where women undertook *johar*, usually by fire
Jooni-vani	old sayings, speech, history
Kair	bitter fruit eaten in Rajasthan
Kajal	kohl (rubbed in eyes)
Kankut	form of tax assessment of standing crops (Rajasthan)
Karela	bitter gourd—vegetable
Kari	foot ornament
Kartal	cymbals, played together in time to bhajans
Khadi	hand spun and hand woven cloth
Khalisa	land belonging to the state
Kharif	monsoon crop
Khati-chhas	sour buttermilk: a staple part of peasant diet, associated with food taken by the subordinated
Kheda	small village
Khyat	chronicle of fame
Killedar	fort-keeper
Kirtan	collective singing of devotional songs, accompanied by music
Kos	unit of measurement, to about one and a half miles
Kukkut	cockerel
Kul	clan
Kuldevi	clan goddess
Kul-nasi	a destructress of the clan
Kum-kum	red powder applied to forehead by women, as a sign of marital status
Lag-bag	cesses, applies to forced labour too
Lok devta	peoples' deity: only tangentially incorporated into the Hindu pantheon of gods
Lok-geet	folk song
Lok sants	those who set responsible moral and social principles, revered by the people
Mahajan	merchant or moneylender
Maha-	the 'great' sect. In Saurashtra, refers to

panth	the Tantric inspired *shakta* sect
Mahmudi	a silver coin originating in the times of the Gujarat Sultans (about fifteenth-sixteenth century), which was being minted in the eighteenth century in Gujarat
Mandal	circle
Mandap	wedding pavilion
Mandir	temple
Mandli	organized group of bhajan singers
Manjira	small cymbals, played to accompany bhajans
Mantra	magical, religious chant
Marjad	bounds of propriety, decorum
Maud	a crown made of reeds, worn by bride on day of wedding
Maukhan	feast
Mausi	aunt, mother's sister
Mindhod	fruit of the plant *randia dumetorum*, tied to the wrist of a woman on her wedding day
Mohalla	street or neighbourhood in a city
Mooli	white radish
Mota-gharan	prestigious house-hold
Multani	merchant from Multan
Murti	image of a god, an icon
Murti puja	ritual worship of an image
Nath bava	an ascetic of the Nath sect
Natrayat	allowing widow remarriage
Nugra	person who has never been initiated by a guru
Odhni	upper garment worn by a woman. To wear an *odhni* sent by a particular man is to be betrothed to him
Paan	betel leaf, eaten with chopped arecanut and other condiments
Pachedi	cloth covering, worn by a woman
Paghdi	turban
Palla/ pallav	edge of saree: connotes honour, status

Panch/ *Panchayat*	caste assembly
Panch pirs	five *pirs*, a common number of revered religious figures found in different regions of India
Panchi	bird, a symbol for the human spirit
Pandas	Brahman priests in centres of pilgrimage, who earn a living by exploiting pilgrims
Pandal	pavilion within which wedding ceremony takes place
Panth	path, a community of believers who adhere to particular doctrines
Paos-ala	rain's coming (Marathi)
Papiha	cuckoo, brain-fever bird, whose call symbolizes the pining after a beloved
Pargana	Mughal tax-division
Paricayi	writing which provides knowledge of a person
Patidev	elevation of husband as god
Pativrata	woman leading a life in devotion to her husband
Pratishtha	prestige
Patlo	low, wooden seat: stool upon which the bride and groom sit during wedding ceremony
Pee kahan	the call of the *papiha* (where is my beloved?)
Phool	medallion
Pir	Sufi saint, mystic, revered religious figure
Pithi	turmeric paste rubbed on the body of the bride on her wedding day
Piu	beloved
Piu-piu	call of the *papiha*
Pucca	durable, long-lasting, stone and cement (of house)
Puja	ritual worship
Purdah	veil: much more, the close confinement of women, and restrictions on movement
Qawwals	Sufi devotional singers
Rabi	winter crop
Rajvi	royal
Rabab	stringed instrument
Ragas	set of musical notes on which a melody is based

Rana	ruler of the state of Mewar
Rand	widow, term used for prostitutes too
Ras	juice, essence
Rasik-ras	erotic mood, essence
Ravan-hatho	stringed instrument
rotla/roti	generally described as unleavened 'bread', made out of millet flour, corn flour, wheat flour, etc
Saathin	woman comrade
Saar	essence, meaning
Sadavrat	place which regularly distributes food to the poor
Sadhu/sadhuda	ascetic
Sadha	ascetic, saint, the good (plural, Rajasthani)
Sadhna	method by which a particular religious stage is achieved
Saga	related
Sahajiya	those adhering to a belief in the 'sahaj', the essential and 'easy' path to salvation. Here, it refers to those adherents in Bengal who, heavily influenced by Tantricism, evolved a distinctive set of Vaishnav practice and philosophy
Sakhi	couplet, bearing authoritative witness
Samadhi	means whereby one's life-force is expired voluntarily
Sammdharma	duty to a feudal ruler, over-lord
Sampraday	religious sect
Sanyas	renunciation
Sanyasini	woman renunciator
Sant	'one who knows the truth', the just, the poor and the good
Sant-sahitya	literature on *sants*
Sarangi	stringed instrument, played with the bow
Sardar	chief

Sati	widow immolation
Satimata	worship of immolated women as goddesses
Satya-graha	truth-force, word coined by Gandhi to describe his form of non-violent resistance
Sat-guru	worthy preceptor
Sevak	temple servant, attendant
Shaktas	worshippers influenced by Tantricism, undertaking ritual sexual activity
Shakti	power
Shami	plant, *prosopis spicigera*
Sharad purnima	full moon in the month of Ashvin, (around October)
Strimay	full of a woman i.e. become one
Stri vachya	in the feminine voice
Shudra	member of the degraded caste in the hierarchical system
Svati	the fifteenth of the twenty-seven constellations, which appears but rarely
Tadha tukda	pieces of stale food. As a phrase, it denotes poverty
Taka	a copper coin
Talab	village pond
Taluka	sub-division of a district
Tanpura	stringed instrument
Tapas	austerities
Tapas-charya	to practice austerity/penance
Thikana	an estate
Tika	mark on forehead, denoting a woman's marital status
Tikayat	head (person)
Tooti tapri	broken down hut
Tu	familiar form of address, used amongst equals, to those who are intimate, and those who are inferior in status
Tulsi mala	garland worn round the necklace signifying

	renunciation of wordly things
Vair	vendetta
Vairag/ vairagin	renunciation, woman renunciator
Varna	four-fold hierarchy of stratification in Indian society
Varna-samkara	children born between people from different castes
Varnash-ram-dharma	the caste system as laid down in the Hindu scriptures
Varta	narrative
Vas	locality
Veskar	gate-keeper, watchman, usually an untouchable, in Maharashtra
Vigat	detailed chronicle
Vigha	area of land, normally less than an acre
Viraha	pain of separation
Virahani	song of *viraha*
Viyogan	woman separated from her beloved
Yugas	four ages namely Satyuga, Tretayuga, Dvapar and Kali

Bibliography

Primary Sources

1. Unpublished Government Records
Maharashtra State Archives, Bombay:
- District Administration Reports, Kaira District, 1902-3 to 1912-13.
- Revenue Department Records.

Rajasthan State Archives, Bikaner:
- Jodhpur State Mehkma Khas, Social; File no. 4, Office Notes 1923-8.

2. Government Publications
Bombay Government:
- *Progress Report of the Archaeological Survey of Western India for the year ending 30 June 1905* (Bombay, 1905).
- *Gazzetteer of the Bombay Presidency*, Vol. VIII, *Kathiawar* (Bombay, 1884).
- *Saurasthrani Pachat Komo*, Vols. 1 & 2 (Saurashtra Pachat Varga Board, Rajkot 1957 & 1958).

Government of India:
- Annual Report of the Director General of Archaeology for the year 1903-04, part 1 (Calcutta, 1905).

- *Census of India 1901*, Vol. XXV, *Rajputana* (Lucknow, 1902).
- *Census of India 1931*, Vol. XIX, *Baroda*, pt. 1 (Baroda, 1931).

Government of Marwar:
- *Mardumshumari Raj Marwar [Census of Marwar] 1891*, pts. 1 & 2 (Jodhpur, 1894).

Government of Rajputana:
Rajputana Gazetteers, Vol. II-A, *The Mewar Residency* (Ajmer, 1908).

Secondary Sources

Abbott, Justin E., *Tukaram: Translation from Mahipati's Bhaktalilamrita* (Scottish Mission Industries, Poona, 1930).

Ali, Salim, *The Book of Indian Birds* (Natural History Society, Bombay, 1972).

Archer, W.G., *The Loves of Krishna in Indian Painting and Poetry* (George Allen & Unwin, London, 1957).

Barz, R., *The Bhakti Sect of Vallabhacharya* (Thompson Press, Faridabad, 1976).

Baskaran, S. Theodor, *The Message Bearers: Nationalist Politics and the Entertainment Media in South India, 1880-1945* (Cre-A, Madras, 1981).

Bhadani, B.L. [appears to be same author as Bhidwani, below], 'Economic Conditions in Pargana Merta (Rajasthan), 1658-63', in G.L. Devra, *Socio-Economic Study of Rajasthan* (Rajasthani Granthagar, Jodhpur, 1986).

Bhatti, Hukamsinha, *Rajasthan ke Mertiya Rathor* (Rajasthani Granthagar, Jodhpur, 1986).

Bhidwani, Bhanwar, 'Economic Conditions in Pargana Merta (Rajasthan) (c. AD 1658-63)', in *Proceedings of the Indian History Congress, Aligarh, 1975*.

Briggs, G.W., *Gorakhnath and the Kanphata Yogis* (Motilal Banarasidass, Delhi, 1973).

Chakravarti, Ramakanta, *Vaisnavism in Bengal* (Sanskrit Pustak Bhandar, Calcutta, 1985).

Chattopadhyay, B.D., 'Origin of the Rajputs: The Political, Economic and Social Processes in Early Medieval Rajasthan', in *Indian Historical Review*, Vol. III, No. 1, July 1976.

Chattopadhyaya, Debiprasad, *Lokayata: A Study in Ancient Indian Materialism* (People's Publishing House, New Delhi 1981).

Chaturvedi, Parshuram, *Mirabai ki Padavali* (Sahitya Sammelan, Prayag, 1983).

Chaube, J., *History of the Gujarat Kingdom: 1458-1537* (Munshiram Manoharlal, New Delhi, 1975).

Chaudhuri, K.N., 'European Trade with India', in Tapan Raychaudhuri and Irfan Habib (ed.), *The Cambridge Economic History of India*, Vol. 1, *c. 1200-c. 1750* (Cambridge University Press, Cambridge, 1982).

Chaudhuri, K.N., *Trade and Civilization in the Indian Ocean: An Economic History from the Rise of Islam to 1750* (Cambridge University Press, Cambridge, 1985).

Chicherov, A.I., 'On the Socio-Economic Structure of Pre-Colonial India: Handicraft Production in the Seventeenth to early Nineteenth Century', in *XXII International Congress of Orientalists*, papers presented by the U.S.S.R. delegation (Moscow, 1967).

Cohn, B.S., *An Anthropologist Among the Historians and other Essays* (Oxford University Press, Delhi, 1987).

Datta, K., 'Great Hindu Women in Northern India' in Madhavananda Swami (ed.), *Great Women of India* (Advaita Ashram, Almora 1953).

Das Gupta, S., *Obscure Religious Cults* (Firma Mukhopadhyay, Calcutta, 1969).

De, S.K., *Early History of the Vaisnav Faith and Movement in Bengal* (General Printers and Publishers, Calcutta, 1942).

Deleury, G.A., *The Cult of Vithoba* (Deccan College Post-graduate and Research Institute, Poona, 1960).

Desai, K., *Mirabai: Ten Pictures from the Life of India's Greatest Poetess of the Past* (D.P. Taraporewala, Bombay, 1943).

Dimock, E.C. Junior, *The Place of the Hidden Moon: Erotic Mysticism in the Vaisnava Sahajiya Cult of Bengal* (University of Chicago Press, Chicago, 1966).
Douglass, F., *Narrative of Frederick Douglass, an American Slave: Written by Himself* (Harvard University Press, Cambridge, Mass., 1960).
Du Bois, W.E.B., *The Souls of Black Folk* (Fawcett Premier Book, Geenwich, Conn., 1961).
Dutt, R.C., *The Economic History of India—in the Victorian Age* (Routledge and Kegan Paul, London, 1956).
Dwivedi, H., *Kabir*, (Rajkamal Prakashan, New Delhi, 1985).
Eagleton, T. and Wicker, B., (eds.) *From Culture to Revolution: The Slant Symposium 1967* (Sheed and Ward, London, 1968).
Enthoven, R.E., *The Tribes and Castes of Bombay*, Vols. I, II, III, (Government of Bombay, Bombay, 1920, 1922).
Forbes, A.K., *Ras Mala: Hindu Annals of W. India, with particular reference to Gujarat* (Heritage Publishers, New Delhi, 1973).
Gandhi P., *Bapujiye karavelo Ashram bhajanono swadhyay* (P. Gandhi, Rajkot, 1978).
Gandhi, M.K., *The Collected Works of Mahatma Gandhi*, Vols. I-LXXXVIII, (Publications Division, New Delhi, 1958-1983).
Garrick, H.B.W., *Report of a Tour in the Punjab and Rajputana in 1883-1884*, Vol. XXIII, (Archaeological Survey of India, Calcutta, 1887).
Genovese, E.D., *Roll, Jordan, Roll. The World the Slaves Made* (Pantheon Books, New York, 1974).
Ibid, 'Rebelliousness and Docility in the Slave' in Genovese, E.D., in *Red and Black: Marxian Explorations in Southern and Afro-American History* (University of Tennesse Press, Knoxville, 1984).
Ginzburg C., *The Cheese and the Worms: The Cosmos of a Sixteenth Century Miller* (Routledge and Kegan Paul, London, 1980).
Gramsci A., *Selections from the Prison Notebooks* (Lawrence and Wishart, London, 1976).

Ibid, *Selections from Cultural Writings* (Lawrence and Wishart, London, 1985).
Goetz H., *Mira Bai: Her Life and Times* (Bharatiya Vidya Bhavan, Bombay, 1966).
Gokuldas S., *Meghvansh Itihaas* (Arya Brothers, Ajmer, n.p.d.).
Gopal S., *Commerce and Trade in Gujarat, Sixteenth and Seventeenth Centuries* (Peoples' Publishing House, New Delhi, 1975).
Gupta B.L., *Trade and Commerce in Rajasthan* (Jaipur Publishing House, Jaipur, 1987).
Gupta S., *Rajasthani Lok-Mahabharat ka Sahityaik evam Sanskritik adhyayan* (unpublished Ph.d thesis, Hindi Department, Rajasthan University, Jaipur, 1974).
Gupta, S.P., *The Agrarian System of Eastern Rajasthan* (Manohar, Delhi, 1986).
Gurevich A.J., *Categories of Medieval Culture* (Routledge and Kegan Paul, London, 1985).
Habib I., *The Agrarian System of Mughal India (1556-1707)* (Asia Publishing House, London, 1963).
Ibid, 'Historical Background of the Monotheistic Movement in the Fifteenth Century', paper read at the *Seminar on Ideas, Medieval India* (University of Delhi, Delhi, 15-18 November 1965).
Harlan, L., *Religion and Rajput Women: The Ethic of Protection in Contemporary Narratives* (University of California Press, Berkeley, 1992).
Hawley J.S., 'The Sant in Surdas' in Schomer and Mcleod (eds.), (Motilal Banarasidass, Delhi, 1987).
'Author and Authority in the Bhakti Poetry of N. India' in *Journal of Asian Studies* 47, No. 2, May 1988.
and Juergensmeyer M., *Songs of the Saints of India* (Oxford University Press, New York, 1988).
Hoggart R., *The Uses of Literacy* (Penguin, Harmondsworth, 1962).
Jhaveri, K.M., *Milestones in Gujarati Literature* (Tripathi and Company, Bombay, 1938).

Juergensmeyer, M., *Religion as Social Vision: The Movement against Untouchability in Twentieth Century Punjab* (University of California Press, Berkeley, 1982).
Kalelkar, K., *Bhajananjali* (Navjivan Prakashan, Ahmedabad, 1974).
Karve I., *Kinship Organisation in India* (Asian Publishing House, Bombay, 1965).
Kathavyas N., *Mira Bhajan Sangraha* (Charbhuja mandir, Merta city, n.p.d.).
Katz B., *The Social Implications of Early Negro Music in the U.S.* (Arno Press and the New York Times, New York, 1969).
Khare R.S., *The Untouchable as Himself: Ideology, Identity and Pragmatism among the Lucknow Chamars* (Cambridge University Press, Cambridge, 1984).
Kishwar M. & Vanita R., 'The Burning of Roop Kanwar', *Manushi*, No. 42-43, Sept-Dec 1987.
Kishwar M. and Vanita R., 'Poison to Nectar: The Life of Mirabai', *Manushi*, No. 50-52, Jan-June 1989.
Kosambi D.D., *An Introduction to the Study of Indian History* (Popular Book Depot, Bombay, 1956).
Ibid, *Myth and Reality: Studies in the Formation of Indian Culture* (Popular Prakashan, Bombay, 1962).
Ibid. 'The Culture & Civilization of Ancient India in Historical Outline', 1965, Routledge and Kegan Paul, London.
Lenin V.I., 'Leo Tolstoy as the Mirror of the Russian Revolution' in *On Religion* (Progress Publishers, Moscow, 1978).
Lyall A.C., *Asiatic Studies: Religious and Social*, First Series, (John Murray, London, 1899).
MacMurdo J., 'Journal of a Route Through the Peninsula of Gujarat, from Malia to Radhanpura, 1809-1810' in *Selections from the Record of the Bombay Government*, No. XXVII, New Series, (Government of Bombay, Bombay, 1894).
Maheshvari H., *History of Rajasthani Literature* (Sahitya Akademi, New Delhi, 1980).
Manuel P., 'Andalusian Gypsy and Class Identity in the Flamenco Complex' in *Ethnomusicology*, Vol. 33, No. 1, Winter 1982.

Manushi special issue on Women Bhakta Poets, Jan-June 1989.

Marx K., 'Introduction to the Contribution to the Critique of Hegel's Philosophy of Right' in Marx K. and Engels F., *'On Religion'* (Progress Publishers, Moscow, 1975).

Mukhya H., 'The Ideology of the Bhakti Movement: The Case of Dadu Dayal' in Chattopadhyay D.P. (ed.), *History and Society: Essays in Honour of Professor Nihar Ranjan Ray* (K.P. Bagchi, Calcutta, 1978).

Mukta P., 'Dalits Take Over' in *Economic and Political Weekly*, 19 December, 1987.

'Ram Janmabhoomi Comes to Milton Keynes' in *Economic and Political Weekly*, 4-11 November 1989.

Munshi, K.M., *Gujarat and Its Literature from Early Times to 1852* (Bharatiya Vidya Bhavan, Bombay, 1967).

Nabhadas, *Bhaktamal* (Lucknow, 1801, MS number 035 in Wellcome Library, London).

Nainsi M., *Marwar ra Pargana ri Vigat* (Rajasthan Oriental Research Institute, Jodhpur 1968-1974).

Omvedt G., 'Caste, Class and Women's Liberation' in *Bulletin of Concerned Asian Scholars*, Vol. 7, No. 1, January-March 1975.

Oman J.C., *Cults, Customs and Superstitions of India* (Vishal Publishers, Delhi, 1972).

Pelsaert F., *The Remonstratie*, translated by Moreland W.H. and Geyl P. as *Jahangir's India* (W. Heffer, Cambridge, 1925).

Prasad M., *A Gandhian Patriarch: A Political and Spiritual Biography of Kaka Kalelkar* (Popular Prakashan, Bombay, 1965).

Priyadas, *Commentary on the Bhaktamal* (Lucknow, 1801, MS number 035 in Wellcome Library, London).

Qadeer I. and Hasan Z., 'Deadly Politics of the State and its Apologists' in *Economic and Political Weekly*, 14 November, 1987.

Rajyaguru N., 'Mahapanth ane tena Santo' in *Urminavarachna*, special issue on *'sant sahitya'*, March 1986.

Ram P., *Madhyakalin Rajasthan mein Dharmic andolan* (Ram P., Ajmer, 1977).

Agrarian Movement in Rajasthan: 1913-1947 A.D. (Panchsheel Prakashan, Jaipur, 1986).

Rawal R., *Kala-chintan Ravishankar Rawalna nibandho, charchayo, avlokno ane vicharo* (Bharatiya Sahitya Sangh, Bombay, 1947).

Ray, R.K., 'Mewar: The Breakdown of the Princely Order' in Jeffrey R. (ed.) *People, Princes and Paramount Power* (Oxford University Press, Delhi.

Roy, D.K., *Among the Great: Conversations with Romain Rolland, Mahatma Gandhi, Bertrand Russell, Rabindranath Tagore, Sri Aurobindo* (Nalanda, Bombay, 1945).

Chaitanya and Mira: Two Plays (Aurobindo Ashram, Pondicherry, 1979).

Sangari, K., 'Mirabai and the Spiritual Economy of Bhakti' in *Economic and Political Weekly,* July 7 and July 14, 1990.

Sanyal H., 'Social Mobility in Bengal: Its Sources and Constraints' in *Indian Historical Review*, Vol. II, No. 1, July 1975.

'Trends of Change in the Bhakti Movement in Bengal, *Occasional Paper No. 76*, Center for Studies in Social Sciences, Calcutta.

Sarda H.V., *Maharana Kumbha: Sovereign, Soldier and Scholar* (Vedic Yantralaya, Ajmer, 1932).

Sarkar S., *Modern India 1885-1947* (Macmillan, Delhi, 1984).

Schomer K. and McLeod W.H. (eds.), *The Sants. Studies in a Devotional Tradition of India* (Motilal Banarasidass, Delhi, 1987).

'Introduction' in Schomer K. and McLeod W.H., (eds.), (Motilal Banarasidass, Delhi, 1987).

The Doha as a Vehicle of Sant Teaching' in Schomer K. and McLeod W.H., (eds.), (Motilalal Banarasidass, Delhi, 1987).

Seshu G., 'The Making of a Dangerous Myth' in *The Indian Express*, 1 November, 1987.

Shabnam P., *Mira, ek adhyayan* (Lok Sevak Prakashan, Benares, 1951).

Sharma D., *Rajashtan Through the Ages: From the Earliest Times to 1316 AD*, (Rajasthan State Archives, Bikaner, 1966).

Sharma G.D., *Rajput Polity: A Study of Politics and Administration of the State of Marawar, 1638-1749*, (Manohar, Delhi, 1977).

'Urban Social Structure: A Case Study of the Towns of Western Rajasthan during the Seventeenth Century' in Grewal J.S. and Banga I. (ed.) *Studies in Urban History* (Guru Nanak Dev University, Amritsar, 1981).

Sharma G.N., *Social Life in Medieval Rajasthan: 1500-1800 AD* (Lakshmi Narain Agarwal, Agra, 1968).

Shaktawat L., *Mira Darshan: Jivani tatha bhajan* (Lalsinha Shaktawat Trust, Udaipur, 1982).

Shekhawat, K., *Mirabai ka Jivanvrat evam Kavya* (Hindi Sahitya Mandir, Jodhpur, 1974).

Shyamaldas Kavi, *Vir Vinod*, part II, Vol. I, (Motilal Banarasidass, Delhi, 1986).

Singer, M., 'The Great Tradition in a Metropolitan Centre: Madras' in Singer, M., *Traditional India: Structure and Change* (American Folklore Society, Philadelphia, 1959).

Singh, *'Sant Ravidas Ramayan'*.

Singh, D., *A Study of Bhakta Ravidas* (Punjabi University, Patiala, 1981).

Sow Fall A., *The Beggars' Strike* (Longman African Classics, Essex, 1986).

Sukul, L., *Mira Smriti Granth* (Bangiya Hindi Parishad, Calcutta, 1949).

Swarup Anand Swami, *Mira Sudha Sindhu* (Shree Mira Prakashan Samiti, Bhilwada, 1958).

Thakar J., 'Okhamandal: Udti Najre' in *Dwarka Sarvasangraha* (Gujarat Itihaas Parishad, Dwarka, n.p.d.).

Thapar R., *Ancient Indian Social History: Some Interpretations* (Orient Longman, Hyderabad, 1984).

'Historical Realities' in *Seminar*, Annual Number, January 1987.

Thompson E.P., 'Anthropology and the Discipline of Historical Context' in *Midland History*, Vol. I, No. 3, Spring 1972.

Times of India, Ahmedabad edition, 'Eight hurt as Harijans enter temple at Nathdwara', 11 August, 1988.

'To Enter God's House', 13 August 1988.

Tod J., *Annals and Antiquities of Rajasthan, or the Central and Western Rajput States of India*, Vols. I, II and III (Motilal Banarasidass, Delhi, 1971).

Tripathi, G., *The Classical Poets of Gujarat and their Influence on Society and Morals* (Tripathi and Company, Bombay, 1892).

Twomey M., 'Employment in Nineteenth Century Indian Textiles' in *Explorations in Economic History*, Vol. 20, 1983.

Vaudeville C., *Kabir*, Vol. I, (Clarendon Press, Oxford, 1974).
'Sant Mat: Santism as the Universal Path to Sanctity' in Schomer K. and McLeod W.H. (eds.), (Motilal Banarasidass, Delhi, 1987).

Walker A., 'Measures adopted (commencing with the year 1805) by Lt. Col. A. Walker, Resident at Baroda, for the suppression of female infanticide in *Selections from the Records of the Bombay Government*, No. XXXIX, Bombay, 1856.

Warner M., *Joan of Arc: The Image of Female Heroism* (Penguin, Harmondsworth, 1983).

Williams R., *The Long Revolution* (Penguin, Harmondsworth, 1961).
Marxism and Literature (Oxford University Press, Oxford, 1977).
Keywords: A Vocabulary of Culture and Society (Flamingo, London, 1983).

Wilson H.H., *Religion of the Hindus*, Vol. I, (Trubner, London, 1862).

Zelliott E., 'Eknath's Bharuds: The Sant as a Link Between Cultures' in Schomer K. and McLeod W.H., (eds.), (Motilal Banarisdass, Delhi, 1987).

Ziegler N.P., *Action, Power and Service in Rajasthani Culture: A Social History of the Rajputs of Middle Period Rajasthan*, (unpublished Ph.d thesis, University of California, 1973).
'Marwari Historical Chronicles: Sources for the Social and Cultural History of Rajasthan' in *Indian Economic and Social History Review*, Vol. XIII, No. 2, April-June 1976.
'Some Notes on Rajput Loyalties during the Mughal Period' in Richards J.T. (ed.) *Kingship and Authority in S. Asia* (University of Wisconsin, Madison, 1978).

Index

Abhangs, 38
Abu, 55
Achut Kanya, 204
Ad Dharm movement, 82–3
Adhikari, Krishnadas, 24
Agolai, 101, 103
Agra, 53
Ahirs, 7, 74, 159, 166
Ahmedabad city, 148, 198–200, 221
Akbar, 15, 54, 56, 204–5, 226
Akincanadas, 41
Akka Mahadevi, 38, 40
Ambarbai, 35, 158–9
Ambedkar, B., 109
Amritsar, 198–9
Anjania Patels, 70, 74, 84, 96, 130, 134
Annals and Antiquities of Rajasthan, 50, 173
Arab nationalism, 195
Artisan communities, 75–80, 105
Arya Samaj, 175
Ashamli village, 152
Ashram Bhajnavali, 148–9, 191–2
Aurobindo Ashram, Pondicherry, 30

Babur, 53, 55
Badi Didi, 204
Badnor, 54
Bahinabai, 35
Bakshidas, 82
Bala yogini, 204
Bambhis, 76–9, 81, 98–100, 113, 134
Bami Kirtani, 180
Banias, 179
Bappa Rawal, 54, 56, 64
Barmer, 51
Baroda city, 221
Basi Village, 70
Bat, 26

Bauris, 113
Benares manuscript, 23
Bengal, 39, 41, 158, 180
Bhadani, B.L., 76
Bhadrajun, 51
Bhagtans, 180
Bhakta Chetha, 204
Bhaktas, male, 87, 116–17
Bhakti, 20, 29, 31–2, 34–38, 72, 87–90, 141, 186–7, 190, 211–21, 227
  life of, 15
  suspicion of by, elites 32–3
  world of, 25, 64, 221
Bhajan:
  Gatherings, 4, 7, 11, 31, 70, 107, 138, 144, 211–23
  mandalis, 3, 94, 96–7, 130, 221
  singing, 38–9, 42–3, 87–90
Bhajans, 4, 42–3, 183, 202, 208–9
  See also Mira bhajans
Bhajniks, 3–4, 7, 70–114
Bhaktamal of Nabhadas, 19–21, 26
Bhangi Women, 3, 91
Bhangis, 133–4, 163
Bharathari, 162
Bharuch town, 122
Bhattnagar, 69
Bhavanibai, 215–16
Bhayani, Harivallabh, 179
Bhils, 54–5, 84
Bhindar, 112
Bhoj, prince of Mewar, 26, 120
Bhopalsing of Mewar, 177
Bikaner region, 51
Bisnois, 154, 163
Bombay, 53, 109, 197, 200
Borunda village, 100, 104, 112, 121, 124
Bostom Vaishnavs, 39

Brahma, 79
Brahmanical:
  hegemony, 106
  tradition, 42
Brahmans, 36, 39, 77–8, 89, 106, 117, 158, 180, 204, 210, 226
  Aboti, 143
  Guali, 148, 221
  Nagar, 39
Braj, 226
Braj *mandal*, 21
British colonialism, 50, 53, 158
Budha, gautam, 185
Buddhism, 95, 109
Bunkars, 75

Calcutta, 200
Capitalist hegemony, 120, 201–10
Cassettes (audio), 12, 103, 208–9, 222
Chaitanya, 39–40, 65, 116, 156, 158
  sampraday, 21, 25
Chakar, 62
Charbhuja temple, Merta, 209, 220–1
Charmars, 70, 73, 75–80, 98, 106, 110–1, 138, 146, 177, 233–4
Chaturvedi, parshuram, 119–20
Chaudhri, Gogadevi, 101
Chauri Chaura, 199
Chauriasi vaishnavo ki Varta, 24
Chavan, Chandabai, 97
Chavan, Phulibai, 97
Chittorgarh, 1, 24, 26, 54–6, 60–1, 64, 66, 69–70, 84, 93, 105–7, 110, 113–14, 129, 140, 147, 151, 155, 160–1, 173–80, 186, 202, 204–5, 217, 226, 234
Chokhamela, 39
Chundawat, Himatkumari, 217
Classical music, 202–3
Colonial period, 12
Commercial art, 201–10
Communitas, 37–8, 40
Community life, 7, 39, 99–100

Dadu, 88

Dagla Ka Keda village, 179
Dakor Mnuscript, 23
Dalits, 4, 39, 44, 58, 70, 73, 80–3, 105–8, 190, 204, 210
Damanis, 217
Damami, Jashodra, 217
Dangawas, 81
Dangis, 74
Dasi jeevan, 89
Data, kalinikar, 29
Dechara Village of Mewar, 4, 70, 96, 127, 130
Deforestation, 11
Delhi, 52, 55, 78, 197, 200
Deogarh, 70, 84, 91
Desai, Mahadev, 186
Deval, Ranjanabehn, 212–13
Devdas, 204
Devi, Indira, 30
Dhadhis, 163
Dhakars, 70, 74
Dhanagaji village, 179
Dhani, 62
Dhanna, 105
Dharmashastras, 32
Dheds, 58, 77, 81, 163
Dhobis, 162
Dhola maru ra Duha, 64
Dholis, 163
Dhruv, 139, 142, 144
Dimock, E.C., 41
Domestic sphere, 28–30, 34
Doordarshan, 205
Douglass, Frederick, 43
Drought, 7–11, 143
Du Bois, W.E.B., 43
Duda, ruler of Merta, 52–3, 113, 118, 233, 234
Dudhrejiya, bachudas, 104, 136, 144
Dungarpur State, 85–6
Duniya na mane, 204
Dutch, 75
Dwarka, 21, 24, 41, 148, 155–7, 164, 207, 209, 212, 221, 226–8, 231

Index

East India Company, 75
Eklingji, 56, 81
Ekanath, 77–8, 89
Eknath, 204

Female infanticide, 152
Feudal:
    Princely domain, 44
    privilege, 12
    relationships, 35
    social hierarchy, 74, 86
    society, 19
    taxes, 84–6
    values, 2, 57, 92–3, 98
    warfare, 14
Films, 12, 201, 203–6, 221–2

Gandhi, Kasturba, 190
Gandhi, Mohandas, 1–2, 12, 29, 225, 117, 119, 148–9, 182–200, 206
Gandhi, Prabhudas, 183
Gandhian ashrams, 148–9, 183, 190–2, 194, 202
Ganga river, 106
Garudas, 79, 134
Gaudiya Vaishnav *sampraday*, 21, 156
Ganvri, Gulabbai, 97
Genovese, Eugene, 43
Ghanti village, 91, 94, 130
Ghose, Aurobindo, 30
Giridhar, 21
Girnar, 164
Gitagovinda of Jayadev, 65
Godvad pargana, 147
Goetz, Hermann, 22–3, 105, 156–7, 227
Goga, 57–8
Gopi Mandli of Dwarka, 148, 221
Gopichand, 162
Gopis, 21, 65, 183
Gora, 39
Gorakhmadhi, 158
Gramsci, Antonio, 45, 72

Gujarat, 28, 37–8, 43, 53, 57, 74, 80, 148–9, 192, 197–8, 202, 207, 222
    Government, 206
    Vidhyapith, 206
Gujarati:
    literature, 29
    middle classes, 1–2, 12, 119, 192, 208, 211–23
    novelists, 27
    poets, 28
Gulzar, 205

Habib, Irfan, 79
Harishchandra, 162
Harlan, Lindsay, 13–16
Hawley, J.S., 33–4
Hegemony, 2
Hindi Film songs, 203–5, 221–2
Hindi literature, 29, 217
Hindu polity, 49–50
Hinduism, 30–1, 196
Historiography, 25–33

Idar, 54
Indian nationalism, 1–2, 12
Individualism, 20, 23, 27–9, 35

Jadejas, 152
Jagdish temple, Udaipur, 209
Jaimal Rathor, 54, 56
Jainism, 95, 222
Jaipur:
    city, 1, 14
    state, 76, 152–3
Jaitaran, 74
Jalor state, 147
Jalota Anup, 203, 209
Jamnagar:
    district, 127, 138
    town, 222
Janabai, 39
anma Patri of Mira, 112–14, 136, 233–4
Jatiyas, 108

264   THE COMMUNITY OF MIRABAI

Jats, 11, 52, 74, 81, 101, 134, 146, 163
Jayadev, 65
Jesal, 162
Jhali, Rani of Mewar, 105–6
Jhaveri, K.M. 29, 33
Jiva Gosain, 25, 183
Jnanesvar, 156, 158
Jodha, Rao of Marwar, 51–2, 54
Jodhpur:
    city, 14, 51, 54, 81, 101, 205, 218
    district, 108, 124
    state, 52–3, 56, 155
Johar, 56
Joshi, Vinodbhai Dosa, 143–4, 160, 165
Juergensmeyer, M., 83
Julahas, 75–6
Junagadh:
    district, 104, 110, 136, 144
    town, 156–7

Kabir, 32, 79–80, 82, 88, 105–6, 116, 143, 156, 158, 194–6, 217, 222
Kabirpanthis, 94, 112
Kabirvad, 222
Kalal, Kankubehn, 219
Kalal, Lachamibai, 219
Kala, Sivri, 218
Kalas, 218–20
Kalelkar, D.B., 191
Kali, age of, 21
Kamadia, 100
Kamads, 113, 124
Kamali, daughter, of Kabir, 82
Kamladasi, 112
Kanadde, Rao of Jalor, 147
Kanauj, 55
Kanhoptra, 39
Kapdi, Govindram, 138
Kashi, 81
Kemble, Frances Anne, 44
Keshav village, 104, 136, 144
Khadi, 196–7
Khare, Narayan, 148, 202

Kharvas, 111, 13, 138, 141, 160, 165
Khataravada, Kunjibhai, 160
Khatumbha village, 143
Khed, 51
Kheda District, 151–2
Kherwara, 91
Khetsingh, Rana of Mewar, 81
Khilafat movement, 195
Khayat, 26
Kir, Gulabbai, 123–4
Kirtan, 38–40
Kodra, 51
Kolis, 74, 110, 135
Kotwal, Khimdio, 108–9, 138
Krishna, 2, 19, 22, 30, 62, 65, 88–9, 97, 111, 115, 117–18, 120–3, 140–1, 174, 205, 227–8
    murti, 16, 21, 105, 117–18, 120, 177, 206, 215, 226–8
    worship, 32, 35, 56, 65, 117–18, 173, 175, 211–21
Krishna Kunwari, 152–3
Kshatriyas, 50
kul, 21, 35, 49, 58–61
Kuldevi, 13–14, 22
Kumbalgadh, 55
Kumbha, Rana of Mewar, 26, 54–6, 64, 173–5, 184, 186, 190–1
Kumbhar, Jawalaram, 102
Kunbis, 83, 91, 94

Ladha, Mrs. 217
Lakha, Rana of Mewar, 81
Lal Ded, 38, 40
Langas, 121
Lenin, V.I., 187
Lingayats, 154
Lions Club, 217
Lirbai Mata, 136, 158
Lok Devtas, 58
Lok Mahabharat, 113
Luhanas, 158
Luna, wife of raidas, 106
Lyall, A.C., 61

Index

MacMurdo, James, 157
Madhavacharya, 156
Madhopur village, 107
Madhya Pradesh, 57
Madras, 31
Mahabharata, 113
Mahapanth of Saurashtra, 158–9
Maharashtra, 39, 77–8, 109, 116, 202, 204
Mahars, 39, 77–9, 89
Mahewa, 51
Mahmud Khilji, 175
Mahmud Shah I (Mahmud Begadha), 156–7
Mahuva town, 179
Maldeo, Rao of Marwar, 52–4, 57
Malini, Hema, 205
Malwa state, 55
Man, Rao of Marwar, 152–3
Manaklav village, 108
Mandore, 54, 64, 80
Manek, Hothiba, 127
Manek, Pacchabha, 166
Manek, Ranmalbha, 127
Manek, Vidhabha, 167
Manganiyaras, 104
Mangeshkar, Lata, 203
Manushi, 34
Marriage, customs of low castes, 133–5, 145–9
Marwar:
    region, 4, 11, 41, 55, 77, 228
    state, 50–3, 56–7, 80, 152–3
Marwaris, 109–10
Marxist writers, 27
Mathura, 36
Maya, 32
Mayo the dhed, 81
Mecca, 157
Meghani, Jhaverchand, 208
Meghchand, 78
Meghwal, Jamkhubai, 108
Meghwal, Mahachandra, 81
Meghwal, Manna, 81
Meghwals, 57, 77–8, 108, 134

Mercantilist mentality, 22–3, 28, 30
Merchant community, 21–2, 53, 157–8
Mers, 51, 55, 74, 104, 110, 136
Merta, 22, 49, 51, 53–4, 63, 75–6, 81, 91–3, 100, 118, 150, 155, 209, 215, 220–1
Mewar:
    region, 3, 11, 15, 40, 61, 71, 90–7, 228
    State, 1, 13, 49–66, 69, 76, 84–5, 155, 173
Mewat region, 179
Middle East, 157
Migrants, 7–11
Minas, 84, 91
Mira:
    and Gandhi, 12, 182–200
    and poison cup, 1, 19, 21, 60, 92, 150–1, 181, 207
    and Rohidas, 82, 105–14
    animosity of Vallabh *sampraday* towards, 24, 183
    as exile, 41, 114, 155–69, 207
    as mendicant, 41, 155–69
    as poetess, 27–9
    as rebel, 40–1, 155
    bhajans, 3–4, 11, 14, 23–4, 26, 33–5, 37–8, 40, 43–5, 66, 69–72, 82–3, 87, 90–114, 120–31, 135–45, 148, 160, 164, 166, 178, 182–4, 190–4, 203, 209–10, 215–20, 225
    bhakti, 2, 11–12, 15, 37, 40, 65–6, 72–115, 174, 219–20
    biographies of 19–30, 35
    community of 37–45, 135–6, 145, 182, 190, 183, 209–10
    death of, 225–31
    described as *rand*, 24, 148–9, 180, 192
    domestication of, 28–9
    films, 203–6
    in Punjab, 82

266   THE COMMUNITY OF MIRABAI

  incorporation of Rajput tradition,
     13–6, 173–81, 226–7
  mandir in Chittorgarh, 2, 273–7
  mandali, 3, 97
  marriage of, 22, 113–14, 118–23,
     128–31, 136–44, 148, 216,
     233–4
  paternal home of, 51–2, 113, 223
  play, 30
  positivist understanding of, 25–33
  rejection by Rajputs, 1–3, 14–69–71,
     150, 178–81
  rejection of caste values, 105–12
  rejection of Rajput values, 105–12
  religiosity of, 32
  sect, 36
  worship of, 1
Mira Smriti Granth, 30
Mirabai (*see* Slade, Madeleine)
Mithapur village, 143
Misogyny of bhaktas, 116–17
Mochis, 75, 162
Modhvada village of Saurashtra, 4,
   110
Moholel village of Kheda, 152
Mokal, Rana of Mewar, 64
Morality of the people, 45
Mother India, 30
Mughals, 26, 50–5, 204
Muktabai, 35
Munshi, K.M. 29
Muslim:
  invasions, 49
  rule, 50
Muslims, 121, 156, 195, 198, 203

Nabhadas, 19–22, 26
Nagda, 54
Nagpur, 109
Nagri village, 123, 180
Nahad, Rao of marwar, 81
Naidu, Sarojini, 203
Mainsi, Muhnot, 26, 52, 75–6
Nair, Kanharam, 101, 103
Namdev, 39

Nanak, 156, 195–6
Narahari, 39
Narasinha Mehta, 27, 39, 65, 117,
   162, 184, 193
Nat, Chothuji, 178–9
Nath bavas, 162
Nathdwara, 36, 82
Nathpanthi sect, 31–2, 57, 158–9
Navadvip, 39
Nirgun, 32
Nivritinath, 158
Od, Pratapi Modhu, 70
Od women, 70
Ods, 146
Okha town, 143–4, 160, 165
Okhamandal, 11, 143
Orientalism, 22

Pabu, 57–8
Padh, Manglaben, 212
Pali, 51
Paluskar, Vishnu Digambar, 201
Palval, Purushottam, 180
Pandarpur, 91
Parab Vavdi village, 159
Pastoralists, 7
Patan, 81
Patel, Hakra Nanaji, 127
Patel, huki Kodra, 70, 96
Patel, Raojibhai, 185
Patel, Ruplal Hakraji, 130
Patidars, 151–2
Pativarata, 15–16
Patnish, Jagdishbhai, 110
Patriarchy, 40, 186–90, 211–12, 220
   (*see also* Rajput Patriachy)
Pavagadh, 156
Persian chronicles, 26
Phoenix Ashram, 183
Pippa, 105
Pondicherry, 30
Porbandar, 110, 141, 210
Portuguese, 75
Positivism, 25, 32
Positivist history, 20

Post-Enlightenment writers, 32–3
Prahlad, 139, 142, 144, 184–5, 198–9
Pratabgarh, 70
Pratap, Rana of Mewar, 50, 178
Premvilas, 42
Priyadas, 19–22, 34
Punjab, 79, 82–3, 105–6, 197–9
Puranas, 32
Purohit Ramdas, 24
Pushkar, 92–3

Rabaris, 7, 159
Radha Krishna of Udaipur, 175–7
Radio, 12, 14, 167, 209
Raghupati Raghav Raja Ram, 202
Raidas, 4, 70, 73, 76, 79–80, 82–3, 105–14, 131, 138, 177, 233–4
Raidasis, 106
Raikas, 58, 74, 163
Raja Harishchandra, 208
Rajasthan, 1–2, 4, 7, 11–3, 26, 31, 35, 37–8, 42–3, 49–66, 73–4, 80, 94, 104–5, 108, 115, 127, 130, 163, 169, 174, 179, 211, 222
Rajasthan Legislative Assembly, 177
Rajasthani studies, 27
Rajput:
    bhaiyad, 49, 58–61
    chronicles, 27, 230
    clans, 26, 50, 58–61
    dharma, 15, 49–50, 56–8, 61–6
    hierarchy, 61–2, 147
    history, 12
    honour, 1, 69, 151, 153, 178
    landlords, 107
    marriage customs, 63–4, 128–9, 132–3, 147
    nobility, 15, 27, 217
    patriarchy, 13, 15, 41, 58, 153, 173–4
    peasants, 61, 178–9
    polity, 41, 49, 84–6, 173
    rulers, 42, 49–66, 93, 174, 204
    states, 35, 49–66, 80, 84–6
    the term, 49–51

vendetta (*vair*), 63, 132, 230
women, 13–16, 56–7, 63, 133, 153, 179, 216–17
Rajputs, 2–3, 12–16, 26, 37, 44, 49–66, 102
Ramanand, 38
Ramanuja, 38
Ramayan, of Valmiki, 77, 213
Ramdev Pir, 57–8, 71, 81, 96, 100, 104, 124, 136, 138, 143, 165
Ramlila, 162
Ran mal Rathod, 64
Rana of Mewar, 1, 22, 26, 28, 40–1, 50–66, 84–7, 90–7, 100–4, 106–7, 110, 113–15, 118–23, 127, 129–31, 135, 138–40, 142, 144, 147, 160, 166–7, 186, 186–8, 190, 192, 199, 216–17, 225–6, 230, 234
Ranchhodji temple, Dwarka, 156–7
Ranchhor, 36
Ranuja, 71
Ratan Singh, father, of Mira, 53, 55
Rathors, 49, 51–4, 64, 118, 216
Ravi Bhan *sampraday*, 4
Ravidas, (*see* Raidas)
Ravidas Ramayan, 82
Ravidasis, 82
Rawal, Ravishankar, 206–7
Ray, Rajat, 50
Regars, 75, 78, 106, 180
Religion of slaves in United States, 43–4
Riddles of Hinduism, 109
Rohidas, *see* Raidas
Rohidas ki parchi, 105
Romantic tradition, 27, 174
Rowalatt Satyagraha, 197–8
Roy, D.K., 30–1
Rupa the Vaishnav gosain, 41–2

Sadhna, 41–2
Sagun, 32
Salet, kanjibhai Punja, 141
Salvi, Devaram, 70

Sanga, Rana of Mewar, 22, 26, 50, 53–5, 105, 175
Sangari, Kum Kum, 32, 34
Sant, the term, 90–1
Sant Ravidas Mahatmay, 82
Sarvodaya movement, 202
Sati, 16
satimata, 13–14
Saurashtra, 4, 7, 12, 31, 39, 41–2, 58, 74, 89, 108, 110–11, 115, 127, 134, 136, 140, 142, 148, 155–59, 208, 211
Satvaras, 74, 111, 135
Satyagraha, 184–7, 196–7, 200
Schomer, K. 90
Sela Amba village, 112
Sena, 39
Shaktawat, Lalsinha, 175–7
Shankracharya of Dwarka, 156
Sharma, G.D., 179
Sharma, G.N., 36
Sharnam, Hari Om, 203, 209
Shatrunjaya, 164
Shiv, 56
Shivaji Park, Bombay, 109
Shivrajpur village, 127, 166
Shreenathji, 24
Sidhraj Solanki, 81
Sindhia, 153
Singer, Milton, 31
Singh, Arvind, 15
Sirohi, 55
Sisodiya:
    clan 1–2, 12, 44, 54–6, 60–3, 91–2, 150, 152, 174, 177–9, 186, 225–6, 229
    dynasty, 13, 49, 51, 54–6
    Kings, 26, 44, 53–6, 73, 115
    Kuldevi, 22
Slade, Madeleine, 191
Smritis, 32
Social reformers, 27
Sojat, 75
Sojawas, 81
South Africa, 182–4

South Gujarat, 7
Subbulakshmi, M.S. 203–4
Subhashnagar, 141
Subramanyan, K. 204
Sufis, 158, 196
Sunars, 163
Surdas, 24, 217
Suthars, 96
Swadeshi songs, 203

Tagore, Rabindranath, 2
Tamil, 203
Tantrism, 108, 158
Teja, 58
Telis, 146
Thakur, Omkarnath, 202
Thapar, Romila, 95, 151
Thoris, 57–8
Tod, James, 12–13, 50, 54, 56, 60, 64, 152–3, 173–4, 190
Tolstoy, Leo, 187
Toral, 35, 158, 162
Trade in Rajasthan, 53
Trimbak, 158
Tripathi, Govardhanram, 27, 32–3
Tukaram, 116, 158
Turis, 162–3
Turkey, 195

Udai Singh, Rana of Mewar, 226
Udaipur
    city, 1, 3, 14–15, 70, 91, 97, 177, 180, 209, 212–13, 216, 226, 229–30
    district, 127, 130
Untouchables, (*see* dalits)
Upper castes
Uttar Pradesh, 82, 105, 107, 158

Vaishnavism, 2, 39, 56, 118, 161, 180
Vallabhacharya, 24
Vallabh *sampraday*, 24–5, 36, 156
Valmiki, 213
Valsad Vapi, 7
Vande Mataram, 202
Varkari Panth, 91

Varta, 26
Varvada village, 138
Vasai village, 167
Vaudeville, Charlotte, 90–1
Vedantic Philosophy, 30–1
Vedic tradition, 41
Vigat, 26
Vikramaditya, Rana of Mewar, 26
Vir Vinod, 227
Viramde, 147
Viramdeo, ruler of Merta, 53–4
Vithoba, 39
Vivarata-vilas, 41

Vrandavan, 21, 36, 156, 183
   gosains, 38, 41

Waghers, 74, 110, 127, 157–8, 166
Widows, 36, 39–40, 145–9, 190–2, 204, 208, 215
Williams, Raymond, 168
Wilson, H.H., 36

Yeravda jail, 191
Yugaldas, 42

Zelliot, E. 77